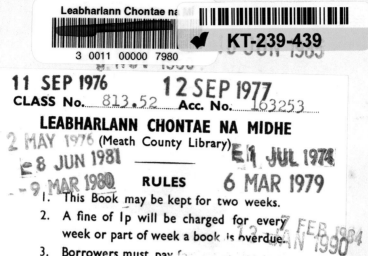

BRIGHT BOOK OF LIFE

Books by Alfred Kazin

ON NATIVE GROUNDS

A WALKER IN THE CITY

THE INMOST LEAF

CONTEMPORARIES

STARTING OUT IN THE THIRTIES

BRIGHT BOOK OF LIFE
American Novelists and Storytellers
from Hemingway to Mailer

Editor

THE PORTABLE WILLIAM BLAKE

F. SCOTT FITZGERALD
The Man and His Work

THE STATURE OF THEODORE DREISER
(with Charles Shapiro)

MELVILLE'S *Moby-Dick*
(Riverside Edition)

RALPH WALDO EMERSON
A Modern Anthology
(with Daniel Aaron)

THE OPEN FORM
Essays for Our Time

THE SELECTED STORIES OF NATHANIEL HAWTHORNE

HENRY JAMES, THE AMBASSADORS

BRIGHT BOOK OF LIFE

American Novelists and Storytellers
from Hemingway to Mailer

ALFRED KAZIN

SECKER & WARBURG
London

First published in England 1974 by
Martin Secker & Warburg Limited
14 Carlisle Street, London W1V 6NN

Copyright © 1971, 1973 by Alfred Kazin

SBN: 436 23202 2

Lines from "East Coker" in *Four Quartets*,
by T. S. Eliot, copyright 1943 by T. S. Eliot,
copyright 1971 by Esme Valerie Eliot.
Reprinted by permission of Faber and Faber Limited.

To My Novelists and Storytellers

And being a novelist, I consider myself superior to the saint, the scientist, the philosopher, and the poet, who are all great masters of different bits of man alive, but never get the whole hog.
The novel is the one bright book of life.

— D. H. Lawrence,
"Why the Novel Matters"

It is with fiction as with religion. It should present another world, but one to which we feel the tie.

— Herman Melville,
The Confidence Man

Acknowledgments

To Peter Davison and Esther S. Yntema, my editors at the Atlantic Monthly Press, whose interest in this book has been the breath of life to me.

To Gordon N. Ray and the John Simon Guggenheim Memorial Foundation, for their generous support.

To Yaddo — and to Mrs. Elizabeth Ames, its first director, for her friendship over the years.

To my wife Ann Birstein, for more than twenty years of conversation about the novel and her fellow novelists that made this book possible.

Chapters of this book in early drafts were delivered as the Ewing Lectures at the University of California, Los Angeles, 1969. Sketches for some sections of the book were published as articles, or parts of articles, in *The Atlantic, Harper's, The Saturday Review, The New York Times Book Review, The New York Review of Books,* and *The Mediterranean Review.* Nonetheless, for over three years, whether in the reading that prepared for its composition or in the writing itself, this book has been conceived as an integrated account of the fiction written in the United States since the outset of the World War II, a fiction that has reflected and embodied, more variously and truthfully than any other form of written art, the nature of our American experiences.

Contents

1

A DREAM OF ORDER
Hemingway

I want to write scenes that are frightening and inimitable. I don't want to be as intelligible to my contemporaries as Ernest, who as Gertrude says is bound for the Museums. I am sure I am far enough ahead to have some small immortality if I can keep well.

— F. Scott Fitzgerald

I N HIS LAST YEARS he called himself "Papa"; he had an authority so great that he had not been able to live up to it in years. Before he died — before he turned even the shotgun in his mouth into the expected, the last great Hemingway short story — he rewrote what was by now the classic story of a novelist's accomplishment and defeat as that of a dying American colonel unable to make love, as a totally alone Cuban fisherman losing the greatest single catch of his life to ravenous sharks, as an innocent young writer in the Paris of the Twenties discovering his talent but falling prey to a rich bitch who takes him away from his first wife, as a painter all alone on a Caribbean island whose three sons all die and who now makes a good death chasing Nazi subs from his private boat.

In all these last books Hemingway attempted that absolute identification of life with literature, in the name of precision of feeling, that was the hallmark of the moderns and their *grande époque*. He was the last great embodiment of the belief that experience can look entirely to literature for its ideal. After World War II writers would no longer understand this; Hemingway went to pieces because even he, to whom precision of feeling was writing and writing was everything, could no longer practice it with the old conviction.

"Make all that come true again," he said, trying to squeeze something more out of Spain in the Epilogue to *Death in the Afternoon*,

> *throw grasshoppers to the trout in the Tambre on the bridge in the evening; have the serious brown face of Felix Merino at the old Aguilar; have . . . Litri, like a little rabbit, his eyes winking nervously as the bull came; he was very bow-legged and brave and those three are all killed and never any mention made about the beer place on the cool side of the street underneath the Palace where he sat with his father and how it is a Citroën show room now. . . .*

It was not time alone that he was praying back: "the one year every one drank so much and no one was nasty"; it was a time-spirit in which a writer could feel that he had art by the tail, was completely the master and dominator of its necessary effects so long as each detail was so lovingly enumerated:

> *the Prado, looking like some big American college building, with sprinklers watering the grass early in the bright Madrid summer morning; the bare white mud hills looking across toward Carabanchel; days on the train in August with the blinds pulled down on the side against the sun and the wind blowing them . . .*

and promised as concrete an effect. Hemingway had discovered very early in his career the reductive principle with which he was to identify everything that promised success in his art. Even in his last books his famous style was the mold into which everything else had to fit. *The Old Man and the Sea, Islands in the Stream, A Moveable Feast, Across the River and into the Trees* were all extraordinarily centered, as usual, around a dominating all-absorbing self whose sensations and reflections gave pattern to the story. Even in the indulgent tenderness of *A Moveable Feast* and the suddenly rhetorical simplicities of *The Old Man and the Sea*, there was that extraordinary concentration of subject, place, mood, that enumeration of the world in Hemingway's special style, that was his trademark, his secret — and in a writer so superstitious, anxious, competitive — his rabbit's foot.

Unbeatable definiteness of detail, guaranteed precision of effect. The objective correlative in Hemingway's sure-fire version. One by one *his* beasts entered the ark, and so this Noah knew where he was.

Nothing extraneous, nothing vague. Line was everything. It was unflagging concentration, with its implicit guarantees, that from his first stories, *In Our Time*, gave the "stamp," the magical thing-ness, the determinable and irreducible compressiveness, to Hemingway's writing. A story was a unit of narrative, held together by a centered persona who seemed to hold his life in his hands, to be gambling it for the highest possible stakes. So you always knew where you were. There was a mental warding off of death. But within this context of danger there was a value to the moments, works and days of the hero's existence, a golden savor, that was somehow (just barely) achieved by the fiercest elimination, by the fierceness of reduction. When it worked, there was a luminous, glowing, sacred center of things that was one's intactness. The Heming-

5

way hero comes to regard himself, to cherish himself, by achieving control over a disorder that is different in kind from himself. Everything is founded on the struggle that gives one back to oneself. Faulkner paid his tribute to the modern sense of purposelessness by speaking of "one anonymous chance to perform something passionate and brave and austere not just in but into man's enduring chronicle . . . in gratitude for the gift of time in it." Hemingway jeered at all noble pronouncements, but gave the heroic version of himself what looked like archaic military dignity. He pitted his persona against situations that remained his definition of them — *In Our Time, Winner Take Nothing, Men Without Women*, A Lost Generation, A Separate Peace, "The Killers," All Is Nada, Hail Nada.

These stories and sayings were produced in what Eliot in "East Coker" (1940) was to call "the years of l'entre deux guerres." It was a period that for Hemingway, as for Eliot and so many of the modernist generation, was not "twenty years largely wasted" but the last great practice of a confidence in the purpose of literature that now seems as privileged as aristocracy. The works that made Hemingway famous had cleared his mind of everything past, false, inflated, in order to set the stage for heroic combat between the individual and "in our time." More than anyone else in that great generation that believed in "the religion of the word," Hemingway managed, by one word after another, to make the world as linear as his prose, as stripped as a prize ring, as "clean" as an operating room. You were always aware, reading those beautiful early stories, of someone writing with a desperate grace without which there was nothing, of a world so *made* that it flashed out into positiveness only as a fable in relief, cut like an intaglio, sharp as the Sforza face in the painting by Piero della Francesca, dominating the landscape that he owned, and whose hard-won harmonies expressed *him*.

Confidence was won, just barely, when the "truth" of one's words showed the "precision" of one's feelings, and so won the battle over the "shapelessness," the "mere anarchy," "the panorama of futility and anarchy that is contemporary history." There was, Hemingway liked to say, "a real thing, a fourth or fifth dimension that can be won. . . ." The secret was writing "truly." There had to be a one-to-one correspondence between the object described and the reaction-feeling it stimulated. Even in his last books, where the world would no longer *hold* for him as it once had, where it had plainly shifted out of his control, so that taken as books, his dogged enumeration of "facts" one by one seemed an imposture, rhetorical rather than the "moment of truth," his perfect passagework could move one by its fierce insistency.

Then he thought, think of it always. Think of what you are doing. You must do nothing stupid.

He took all his pain and what was left of his long gone pride and he put it against the fish's agony and the fish came over onto his side and swam gently on his side, his bill almost touching the planking of the skiff and started to pass the boat, long, deep, wide, silver and barred with purpose and interminable in the water. [The Old Man and the Sea]

7

*It was wonderful to walk down the long flights of
stairs knowing that I'd had good luck working. I always
worked until I had something done and I always
stopped when I knew what was going to happen next.
That way I could be sure of going on the next day. But
sometimes when I was starting a new story and I could
not get it going, I would sit in front of the fire and
squeel the peel of the little oranges into the edge of the
flame and watch the sputter of blue that they made. I
would stand and look out over the roofs of Paris and
think, "Do not worry. You have always written before
and you will write now. All you have to do is write one
true sentence. Write the truest sentence that you know."*
[*A Moveable Feast*]

The "precision of feeling" here was unanswerable, but
this was so because it was one man's intimate experience
of danger, dread, anxiety, hope. It spoke for that experience and nothing else: "precision" had been won at the
cost of sacrificing anything beyond the quality in danger,
the crisis-point, the importance of what the self says it
feels. The vividness, timing, tonality, echoing repetitions
— Dr. Johnson said that waiting to be hanged concen-
trates a man's faculties wonderfully — point back to the
ordeal. The hero's sense of his own existence, the fierce
presentness of his emotions or feelings, were always more
convincing in Hemingway's stories than in his novels; the
"moment of truth" is always more than the plot. It was
only in his greatest "pieces," as one must call them, that
his self-obsessed stories were as dramatically convincing
as they were emotionally powerful. One believed in the
swamp and the haunted soul behind Nick Adams's fishing in "Big Two-Hearted River" as one could not believe

that other people are desperately fighting for their lives in Hemingway's flip introduction of himself into *their* war. "The Germans came over the wall. We shot them one after another, just like that." But when he wrote out of history, out of the confidence that war was a school of style, his sureness expressed itself in rhythms that showed history in the service of art — "Troops went by the house and down the road and the dust they raised powdered the leaves of the trees. The trunks of the trees too were dusty and the leaves fell early that year and we saw the troops marching along the road and the dust rising and leaves, stirred by the breeze, falling and the soldiers marching and afterward the road bare and white except for the leaves." Caporetto, the great episode of the Italian officers being taken out of the line of retreat and shot by military police, stands out in *A Farewell to Arms* because it is a Goya painting of the horrors of war. The expected response is built into the material. The emotions involved are purely tragic, never disturbing, confusing, uncertain. Hemingway's greatest stories, "The Killers," "Fifty Grand," "My Old Man," all present someone else's disaster as so precisely satisfying to the present causes of it that the matter is clinched, the reader is dramatically satisfied; he can never believe in Jake Barnes's supposed inability to make love to Lady Brett, Frederic Henry's ability to make a "separate peace," Thomas Hudson's being a painter, or the old man's being a Cuban fisherman.

Still, painting and fishing as work toward a specified object interested Hemingway more than the novel as a many-sided form. For his own novels he never thought

9

of plot as a structure with an interest of its own. He made do with the all-important instances of the self doggedly achieving its passage through life, the lyric emphasis of consciousness on itself. The sovereignty of the storyteller, of which Dickens and Balzac were equally conscious, became for Hemingway the *matter* of fiction. When he announced that all modern American writing comes out of *Huckleberry Finn*, he was obviously thinking of spoken style. He praised James formally, as one plenipotentiary to another, but not as a deviser in fiction. He had many things to say about Fitzgerald's "weak" character, but the role of coincidence as an agent of disaster in *The Great Gatsby* never interested him any more than did the social contraption that Dos Passos rigged up in *U.S.A.* to mirror History to itself, or the interlocking sagas of family history and Southern history in Faulkner. Hemingway was by no means the first or the last American writer of fiction to be so much his own presiding situation. But what made the immediate matter in hand excitingly tense, dramatic, always a combat (even when the opponent is rigged and the horrors of war just another battle scene) is Hemingway's fervent belief that if a tragic cause is established, the response is guaranteed — art comes out of style, style out of combat.

The fighter in "Fifty Grand" thinks, "It looked like half a mile down to the ring. It was all dark. . . . Just the lights over the ring." The circumscribed narrow world, the tightening of nature to design as in painting, the handling of weapons, the prize ring, the arena, the making and unmaking of camp, the use of any moment to show only the ultimate responses to life, the line of words in Indian file that is exciting because it conveys the ordeal of consciousness to itself. One item succeeding another with the tread of time itself, Hemingway looking at Nick Adams as Nick Adams looks at his can of beans, the head looking always just one way, directed to nothing but the occasion. The extraordinary replacement of dramatic complexity by a successiveness of words that is the immediate physical experience, the curtailing of everything to the handling of things, the getting on top of difficulties. All these identify obsessive patterning of the smallest experience *with* the deliberate effort it takes to keep alive. The individual person in all his idiosyncrasy, that famous single character as character who had reflected the middle-class tradition of the novel, has been contracted in Hemingway's work to a certain obsessive watchfulness and mindfulness — to a burden of consciousness so haunting and limiting that it makes any complex dramatic structure unnecessary to Hemingway. Even his novels soon came down to one character haunted by danger, reviving each time he could recover his balance by handling each detail in his path with the gravest self-importance.

Hemingway gave a particular and somehow fatal emphasis to the self as the necessary end product of literature. But a belief in the self as the essential *form* of literature was typical of that group of friends — Hemingway, Fitzgerald, Dos Passos, Cummings, Wilson — for whom the right words in the right order were the immediate act that cut away the falseness and inconsequence of the world — "the lies, the lies!" as one battle-weary character cried in Dos Passos's *Three Soldiers*. And left oneself intact. The near was the self. The far-off was the world. Only what was near could be trusted. Because it alone could be used?

In 1940 T. S. Eliot was to say in "East Coker":

So here I am, in the middle way, having had twenty years —
Twenty years largely wasted, the years of l'entre deux guerres
Trying to learn to use words, and every attempt
Is a wholly new start, and a different kind of failure
Because one has only learnt to get the better of words
For the thing one no longer has to say, or the way in which
One is no longer disposed to say it. And so each venture
Is a new beginning, a raid on the inarticulate
With shabby equipment always deteriorating
In the general mess of imprecision of feeling,
Undisciplined squads of emotion. . . .

There is only the fight to recover what has been lost
And found and lost again and again: and now, under
   conditions
That seem unpropitious . . .

"Mystical" as these lines were to become in the total context of *Four Quartets*, Eliot the lawgiver of his generation was here summing up the most personal of his accounts, writing his confession as an artist. Eliot was moving between memories already faint with too much use and the God of perfect love, whose features were becoming dim and impersonal, more a principle than a person. The "perfect balance" on which Eliot had relied as a critic of literature past and present, the balance he had indeed in so many poems, the perfect balance between precision of words and feelings that Hemingway believed in as he believed in nothing else — this was now to go, as so many more established things were now to go.

The key was war, the two wars and the difference between them that was soon to make a legend of the "twenty years." Eliot's confession called them "largely wasted," but after the disrupting, utterly murderous war that lay ahead, *l'entre deux guerres* would become a celebration of freedom, a fixed point of greatness — not least for Hemingway himself and Scott Fitzgerald dying in 1940, all of whom had been crying out in their works, Make All That Come True Again! The key was not the Twenties, the end of a period, the end of the bourgeois nineteenth century: it was war and the difference between the two wars.

For Hemingway, as for all the best writers of his generation, the great thing about war had been that it was an object lesson for writers and "unmistakable." To be "unmistakable" was Stephen Crane's only rule for "good writing." From the perspective after 1945, Hemingway the Red Cross driver and dilettante of violence was to seem as much a student of other people's wars as Stephen Crane (born 1871) had been of the Civil War.

The first World War was not only a great "experience" for Fitzgerald, Dos Passos, Cummings, Wilson — it was also a school of writing in that most famous of schools for writing, France. Faulkner, who in any event never belonged to this group and had his war experience cracking up an old crate in the Royal Flying Corps in Canada, obviously did not model *Soldiers' Pay* on clean French prose. And 1917–1918 was always to seem less significant to Faulkner than 1861–1865. But looking back now on Hemingway and his nearest friends and rivals, a "lost" generation that found its greatest possible chance in literature by getting to the "Great War" as ambulance drivers, we can see that the famous directness, concreteness, precision so fundamental to these writers arose from the assurance that war was just another tragedy in man's experience. And tragedy was enough to carry a writer in those days, for in tragedy the self was not destroyed from within. With tragedy you knew where you were, always in mortal combat. Death was the only enemy. Constantly facing the greater power of nature and the universe, a man could rise to heroism just as he rose to a clear knowledge of the odds against him in a well-defined godless universe. In tragedy, there was still that instinctive unconscious connection with nature which Hemingway always celebrated lyrically; there was a necessary connection between his sense of the "unmistakable" and the writer's own strength. The "unmistakable" kept man and history in order by keeping them apart. The desired clarity of the lost generation can now be seen as the last example of the pure tragic sense in our literature. The combatants — man and his unfriendly destiny — were like actors well-practiced in the tolerable roles of Achilles and Hector lined up against each other through all eternity.

Hemingway's was the perfect reduction, the ultimate logic, of this modernist faith: what was unmistakable would be indestructible. Immortality existed, for artists. Dos Passos, with the same esthetic, was able to organize this special gift for one-to-one definition into the mechanics of *U.S.A.* The same urgency of form explains the felt excitement behind Fitzgerald's fiction — "the stamp that goes into my books so that people can read it

blind like Braille." In the opening of *Tender Is the Night*
(as published in the original edition), the honeyed words
about the hotel and "its bright tan prayer rug of a beach,"
one sees that same love of what oneself has made, that
ardor of precision, that achieved separateness of the
made world from the decadent world that has died from
our vision in giving birth to this beauty. As a style in the
largest sense, a way of putting everything into succession,
this dream of literature as perfect order was to show
itself in the design-typography with which E. E. Cummings's lines fell into place, in the excision of whatever
was "vague," "religious," "shadowy," like Kafka, from
Edmund Wilson's critical admiration. These writers were
the last embodiment and justification of their fathers'
rugged individualism. They had class in both senses of
the word, and they had social confidence, for they still
believed in civilization — a community of mind with their
adoring readers. Everything about them suggested an ir-
resistible quality of both nostalgia and regret for the
American past. Better than anyone else, Scott Fitzgerald
gave voice to this in the elegies that round out *The Great
Gatsby*.

This severe modernist esthetic, this faith in a conscious
perfectibility through the right ordering of words, was the
property of rebellious privileged children of the upper
middle class. Hemingway, Fitzgerald, Dos Passos, Cummings all had the strongest possible sense of the breakdown of *their* moral inheritance — "you are all a lost
generation" — and of their own exceptionality and luster
as individuals. As Nick Carraway said in *The Great
Gatsby*, "I am a little complacent from growing up in a

town where houses are named after the people who have always lived in them." Society was corrupt but intact. There was invisible support in what Dos Passos was to remember as "the best of times." The word is central when continuity is assured. Art was rebellion against one's fathers, and when you beat them, there was the immortality not known to businessmen, doctors, lawyers and professors. Hemingway, Fitzgerald, Dos Passos, like their patron saints Eliot, Pound and Joyce, believed that writers are cleverer and more prophetic than anyone else — "antennae of the race," said Ezra Pound, who knew exactly where the future was heading.* They were the orphic leaders, they had the ruling instinct, they knew what made writing *writing*. And above all, they believed in glory.

When the going got just a little tough, in the early Thirties, Hemingway knew that "The great thing is to last and get your work done and see and hear and learn and understand. . . . Let those who want to save the world if you can get to see it clear and as whole. Then any part you make will represent the whole if it's made truly."

No one else bet so assuredly on the future as did Hemingway. No one else came so much to identify literature with the *act* of writing, writing as the word-for-word struggle against the murkiness of death. Getting it right subjected Hemingway so rigorously to its code that in his last years a novel became wholly a series of symbols for Hemingway and his material. He preserved a look of dogged clarity even when the single words swelled and

---

* "This wouldn't have happened if they had read *L'Education sentimentale*," said Flaubert after the Paris Commune.

broke. Like the world in which he was now writing, he was being pulled out of orbit. In *The Old Man and the Sea* the reader is conscious of Hemingway's despairing will, of what was always most distinct in Hemingway and remained beautiful to the end — his power to invest a passage with the force of his effort.

> *Before it was really light he had his baits out and was drifting with the current. One bait was down forty fathoms. The second was at seventy-five and the third and fourth were down in the blue water at one hundred and twenty-five fathoms. Each bait hung down with the shank of the hook inside the bait fish, tied and sewed solid and all the projecting part of the hook, the curve and the point, were covered with fresh sardines. Each sardine was hooked through eyes so that they made a half-garland on the projecting steel. There was no part of the hook that a great fish could feel which was not sweet-smelling and tasty.*

Clarity was held in these words, but would more than the word live in these words? The idea of "a separat peace," of a certain privilege created by tradition, would not be sustained by what now showed itself as the destructiveness — not the mere "corruption" — of contemporary history.

After Hemingway, the "unmistakable" as the point of style, his special clarity and grace, was to become a faint memory in the violently flashing images with which Nathanael West rendered the atomized emotions of *Miss Lonelyhearts* and the surrealistically overpainted Hollywood of *The Day of the Locust*. West was as prophetic of a new consciousness in fiction as Hemingway had been in his day; his instinct about the ever-growing disturbance around him was to survive him (he was killed speeding to Scott Fitzgerald's funeral in 1940), although even his best writing was impatient, unsteady, and composed by violently oscillating passages, like action painting twenty years later. But the emphasis on prose fiction as "one great form" that had grown out of the connection of narrative rhythms with poetry (both Hemingway and Faulkner felt themselves to be failed poets) was to have one amazing revival, after the war, in Malcolm Lowry's *Under the Volcano* (1947). This extraordinarily accomplished, complex, thoroughly woven novel, one of the last great tributes to high art in the contemporary novel, sets the disintegration of "the Consul," an English alcoholic in Mexico, a kind of historical-musical motif in the style of *The Magic Mountain*, into the darkening atmosphere of fascist triumph that climaxed in Hitler's war.

Under the Volcano is a novel of twentieth-century political hell which in its complex structure, its use of simultaneity on all levels, its desperate fullness of language and occult learning, constantly seeks to explain the individual's despair by the disintegration of the established order. It is a novel about the triumph of evil, on "the Day of the Dead" in Cuernavaca, that constantly asserts itself as the most expressive form of conjunction between man's inner and outer worlds. Far from seeking to exclude and to reduce, in Hemingway's tradition of scornful understatement, Lowry weaves together, in sentences, chapters, sections, in his use of punctuation and paragraph structure, the ominous involvement of the most intimate body sensations with the world crumbling within him. The Consul's drunkenness is a magnetic field where everything is driven toward its inescapable link with everything else. Like the physical Mexico that constantly excites and unsettles him, the Consul's moral world is maddeningly part of something more. This is Lowry's theme, his political intelligence, the obsession behind the unresting conjunctions of his style. It is this desperate unity of the book that links *Under the Volcano* with *The Magic Mountain, Journey to the End of the Night* and so many earlier twentieth-century epic novels rather than with Hemingway's glistening monads of wholly personal experience. The correspondence between the lethal surrender of the Consul to his drunkenness and the Mexican fascists who contemptuously get rid of him as if he were a piece of dirt is what Lowry seeks for his novel more than anything else. The circles ringing poor Geoffrey Firmin round and round are circles of heaven and hell that he has studied in cabalistic books. But Heaven and Hell are now as close to Geoffrey as they were to Swedenborg and Blake. The whole novel represents a magnification of abilities, betrayals and despairs to the point when they are felt as cosmic events. When Yvonne, the Consul's ex-wife, is stomped to death by a runaway horse, the planets come into her death gasp. And this is convincing, part of the furiously grasping consciousness linking together political nemesis, the physical face and terror of Mexico, and the fascist thugs of the late Thirties, in love with evil and rushing everyone else to war.

Hemingway's faith in the "unmistakable," the linear, was to become an heirloom that could not be passed on. It would be remembered — it would earn Hemingway the immortality reserved for one who had known how to treasure the moment, how to make style a preservative of one's own sacred experiences. But even before 1939, this particular style of elegant clarity, of confident American downrightness, had been upstaged by Kafka in those books that were to have a greater influence in English than they would ever have in German, by Jean-Paul Sartre in *Nausea*, by Joyce in the ultimate post-novel that is *Finnegans Wake*. Perhaps the greatest challenge to Hemingway was to come from Faulkner, whose unselfconscious originality of technique, his absorption in the one many-sided story he had to tell, showed narrative not as a triumph *over* experience, but as the struggle of language to find support for the mind in its everlasting struggle with the past.

Hemingway said that he was proud of not writing like "the author of the Octonawhoopoo stories." But Hemingway died of Faulkner as much as he died of Hemingway. In Hemingway's last years it was Faulkner, coming up after having been ignored so long, who was to be a constant shock and bewilderment to Hemingway in the new age of ambiguity. Faulkner was another name for a world — for history — that could not be reduced to a style.

2

THE SECRET OF THE SOUTH
Faulkner to Percy

The eternal mystery of the world is its intelligibility.

— Albert Einstein

FAULKNER SLIPPED OUT OF LIFE with his usual indifference to what people thought. It was an unexpected, a wholly private death, unrelated to literature, even to his literature, and to what some people might have counted on in the manner of a great man's death. A year after Hemingway died on the front page, Faulkner went off after a binge, as if dying was nobody's business but his own.

Flem Snopes's wife in *The Town* shot herself out of sheer boredom. There was a familiar elusiveness about Faulkner even at the end; he had always made a point of being completely private, the most inaccessible and unassimilable writer in the United States, the last countryman in America, the uncompromised product of the poorest, most violent, most scandalously backward state in the Union, an "aristocrat" in a mobocracy. A school principal in Oxford said to a friend of mine: "You can tell from his writing Mr. Faulkner never had a proper education." Faulkner once wrote to Malcolm Cowley: "I think I have written a lot and sent it off to print before I actually realised strangers might read it." Where Hemingway always wrote straight at the reader, to present him with a picture, Faulkner's books seemed parts of each other, like dreams of the same man. Unlike Hemingway, who trained himself to write, each time, like a champion who must not lose, Faulkner gave the impression first of not writing for anybody, then of not knowing whether he had an audience, and finally of not caring what this audience thought. He stood apart, musing, questioning, engaged in some surrender to his own thought in all its ramifications and considerations. Wherever his thought took him, he would go; like Oxford, Mississippi, his mind was a place he could always go back to. Even when he got up to address an audience, he would speak in an inaudible monotone — he would face the audience, but by God he would not make any effort to communicate with it. He just did not function by "communicating"; he could not put himself in the place of an audience.

Yet from the late Forties on, this elusive and unassimilable mind had become the dominating imagination among American novelists, was inspirational and popular while the fierce idiosyncrasy of his genius kept him above the crowd, an intoxication to many storytellers in Europe and America. He was now the embodiment of everything that made Southern writers feel that their time had come — even when, like Flannery O'Connor, they worshipfully complained that "The presence alone of Faulkner in our midst makes a great difference in what the writer can and cannot permit himself to do. Nobody wants his mule and wagon stalled on the same track the Dixie Limited is roaring down."

After years of being the most difficult and supposedly the most unreadable of American novelists, Faulkner had suddenly, in the America after 1945 that had caught up with him, become the most commanding. In Cartier-

Bresson's great photograph, he stood in front of his pil-
lared house in Oxford, looking every inch a Compson,
Sartoris, De Spain, who unlike the Compsons, Sartorises,
De Spains in his books, was making it to the end. He
counted more than Hemingway did now, and Hemingway
knew it. He even pitied Hemingway — "I thought that he
found out early what he could do and stayed inside of that.
He never did try to get outside the boundary of what he
really could do and risk failure. He did what he really
could do marvelously well, first rate, but to me that is not
success but failure . . . failure to me is the best. To try
something you can't do . . . to try it and fail, then try it
again. That to me is success."

Ralph Ellison said that Faulkner, despite *nigger* on
every other page, unlocked his own Southern imagination. Sartre, who found in *The Sound and the Fury* more
universal significance than Malraux had guessed at in
Sanctuary, saw Faulkner's achievement as the most brilliant solution to the problem of time in the contemporary
novel. In these last fifteen years or so of Faulkner's life,
his much derided novels (all out of print when Malcolm
Cowley superbly anthologized him in the *Viking Portable
Faulkner*, a principal instrument of his revival when it
was published in April 1946), became the most intensely
imagined and comprehensive record of separateness,
powerlessness, poverty, mania, defeat, of a pride and
secret renewal unknown to anyone but an isolated Southerner. Faulkner now incarnated boldness of imagination
and force of style, deeply internalized memories and
grievances, the real travail of Southern experience, blood
and soil and trouble. At a time when the Bomb was still

thought to be the exclusive possession of America, when American power was so overwhelming that it seemed that one people could destroy all life on the planet, Faulkner's obsession with the old, the local, the weak but "unvanquished," gave back to America a particular passion, a power of attachment to the outworn and the provincial. Elizabeth Hardwick of Kentucky, living in Boston, complained that the different parts of the country were being ground down to the consistency of cornmeal. At a time when American writers helplessly attacked bigness, commercialism, the facility of mass communications, Faulkner expressed the primeval force at the heart of human conduct, the violence and intractability and mad obstinacy of the human heart. In Faulkner the South justified its last claim to be the great exception. Mark Twain at last had a successor, a spirit as large as his own — who was a far better novelist.

The essential thing in all these books was a sense of havoc and conflict, of human storm, blood madness and the irrational, of the unconscious possessing the human spirit but using it, as Hegel's World Spirit used man, to make history. History always implies meaning. There is a pattern, moral even when it is post-Christian. Everything in Faulkner came back to man as a conflict which pressed for expression as history, not for solution. Faulkner's world was passionate, human, real, was solidly grounded in human violence and the fierce interminabilities of the human will. Facing on every side the consequences of the human tendency to abrupt and fatal action, his characters would go on meditating the consequences of their action — not from any hope of moderating what from the first moment had been beyond them — but from the inevitable need of thought to live with the consequences of action.

The turbulent unstoppable pressure of inner consciousness based on conflict with oneself, others, the "world" as our insufficient home, gives the immediate fiery texture to Faulkner's novels. When you grasp in *The Sound and the Fury* the embattled daily experience of Benjy, Quentin, and Jason Compson, in *Light in August* the futile dream of home obsessing Joe Christmas as he runs in a state of sleep ahead of the posse, you feel that fiction has expressed the unconscious strife of our lives, not a literary personification of *the* "unconscious." There is no more moving expression of unarticulated violence than the idiot Benjy's description in *The Sound and the Fury* of frightening a girl on her way home from school:

> *I was trying to say, and I caught her, trying to say, and she screamed and I was trying to say and trying and the bright shapes began to stop and I tried to get out.*

Each Compson, as he talks his story, is eloquent with a dream that is outside his actual life. Faulkner at his best, in *The Sound and the Fury*, works with authenticity of emotion that comes only when every issue is given its specific weight, style and tone. Even the lack of coherence on the part of Benjy, the idolatry of language on the part of Quentin, becomes a whirlwind of inner creatingness, moves all parts of the Compson family history into being as one of incessant strife. "History" ends up as a book, and the voices of this family live history over and over.

27

What they lived was in fact their own doom; in a sense they all killed each other off. Faulkner liked to say that "the past is never dead. It is not even past." Its reverberations inside the human mind are continuous. All one's efforts as a man must be to understand what *has* been done. Faulkner showed a Shakespearean sense of language as parallel to action, another kind of action, able to write history but not change it. In the beginning was the deed. Man was given that "one anonymous chance to perform something passionate and brave and austere not just in but into man's enduring chronicle . . . in gratitude for the gift of time in it." He could realize his experience only after he had lived it. The doing and the realizing are inaccessible to each other, and this also is the human conflict. The heart is blind, hot, passionate, insatiable beyond anything we admit. Man explodes himself in the service of his passions; his ambition constantly destroys the society he thinks the foundation of moral order. Yet once the deed is done, it is irrevocable; thought alone puts the story together — the artist is a chronicler going back into the havoc that has never ended.

Faulkner's account of the relation between action and thought, violence and literature is of course an apology for the South, but hardly limited to that. Where but from his history can man draw his metaphysics? In "The Bear" the saintly hunter Ike McCaslin and his cousin McCaslin Edmonds, going over the records of the eccentric twin uncles in slave times who did try to alleviate the condition of their slaves, agree with each other that slavery put a curse on the land that had been given to man as God's free gift. Man rushed slaves into the South with the same heedlessness and pride with which he tried to claim the land itself — the land which even the Indians did not "own." The act of appropriation in Faulkner is usually blind; it is the blood speaking, and over the act *heedless* and *proud*, as Faulkner liked to say, the doer later stands *amazed*. Action and recognition are dramatically separated; man is a creature of passions over which his rational will has no dominion. But the retrospect of history is endless, the irrevocability of action, tragic. And the humility and charity that may come with this awareness, symbolized in Ike McCaslin's development from the boy eager to play a man's role in the hunt to the old Ike who detaches himself from all ties and comes to love the wilderness for its own sake, constitutes Faulkner's deepest belief — virtue is powerless, and extreme powerlessness, as in Benjy the "Christ-figure," is virtue. Virtue intervenes when power is gone. The South in 1861, belligerently full of itself, is unconscious of the burdens of war which its descendants will be struggling with in the twentieth century. Faulkner, the great-grandson ·of a slaveowner who was a murderer as proud of being the last gentleman as Colonel Sherburn in *Huckleberry Finn*, feels older to himself than his ancestors do. *His* burden of awareness makes him a seasoned old man by temperament, contemplative and alone by contrast with the Jeb Stuarts and other romantic Confederate leaders who in his work appear dashing, young, suicidally romantic and innocent. *They* rushed into war, they took on an opponent clearly stronger than themselves, they were magnificent in their folly. It was left to their descendants, turned middle class and into writers of books, to tell the story.

No wonder that one hears in Faulkner the wish that the past had never happened — or what for a Southerner can be the same thing, that the Civil War is still in the balance, that the worst hasn't happened yet and perhaps won't. A boy in the South could still wish for that.

> *For every Southern boy fourteen years old, not once but whenever he wants it, there is the instant when it's still not two o'clock on that July afternoon in 1863, the brigades are in position behind the rail fence, the guns are laid and ready in the woods, and the furled flags are already loosened to break out and Pickett himself with his long oiled ringlets and his hat in one hand probably and his sword in the other looking up the hill waiting for Longstreet to give the word and it's all in the balance, it hasn't happened yet. . . .*

The deepest expression of this longing to rerun the past back to a moment before catastrophe is put into the mouth of poor Mrs. Hines, grandmother of the murderer Joe Christmas, when she says in *Light in August*:

> *I am not saying that he never did what they say he did. Ought not to suffer for it like he made them that loved and lost suffer. But if folks could maybe just let him for one day. Like it hadn't happened yet. If it could be like that for one day.*

So intense is Faulkner's belief in thought as rumination over a past completed, final, irrevocable, that in the famous middle section of "The Bear," incidents of slave-keeping are recited from their uncles' account books by Ike McCaslin and McCaslin Edmonds as if they were chanting the past together in wonder and grief. "The Bear" suggests that history is only retrospect; man must tell over and over the story of his fatal deed until he finds the obstinate human touch that sums up every story. At any point, as happens in this middle section of "The Bear," a man can take down the ledgers of the past and uncover the story. But though the past can be stopped like a movie reel and rerun like a film, it can only be meditated and retold. Each of us, as we review the past, becomes as old as thought itself as we look at our younger selves blindly rushing through the past. And this is what makes the final moral development of Ike McCaslin in "The Bear" so beautiful a legend, for admitting that slavery was a curse, Ike lightens himself of its burden; he becomes his own redeemer. This growth is possible only when the chronicle of man's past lives in a man's mind as if he had lived all of it and were now responsible to all of it.

Surely this explains the attempt, in "The Bear," to make a single sentence out of so many pages. This is the most famous instance of what Faulkner described as "my ambition to put everything into one sentence — not only the present but the whole past on which it depends and which keeps overtaking the present." He was accountable only to the laws of his own thought, and there are single units in his writing — sentences, paragraphs, pages, whole narrative sections — which are great waves of passion, recrimination, anguish, and doubt, beating against the rock of man's past. There *was* a great guilt incurred in the South, a curse *was* put on the land that was given to all men freely to enjoy. Faulkner does not excuse this guilt, he does not apologize for it, he does not evade it. He is a Southerner and has a great story to tell. Man's immortality, if he can be said to have one at all, reaches into the past, not into the future: it lies in a candid sense of history, not in the hope offered by orthodox Christianity. The peculiar parallels to Christ that Faulkner finds in his most miserable characters, Benjy in *The Sound and the Fury*, Joe Christmas in *Light in August*, refer to those who have escaped the common guilt by reason of some disability — those who have never lived, because they have always been victims of other people. Those who act, who have power, those who in imagination one can still see riding across the screen of history, can never alter the course of action. Sartre was right when he said of *The Sound and the Fury* that Faulkner cuts off the future. That was necessary to Faulkner, for as Sartre's own erratic development shows, to choose the "future" over everything else makes intellect impatient and manipulative, takes the heart out of art. To be so much bound up with the past, to locate it entirely in one's own work, was a luxury that "modern masters" like Faulkner were able to enjoy before the rate of change overtook the contemporary novel. Faulkner in his greatest works was willingly old in order not to betray those who had been rash in their youth. In no other American writer is this obligation to the past so complex as in this greatest Southern writer — who more than most writers has interrogated the past and has not been able to escape it in one moment of thought.

Faulkner's resurrection in his own lifetime, his all-dominating fame after 1948, came just as the "present" now began to overtake the past. When he was interviewed in Japan, Faulkner recalled the time when he wrote in rapid order *Sartoris, The Sound and the Fury, Light in August, As I Lay Dying.* "I think there's a period in a writer's life . . . one matchless time, when they are matched completely. The speed, and the power and the talent, they're all here and then he is — . . . 'hot' . . ." Faulkner had from the first depended on the vagaries of his own thought, was so much the "sole owner and proprietor of Yoknapatawpha County" that as he mellowed, relaxed in his fame, and began to editorialize about civil rights, the Bomb, honor, to have "ideas," he became a Wisdom Figure rather more entertaining than anything else. Faulkner had always been a great joker, if only by his gift for exaggeration. He could blow up any single human trait in his inimitable style. Luxuriating in his own creations and creatingness, rather than to create new believable stories, he now liked to tell anecdotes about his familiar characters. He often went in for private jokes, self-quotation, a speechifying so clownishly intemperate that he sounded like W. C. Fields chuckling mysteriously over his half-articulated asides.

In these obviously windy books — *Intruder in the Dust, Requiem for a Nun, A Fable, The Town, The Mansion, The Reivers* — the need to complete and round out the design that has carried us this far is actually more pressing now than any particular story. Jefferson is more vivid in *Requiem for a Nun* than the labored rededication of Temple Drake and the self-sacrifice of her servant Nancy Mannigoe. The Negro Lucas Beauchamp in *Intruder in the Dust* is more wise and Olympian than any Negro has been in Faulkner's books, while Faulkner openly discusses the relation of his class to the sudden Negro upsurge with an opinion-atedness that might have shocked the creator of Dilsey. *A Fable* gives us not the old "Christ-figures," Benjy the idiot and Joe Christmas the vagrant, who represent total exposure to suffering, but Christ Himself disguised as a French corporal leading a mutiny in 1917. For Faulkner the most widespread "fable" is now more than the story of an actual man could be. *The Town* and *The Mansion* complete his history of the Snopeses — begun in *The Hamlet* (1940) — by denaturing almost all Snopeses from rapacious peasants into mere freaks. Faulkner had originally conceived the Snopeses — we thought! — as vandals stealing their way into the established order and taking over from the "aristocratic" landowners. But as the rednecks and tenant farmers actually began to rise up to the middle class which the Faulkners had descended to "in order to survive,"* Faulkner's conceit that *Snopeses* were not human — "maybe even a species of pure sons of bitches," as Montgomery Ward Snopes says in *The Mansion* — turned them into Jukes and Kallikaks whose weird, unkillable obstinacy alone explained their hold on Faulkner's mind. To "endure," to persist, to outtrick and outstay had always been the prime human trait to Faulkner. For eighteen years Mink Snopes waits in the Mississippi State Penitentiary to get out and kill his cousin Flem. Yet he allows Flem to trick him into trying an escape in woman's clothes, is

---

* "Past the eighty years (1865–1945), the old reconstructed had died off at last, the strong among the remaining realised that to survive they must stop trying to be pre 1861 barons and become a middle class, they did so, and began to create a literature." [Faulkner to Malcolm Cowley]

promptly given another twenty years, and when he is
finally released in 1946 goes right ahead to kill Flem —
who long before this has turned from a social menace
into a joke, and inertly waits at home for Mink to kill
him.

These last books were not sequels to the great works
— *The Sound and the Fury, Light in August, Absalom,
Absalom!* — so much as they were continuations of an
instinct. Faulkner's insistence on carrying his "saga" to
where there was no saga was based not on the fascinations of one class (or race) accommodating another as
on his belief that people never change. Endurance is all.
Obstinacy is character. He pushed his design through —
he did not carry it out — at a time when even the characters in his own novels were inconsistent with what
they had been, when the novel as a form — his own not
least — was eluding every attempt to identify it with
"permanent" values, the "moral order" behind History.
But in all these last books one sees, along with his new-
found benignity and his surprising use of fiction to
lecture everyone in sight (a little moral advice might
settle the conflict which he felt as a worried Southerner
not unsympathetic to the Negro) the wholly contem-
poraneous belief that American history is a cycle that
may have played itself out. The returns are all in, one
can see with Darwinian completeness the whole scale of
evolution on this continent. The site on which the court-
house stands in *Requiem for a Nun* has seen everything.
So Jefferson is the clue to everything that has taken
place in the New World. Faulkner was not only writing
a conscious final chapter to his own work, but univer-

salizing it, swelling it out with visions of "when the last ding-dong of doom has clanged and faded from the last worthless rock hanging tideless in the last red and dying evening." The doom of man was now becoming a big thing with Americans, and with Southerners long excluded from the native belief in perfectibility, a joke on their old enemies. Faulkner was not the only Wisdom Figure in his own novels; he had lieutenants. Even the sewing machine agent V. K. Ratliff, whose "washed patched collarless shirt" was once so important an image of the South's poverty, has become as big a gasbag as Gavin Stevens as they communicate Faulkner's "amusement" and "quizzical amazement at human folly."

Faulkner now had the field to himself — was not merely the survivor of his great generation but the spokesman to America itself in its now rueful imperial greatness. But these pronouncements seemed a poor substitute for the great novels. The intense sense of place, of the South to itself alone, of human personality for *its* own sake, was being unloosed and undone. It was the self-sufficient thickness of the immediate scene, the unalterable amount of circumstance, a "world" made so by persons who were nothing but themselves, that had made Faulkner's books so right to our minds. It was a world full of persons who had nothing to do but exist in his pages. They were not registers or conductors of anything. Yet they did not conceive of themselves as their own agents and their own highest interest. They knew themselves to be limited, and driven, part of a process, put in motion by the "Player," as Faulkner calls It or

Him at the end of *Light in August*. Life was an *agon* or contest, never a free fall.

"Why has the South produced so many good writers?" Walker Percy was asked when he won the National Book Award for *The Moviegoer*. "Because we got beat." But that was only half the answer, as Percy's stockbroker hero showed in his search for the specific place necessary to the human mind. The Southern writer always knew himself part of History, a larger meaning, whether it was America the colossus, the juggernaut, the great melting pot into which he did not want to melt; or the process of "sin and error," as Southerners liked to say about slavery and more than slavery; or the sheer accumulation of ancestry, history, race superstition as second nature. The Southern writer felt himself expressed by a force larger than himself. There was an unconscious depth to his writing.

In these postwar years, it looked as if "the South" had become the best country for American literature. Readers in the great cities, already weary of civilization, were awed by the "pinewiney silence of the August afternoon," the stillness of the lonely baking mill town, the "dust and the heat" that reminded Camus of his native Algeria, the smoky torches carried by naked mud-caked slaves, the now ghostly always "decaying" mansion, the hysterical baptizings, the revival meetings, the maddened farmers, the redneck in a state of empty mindless choler at the *niggers*, the country store smelling of stale crackers and kerosene, politicians called Willie Joe, dogs called Timmy's Turley, rifles ominously raised from the swamp. There was Katherine Anne Porter, Allen Tate, John Crowe Ransom, Caroline Gordon, Robert Penn Warren, Tennessee Williams, Eudora Welty, Carson McCullers, Randall Jarrell, James Agee, Truman Capote, Peter Taylor, James Purdy, Elizabeth Hardwick, Andrew Lytle, Cleanth Brooks — as soon there would be Flannery O'Connor, Madison Jones, Reynolds Price, Walker Percy, James Dickey, Donald Barthelme, Shirley Ann Grau, Cecil Dawkins.

Southern novelists had just the right landscape; Southern poets and critics, the most corrective ideas. Traditionalist by habit, by affection, and now by opportunity, the brilliant descendants of unsullied Protestants became more Catholic than the College of Cardinals. The emptiness of modern liberalism, humanitarianism, secularism was never so clear as it was to Southern writers admonishing Northern audiences. Reviewing *Brother to Dragons*, Robert Penn Warren's narrative poem about the ghastly butchering of a slave by the brother of Meriwether Lewis, once Jefferson's secretary and then the great explorer with William Clark of the Pacific Northwest, Randall Jarrell wrote with particular satisfaction in the *New York Times Book Review* that

> the live Jefferson had not prepared Lewis for the ignoble truth of man's depravity; the dead Jefferson hammers it home with ignoble avidity. The dead Jefferson looks at the obscene underside of the stone — he can do no other — licks his lips; he knows, now. Most of us know, now, that Rousseau was wrong; that man, when you knock his chains off, sets up the death camps. Soon we

*shall know everything the eighteenth century didn't
know, and nothing it did, and [it] will be hard to live
with us.*

Faulkner, laughing at his own excesses, had described
his style in a letter to Cowley as "oratory out of solitude." Southerners were in fact famous for spilling over,
for talking too much and writing too hard, for a large-
ness and passion of temperament. But Southern poet-
critics were stricter than anyone else in insisting on
"achieved form," "balance of tensions," "the well-
wrought urn," "coordination of effect." The highest
achievement of literature seemed to be a short story in
which no blemish could be detected, a short poem
"perfectly" expressive of the necessary paradox and
ambiguity.

The Southern critics in these years of the "new criticism" created the image of literature as the final and
best word on every human predicament. T. S. Eliot, who
never believed this, had been concerned with pure effect
in modern poetry; his famous early essays cleared the
ground for a closer, more workmanlike study of poetry.
But the Southerners who worked in his light were not
as much at home in Sewanee and Nashville as Eliot was
in London. They found their audience not in the South,
which had never cared for any of the great Southern
writers and certainly did not care for the difficult new
poetry, but in the great universities and intellectual centers of the North, where their classical training, their
passion for poetry, their perfect respect for tradition,
their abounding literary intelligence, to say nothing of

their unreconstructed Southern temperament, made them the most "creative" and convincing indoctrinators of literature-as-religion to American undergraduates who were without either. In Tate, Warren and Brooks literature was literature that could be taught as perfection; literature became a "city of the soul." Literature was somehow the only school of thought: moral, philosophical, Christian, it was presumed more inquisitive than science, more believable than religion. Literature was taught as the Summa of all wisdom to people who still believed that criticism was a counterculture.*

Every experience was fitted to the fashionable terms of criticism. History seemed to Americans peculiarly, unjustly intractable in those years after the war when everything conspired to make liberals "disillusioned" and conservatives paranoid. The kind of intellectual removal more naturally at home in English departments than anywhere else, made it natural to repeat after Joyce that "History is the nightmare from which I am trying to awaken," after Eliot that *Ulysses* showed a way out of "the immense panorama of futility and anarchy that is contemporary history," after Robert Penn Warren in *All the King's Men* that man is conceived in sin and raised in dirt from the didie to the shroud. Corruption was the natural order of things, goodness could rise only out of badness. The images of perfectibility so dear to the more credulous Americans, less experienced in defeat, had to be replaced by the Southern experience.

* Randall Jarrell said during the "Age of Criticism" that certain married couples depended on a favorite literary critic as once they would have depended on a liberal clergyman.

But *whose* experience was this? The Southern writer after 1945 was a prophet speaking against Leviathan and for the old South as the beloved country. He showed up the fiction behind the unwieldy construction "America"; he had evidence long before it became fashionable that America had become too big and powerful for its own good. His prejudice against megalopolis, abstraction, secularism, the soullessness of industrial civilization, rested on his images of the Southern countryside, the Southern small town, the Southern farmer in his old patched overalls. He might not be able to live in the South, he might not even find his audience there, but every Southern writer had this ability to see himself as the South. He was the conscience of his race — where the antagonist of "the South" was the old forces personified by the North. But now these same forces were dominating the South. The Snopeses were becoming more truculently "American" than anyone else. They had already become the South's populist rabble-rousers and spokesmen as they moved ahead of the old genteel, literary, schoolmaster class from which so many Southern writers came. Faulkner's conception of the Snopeses working their way out of Frenchman's Bend, from hamlet to town to mansion — this, brilliantly funny as it was, had not prepared Faulkner to think of a Snopes in the governor's mansion, as a senator in Washington, as a presidential candidate running on nothing but white supremacy. Faulkner thought the Snopeses were a family, not a social mass; genetic monstrosities, they were condescended to as peasants whose one skill was plotting against their betters. Faulkner conceived their malignity as doing each other in rather than as a form of social ascendency. Flem Snopes's whole secret turns out to have been that he was impotent, like Popeye; impotence was Faulkner's symbol for the gangsters from Memphis and Flem Snopes from Frenchman's Bend. The great-grandson of Colonel William Falkner, who wrote *The White Rose of Memphis*, could not use the real war at home — between the Faulkners and the Bilbos, Varda-mans, Huey Longs, Willie Starks and Lester Maddoxes.

Robert Penn Warren in these years put into fiction some concrete social antagonisms. In his most famous novel, *All the King's Men* (1946), Warren took on directly, from his observations of the Huey Long ma-chine while he was teaching at Louisiana State, the worst kind of political oligarchy ever created in the modern South by an ambitious totally demagogic lower-class politician. This was the kind of rough subject which the "Fugitives" and Warren's fellow Rhodes Scholars had rather overlooked in favor of their generalized literary views of the South. But while the particular motif of Warren's fiction (and of his poetry and criti-cism) was original sin, this took the form even in War-ren's fluent, forceful fiction of some unalterable division within the psyche, of the agonizing struggle for goodness within the natural context of sin, corruption, betrayal. Conflict was no more than an idea. Although Warren was to describe with extensive brilliance the social-politi-cal scene in a state very much like Huey Long's Louisi-ana, *All the King's Men* is not about politics. Not only is it not a novel about politics, power, class, bossism; it is a novel about the danger to the South's dreamed stability in sexual transgression; it is an energetic dramatization of Warren's preoccupation with the evil in man that leads him to the wrong bed. There is always a "split in man"; man is a "forked radish."

The most beautiful single section of *All the King's Men*, called "Cass Mastern's Wedding Ring" when it was published separately, is the story of a love affair on the eve of the Civil War between a married woman and her husband's best friend. Cass Mastern's guilt applies also to his indulgence of his mistress's viciousness to a young slave girl who discovered her secret, to the guilt of slavery itself, as this victim of sexual passion tries to atone by getting himself killed in the Civil War. The specific wrongdoing to another human being somehow gets muffled in Cass Mastern's self-concern with guilt. Warren's extremely literary and theoretical conception of social oppression — a pain somehow suffered more by Cass Mastern than by a slave — is shown in the importance given to Cass Mastern's passion for his friend's wife. The most vital situations in the Louisiana of the Thirties somehow turn on the fact that your (sexual) sin shall find you out. Willie Stark orders his assistant Jack Burden to get the goods on a supposedly honorable judge who opposes him; the judge turns out to be Jack's real father and shoots himself. Dr. Adam Stanton shoots Willie Stark after discovering that his sister Anne is Willie's mistress. Adam the innocent is really in love with his own sister but doesn't know enough to admit it; Jack Burden knows his is the burden of "History" as corruption — he is the boss's digger-up of dirt on other people, a coward who loves Anne Stanton and might have saved her from the boss. But he is too conscious of evil all around him, and rather than love Anne Stanton busies himself with condemnations of a generation that believes only in nature and knows not the difference between good and evil.

All the King's Men is a tribute to Warren's literary intelligence and his ability to work up a dramatic situation. But the most obvious quality of the book is the failure of the principal characters to grow believably into the vital situations that are supposed to prove man's disposition to evil. There is no real connection between Willie Stark the naïve political rube and the diabolically clever and ruthlessly all-powerful Willie Stark who takes over the state; no connection between Jack Burden's disgust with his much-married mother and the horror of all that sin in American history that allows him to do Willie Stark's dirty work for him. Nor is the secret liaison between Willie and the patrician Anne Stanton anything but a symbolic expression of the surrender of an aristocrat to an upstart. Machiavelli is Warren's political oracle, but "illicit" sex seems to be the only misfortune of the State. That Willie should be shot down in the Capitol by Adam is a reflection only of Adam's pathological "purity." His social disdain for Willie is not part of the plot, which turns to melodrama. The gap between what Warren thinks of as the "ideal" and the "real" — between one fork of the "human radish" and the other — can be filled in only with bookish themes, Adam's unconscious love for his sister, Jack Burden's Hamlet-like jealousy of his mother, Anne Stanton's surrender of

44

her beauty to the beast. The "rough" characters around the Boss — Sadie Burke, Sugar Boy, Tiny Duffy — are believable only because they are minor actors. The "smooth" characters from an upper class on the defensive — Judge Irwin, Anne Stanton, Jack Burden himself — are unbelievable as major characters because their "corruption" is just pasted on them, symbolizing the helplessness of their class. None of these characters dramatizes anything except Warren's literary, moralistic, psychological conception of personal "motivation."

Yet in *All the King's Men*, as cannot be said of many of his later novels, you hear a voice, you become conscious of an obstinate moral effort, of an urge. Professor Robert Heilman has written admiringly of Warren's "persistent concern with the problem of the 'idea' . . . the ideal or meaning or value which establishes the quality of deed or 'redeems' it — we have the idea as concrete." Perhaps "idea as concrete" expressed it all too well. Since his first and best novel, *Night Rider* (1939), each of Warren's novels has been less interesting than its predecessor. In his early novels one is still aware of Warren the voice, the teacher, the exponent of a traditionalist view of the world that is essentially a philosophy of literature. Warren knows what makes certain literary works great; no critic in our generation has persuaded more people of just what there is to "understand" in poetry and fiction. He tends to *apply* understanding to his own imaginative creations — the understanding is in his voice, his will, his fluent skill. Warren is always in command of the narrative rather than the other way around, expounding the contradictions in human nature and breathing on its symbols. The omnipresent Warren voice, struggling with History, the contradictions of Human Nature and Original Sin as ideas for stories, makes him a sayer of contraries.

The excess and force of so much *saying* is a familiar expression of the Southern writer's identification of himself with the South. The fluency is a stock characteristic of many Southern writers — Thomas Wolfe, James Agee, James Dickey, Truman Capote. The famous, the almost swaggering voice generally combines the easy confidence of upper-class talkers with moral indignation, yet prides itself on being intensely "realistic," on being willing to step into the dirt with the forces that make for so much dirt.

But there is another kind of Southern fiction — Peter Taylor and Walker Percy are current examples, as Carson McCullers and Flannery O'Connor were before them — in which this sometimes overpowering Southern voice is absorbed into the logic of the story itself, in which the prose is entirely close-knit and serviceable, without a breath of fine writing and critical rhetoric. Taylor's fiction takes up directly the subtle moral disarrangements and dislocations within a seemingly immobile middle class. Taylor is all fiction writer and does not seem to want to be anything more. The "little inch of ivory" on which everything is worked out gives his stories an effect of necessity and realization. The shifts are entirely within the stories, do not take us through those harshly contrasting changes of time, scene, history which in many big-writing Southern novelists embody violence to the person even when the novelist seems to be doing all the moving around.

Taylor loves to recite the brand names of candy companies and insurance companies. His subject *is* the executive middle class — its assurances subtly breaking down, the rearrangements being made under the surface. The top middle class seems to be authority in Nashville, but a key situation is the minimizing and subtle reversal of its authority. Authority actually has no power here; the surface of Taylor's stories, entirely domestic, often suburban, conceals the intense Brownian movement of emotions under the surface. Yet these dislocations or rearrangements of authority are more than usually quiet; the manner of a Taylor story is entirely part of the manners it describes, and seems to follow from them; Taylor has just left the party to think it over, but will rejoin it presently. We are in a world where an intense sense of duplication exists from person to person in the same family, from family to family in the same town, from the manner of the story to the matter, from the transparency and pure utility of Taylor's prose to these suburban Southern lives entirely absorbed in the details of living. The closeness of Taylor's workmanship perfectly reflects the habitual unconscious closeness of the group being emphasized here. The crisis usually turns on the sudden awareness of what all this routine has done. Illumination is all. There is almost never any decision forced by violence. There are usually no decisions. There is only the subtle displacement in silent minds still separate from each other.

But the disturbance to the woman in the family, the

central domestic figure, registers the seemingly mild but irreversible shock to a "superior" way of life kept intact by family, money and routine. The "disturbance" to a woman is fundamental. The woman is left with the routine; the men have moved on. The men insist that families and traditions be kept up, but they are not there. In "The Dark Walk," the most concentrated expression of this theme, the widow Sylvia Harrison realizes that "the husbands and fathers in those houses were not the tyrants of another day; . . . it seemed to Sylvia that the husbands had not been there at all . . . . Their lives had been changed in a way that the women's lives were not changed. The men of Nate's time had crossed over a border, had pushed into a new country, or had fled into a new country. And their brides lived as widows clinging to things the men would never come back to and from which they could not free themselves. . . ." Miss Betty in "Two Ladies in Retirement," a story of women as genteel fossils and vestiges, fondly talks about people who had been "prominent in an important way." And Miss Bluemeyer, the old-maid housekeeper to the Wade family in the play *The Death of a Kinsman*, finally speaks out — "I understand a good deal of how this family business works. It makes a woman safe and sure being related this way and that way to everybody around her. And it keeps you from having to bother about anybody else, since they are not 'kinfolks.' " The women are getting mad in both senses of the word. The Negro women servants break out before their men do; in "Bad Dreams" the head of the family reflects that the butler's wife, "a good, hard-working, smart sort of a woman . . .

48

at a moment's notice could get a look so bughouse-wild in her face that you felt you had to talk fast if you were going to keep her calm. Bert's mother had been that sort of woman too. In fact, he felt that most of the women he had ever had much to do with had been that sort. . . ."

There is far less violence in Peter Taylor than there is in Carson McCullers and Flannery O'Connor; but this seemingly intact world in which drama follows only from slight, soundless changes of consciousness has as its center a woman's sensibility precisely because of the contrast between the position she upholds and the slow, inner sapping of her life. The absence of "scenes," friction, strong movement of any kind, is the mark of a good breeding that seems to have worn the material smooth. The craftsmanship, like good manners, makes its points quietly; we are kept in a world in which nothing very much seems to happen only because Taylor is more chivalrous in writing about Southern ladies than they are in writing about themselves. The extraordinary number of talented women writers from the South — Katherine Anne Porter, Caroline Gordon, Eudora Welty, Carson McCullers, Flannery O'Connor, Shirley Ann Grau, Elizabeth Hardwick — also tells us how much Southern fiction springs from families with an intense sense of themselves and their links to the South, families so intricately organized yet extending beyond themselves that a sharp-eyed girl could absorb very early the secrets of the Southern "way of life." The contrast between appearance and reality, the evidence of subtle dissolution along with the hysterical clasping of the past,

49

and above all the dominance of the family, the clan, the group, could give a woman novelist the sense of being in the Southern scene and yet detached from it. She was an expected part and agent of Southern gentility, but no one would be more fascinated with "real" life below it, especially in lonely small towns and on farms.

The extent to which Southern life is composed of deeply woven but separate clans, groups, families, is something that the non-Southern reader carries away most from Southern fiction. Surely it is for the strange foreignness of different races and classes to each other — even when, like black and white, they live closer together than they do elsewhere — the peculiar inhumanness which one group ascribes to another, that explains why the woman who finds her natural subject in the extensive organization of the family also finds herself existing in the space between all the families, in the Southern limbo reserved for its critics and heretics. There is a place for the artist willing to be alone with the South that only certain women have been able to fill.

It is not easy, in talking about two such particularly gifted Southern women writers as Carson McCullers and Flannery O'Connor, to say that the peculiar solitariness from which they wrote, the solitariness (perhaps of another kind) about which they wrote, is due to "the South" — to the contrast between the tradition and the reality. Southern writers have a lot of fables about the South to get over, but no other group has seen life so steadily in terms of fiction, story, legend. The South has

produced writers as the Dark Ages produced saints: the
gifted few who can read the burning letters for themselves in the book of oppression, war, poverty and hate.
Nevertheless there is a Southern book, a Southern legend, created by so much pastness. The South Carolina
gentlemen who in the nineteenth century wouldn't give a
cent to keep a local magazine alive, saying that they
could get all their reading matter from England, were
the same enemy who a century later helped to make
Faulkner independent of Oxford while he wrote about
nothing else. But if we ask to what extent Columbus,
Georgia, helped to make Carson McCullers and Milledgeville, Georgia, Flannery O'Connor, the answer is
less easy to form. Each in her way was doomed from an
early age and knew it; each was dependent on her family
for the sparse numbers of characters in her fiction; each
was a woman novelist in a South that excited her by its
brooding violence, but by its insistent conventions made
her feel that she was a freak.

The terror immanent in their work is not commonplace, is not "social," is not explained, in McCullers, by
the narrowing of all love relationships into solitary ob-
sessions, in O'Connor by the lack of any urgent connection between men and women. One woman was exces-
sively fragile, the other mysteriously impersonal; both
rather specialized in a sense of tragedy, of the over-
powered (mostly feminine) soul, which makes the
strongest character in their work nemesis, some primal
wrongness, — a force which becomes *the* presence as it
so visibly bends them to their subject.

Carson McCullers was a greater myth-maker than she

was a novelist. Her theme was the utter dislocation of love "in our time" and "in our town." Her extreme sense of human separateness took form in deaf-mutes who were also Greek foreigners in the Southern town in which they inexplicably found themselves, Negro doctors maddened by their intellectual isolation, fathers always widowers, and above all a young tomboy who, whether she is too young for sexual love or too odd for it, attributes her own unusedness to everyone else, then projects this "loneliness" against the political terror of the Hitler period and the excessiveness, vacancy, and stillness of summer in the town.

In McCullers what fills the space usually occupied by man-and-woman love is a sensitiveness that charges other people with magical perceptions. She radiated in all her work a demand for love so total that another was to become the perfect giver, and so became magical. The world is so bleak that it is always just about to be transformed. *The Heart Is a Lonely Hunter* (1940) astonishingly comes alive still not only as a virtuoso performance dramatically engaging so many hard solitudes, but also as a novel of the depressed Thirties haunted by the powerlessness of people and the ferocious powers of governments.

McCullers's myth-making power was to fit this obsessive loneliness, this sense of total weakness before real earthly damnation, into the Southern climate, the town in summer, the doldrums of children with nowhere to go. She made many different lacks equal illuminations of the system of life in a Southern town. The bareness, vacancy, inertia seem to come out of the weather; the emotions of solitude flourish crazily in the parched streets; even McCullers's concentration on absolute clarity of style suggests the same still, depressed, vacant atmosphere, produces distinctness as a tragic effect. "In the town there were two deaf-mutes, and they were always together." Unlike the lonelies defeated by convention in *Winesburg, Ohio*, McCullers's girl-children recognize that the town is like themselves. The consistency of her theme absorbed the town into itself, made the immediate landscape hot with silent emotion.

McCullers had the intuition that human beings could be psychic states so absolute and self-contained that they repelled each other sexually. The characters in *The Heart Is a Lonely Hunter* live in another world so insistent as to suggest damnation. They are out of nature. Though she converted this sense of some deep personal unnaturalness into brilliant "atmosphere" (all the more so because her style suggests fright striving for perfect control), the demon of self-damnation, of being utterly locked up, sexually limited, was a subject that fascinated her but which she objectified, as comedy, only once — in *The Ballad of the Sad Cafe*.

The Member of the Wedding, her most popular work, turns the Huckleberry Finn of her first novel back into the children's literature of *Tom Sawyer*; it devalues her most familiarly tragic feelings about sex into cuteness: now she imitates Carson McCullers with an eye on the audience. But in the *Ballad*, emotionally the most detached of her fictions, the distrust of sex which runs all through her work expresses itself as a folktale in which the characters are mostly legends, unnatural and against nature. Everything is seen as a fable; there is nothing of that pervasive cry for sympathy which fills up *The Heart Is a Lonely Hunter* like a gas, numbing us. "The town itself is dreary," she begins, "is lonesome, sad, and like a place that is far off and estranged from all other places in the world."

The now "picturesquely" lonesome state is filled up with a "curious" figure, Miss Amelia Evans, who was once briefly and unsatisfactorily married, and removed from passion has come to exercise a weird power over the town and the chorus of its inhabitants. She is the wonder-working "doctor" to the sick and powerless people; she cures with occult remedies. She also has all the business in town and lives with files. The other characters are childlike in their helplessness. In her fantastic self-sufficiency, Miss Amelia shows what a woman past love can do with her energy. At the end, her exasperated ex-husband, when released from prison, tries to bring her back to his world of passion. She prefers to be a magician — or author — in perfect control. She fights it out with him in a long-drawn-out battle of comic fisticuffs that betrays her desire to lose and her inability to get any profit out of her strength except the solitude which feeds it.

In Flannery O'Connor's fiction we start beyond the line of sexual love; it is never an issue. The characters are recurrently the Mother, the Child, the Brother, and other totally angry people. There are so many angry people, especially if they are landowners burdened by tenant farmers, that the stock elements of human nature — more real to O'Connor than "personalities" — cohere by conflict. What is at once feminine and Southern about her fiction — the original and originating element — is her fatalistic trust in her own truth. Hers is not a world of people made lonely by their freakishness, not simply a rural world that turns people fanatical, but one that subsists on the belief that human beings are absolutely limited.

All people in this uniform condition of silence seem to be the same age. Her stories — more effective in this than her two novels, *Wise Blood* and *The Violent Bear It Away*, which make the same point at greater length — are of a crazy human disposition to error. These stories are as amazing in their stoic self-sufficiency as Stephen Crane's. Their significant fault, rising from the South's intellectual moralism, the need to show that the same legend or fable operates at the heart of everything, is that they are too much alike. The recurrent situation is our fatal disposition to turn petty issues into the greatest possible mistake. Mr. Fortune, an old man who wildly loves his granddaughter, who thinks her the only person at all like himself, tries to absorb her will entirely into his own. He kills her in an hysterical protest against an obstinacy just like his own. A young boy, away from his sophisticated parents in the company of a madly religious baby-sitter, gets baptized. "Where he lived everything was a joke. From the preacher's face, he knew immediately that nothing the preacher said or did was a joke." He returns home but has to get back to the river. "He intended not to fool with preachers any more but to Baptize himself and to keep on going this

time until he found the Kingdom of Christ in the river."
In "Everything That Rises Must Converge" a liberal on
the race question, hopelessly irritated by his mother's
obtuse prejudices, finds after a short bus ride that life
has come to a complete stop. His mother collapses on
the street after being pushed out of the way by a powerfully built, angry Negro woman to whose child she
loftily tried to offer a penny. "The lights drifted farther
away the faster he ran and his feet moved numbly as if
they carried him nowhere. The tide of darkness seemed
to sweep him back to her, postponing from moment to
moment his entry into the world of guilt and sorrow."
In "Greenleaf," Mrs. May's outrageously inefficient
tenant farmer can never keep the bull penned in. She is
finally gored to death through a carelessness on Greenleaf's part that is total hostility.

> She looked back and saw that the bull, his head
> lowered, was racing toward her. She remained perfectly
> still, not in fright, but in a freezing unbelief. She stared
> at the violent black streak bounding toward her as if
> she had no sense of distance, as if she could not decide
> at once what his intention was, and the bull had buried
> his head in her lap, like a wild tormented lover, before
> her expression had changed. One of his horns sank until
> it pierced her heart and the other curved around her
> side and held her in an unbreakable grip. She continued
> to stare straight ahead but the entire scene in front of
> her had changed — the tree line was a dark wound in a
> world that was nothing but sky — and she had the look
> of a person whose sight has been suddenly restored but
> who finds the light unbearable.

Flannery O'Connor's dryness rises to eloquence only in the death-throe. The Pascalian perfection of her phrasing takes us out of time into the last possible thought before death. There is an intense sense of the immediate scenery but the place has been stamped by the South into a universal extract of itself. The place is simply that which backs up this recurrent fault in ourselves, this abysmal disposition to do the wrong thing, to *be* wrong. Her characters are souls in the wrong world, creatures totally resentful, who must express themselves in these ominous silences and ragged figures. Many Southern writers have been grateful for original sin as an explanation of the "guilt" of slavery; Flannery O'Connor really believed in it. She reminds me of that fiercest of all Catholics, Joseph de Maistre, who said that only the executioner keeps man's total untrustworthiness from turning society into chaos.

The fascinations of Flannery O'Connor's work to me are many. She is one of the few Catholic writers of fiction in our day — I omit the convert Evelyn Waugh as being too ideological — who managed to fuse a thorough orthodoxy with the greatest possible independence and sophistication as an artist. Her parish priest in Milledgeville once told me that she was constantly berating him for admiring conventional fiction. Yet her stories show that the Church — which as an institution she used rarely in her work, and then in a relaxed mood of satire at her own expense — was so supreme in her mind as to be invisible. The world of "guilt and sorrow," the light that has been restored but is unbearable — these ultimates are almost Platonic in their severity. The "real" world is the Bible

Belt, an allegory. Reality is sin and error, multiplied by hillbilly fanaticism.

No wonder that the situations are hypnotic, the characters synonymous, the time of the drama anytime. The place is the bull that kills, the river in which you drown, not a place you remember for its tragicomic unsuitability to grace, like the rectories in J. F. Powers's quietly brilliant stories of American priests. Flannery O'Connor's severity is an intrinsic view of the world, the style by which she sees. Her stories remain in your mind as inflexible moral equations. The drama is made up of the short distance between the first intimations of conflict and the catastrophe. They are souls driven into this world and so forced to crash. They rush to their fate in the few pages needed to get them going at all. I am fascinated by O'Connor's severity — by its authority, its consistency, and wonder at its personal source. She inherited the dread circulatory disease of lupus, died of it before she was forty, knew she had it from the time she began to write. Her short career was a progress by dying — the sourness, the unsparingness, the constant sense of human weakness in her work may not need as many translations into theology as they get in contemporary American criticism. As Josephine Hendin pointed out in *The World of Flannery O'Connor,* there was an unreal and even comic gentility to her upbringing in Milledgeville that must have given O'Connor a wry sense of her aloneness as a woman, artist and Southerner who happened to be an Irish Catholic. The local Daughters of the Confederacy liked to babify her as one of Milledgeville's authors, but probably would not have enjoyed her real views about human nature or her mystical, not merely Irish, sense of her isolation as a Catholic in the Bible Belt.

On the other hand, she was so locked up in her body that one can understand why life as well as her faith made her think of *this is my body, this is my blood.* Christianity was sunk in her own flesh. She was a doomed young woman who had nothing to do in her short life but write fiction. There are recurrent examples of The Mother and the precocious, peculiarly neutral figure of The Child who so early sees all, knows all, and forgives no one. The psychological sources of her fiction are so neglected by her closest friends that one might think that Flannery O'Connor wrote fiction only to explain the true religion to the heathen. Yet these are less important than the criticism she makes, as a woman more reduced to inaction than most women, as a Southerner even more suspicious of "America" than most Southerners, of power.

She links power, ownership, authority to violence. People move into violence by a disposition to treat the world as entirely theirs. What Flannery O'Connor is most severe about is the uselessness of mere doing — she is severe about the illusion, not just the traditional male vanity, involved in the despotic show of will. Again and again her stories turn on fights over land and children. People go mad with temper trying to sustain ownership that is supreme — in their own minds. Often the characteristically resentful protagonist is a widow alone in middle age, whose dream is the preservation of property as her authority. The illusion ends in physical smashup. The human quality, at once dull and savage, is as expectable as the animals to which O'Connor goes for her characteristic similes. But what people are most is their disproportion to the world. Human beings are nothing but their moral natures, which sit in them like sacks waiting to be emptied into the world of action. The world is necessarily an empty place for O'Connor; the external is just a trigger. Her art is unhistorical. The only real issue is the primal fault. What people *do* is always grotesque.

To see life with such detachment from the bustling all-consuming power world, the world that dominates and so often hypnotizes the American novelist, is not to satirize the power but to turn one's back on it. Only a Southerner born to the tradition of being "different," off the main road of American progress, could have faced so much relinquishment. In the face of so much glut after 1945, only a woman of an austerity so scriptural as by our present standards to seem mad could have done it. Perhaps Flannery O'Connor owed this "madness" to her sense of many disadvantages. To herself, certainly not to us, she felt like an afterthought even in the most brilliant period of Southern writing. "Nobody wants his mule and wagon stalled on the same track the Dixie Limited is roaring down."

Faulkner ceased to be an influence on Southern novelists when the South at last had its own worldliness to satirize. All modern images of the South had been of the poverty, differentness, resistance with which a writer could identify; suddenly there was a South of stockbrokers and corporation executives who could make a Walker Percy feel as marginal as a Negro or Jew. When Percy's *The Moviegoer* unexpectedly won the National Book

Award for fiction in 1962, the agitation over the prize in
New York — Percy's own publisher had barely heard of
the book — was in sharp contrast with Walker Percy
himself and with *The Moviegoer* — a sardonic, essentially philosophical novel about the spiritual solitude of a
young stockbroker in the New Orleans suburb of Gentilly
who eventually marries a tragically vulnerable young
woman to whom he is distantly related. *The Moviegoer*
was a first novel by an unknown writer in Covington,
Louisiana, who was a doctor of medicine but had never
practiced. The book had not been launched with any great
expectations and was indeed published only because one
editor had stuck with it and with the author through four
drafts.

The Moviegoer was certainly not a book to rouse the
usually bored reviewers of "Other Fiction," or those editors
of Sunday book supplements to whom any book on public
affairs now seems more immediately newsworthy than
any novel not left by Hemingway in a bank vault. By the
early 1960s, the onset of the Kennedy years, the Vietnam
War, the perpetual crisis at home that made this "intellectual" President's fondness for reading history altogether characteristic of the period, "mere fiction" was
getting written off with dismaying ease. *The Moviegoer*
was in any event a book difficult to place. It was a lean,
tartly written, subtle, not very dramatic attack on the
wholly bourgeois way of life and thinking in a "gracious"
and "historic" part of the South. But instead of becoming
merely a satire on the South's retreat from its traditions,
it was, for all the narrator's bantering light tone, an

altogether tragic and curiously noble study in the loneliness of necessary human perceptions.

The narrator and protagonist — John Bickerson Bolling, "Binx" — cleverly increases his income every year and carries on in a mechanical way with one of his secretaries after another. But he has become obsessed with the meaninglessness of everything he is just beginning to *see*, with the despair whose specific character, said Kierkegaard, is that it is unaware of being despair. His father, a doctor, perished during the war; Binx has a distinct sense of fatherlessness, of traditions he is supposed to carry on that he cannot locate or justify in the cozy ways around him. In the secrecy of his own mind he is excited by the possibility of newly looking at life with the special, hallucinated feeling of discovery that he gives to the movies where he spends many evenings. He has become an enraptured observer of the human face, a man who is training himself to look steadily at the most commonplace things in his path. He has found some tiny chink in the wall of his despair — the act of looking, of seeing and discovering. He is a man who can look and listen, in a world where most people don't. His real life, one might say, is dominated by the excitement of conversion. There is a newness in his life. He is a spiritual voyeur, a seeker after the nearest but most unfathomable places of the human heart. He can listen to the tortured girl Kate, who has a powerful attraction to death and belabors him — his ability to give her all his attention constitutes the love between them. He has become the one man around him who seems to want nothing for himself but to look, to be a spectator in the dark. This clinician and diagnostician of the soul trains himself in the movies. The enlarged, brilliantly lighted and concentrated figures upon the screen have taught him how to focus on the secret human places.

The Moviegoer, essentially a sophisticated search of the search for faith in a world that seems almost bent on destroying faith, was not calculated to win great popularity. It was not exactly about going to the movies. It was a brilliant novel about our abandonment, our *Verworfenheit*, as the existentialists used to say — our cast-off state. Yet Binx the narrator and presiding figure was so tart and intractable in tone that one had to be sympathetic to the mind behind it, not impatient with the lack of action, in order to respond. It was, in fact, a book about an outsider for outsiders. Southerners used to call themselves outsiders in respect to the United States because they came from the rural, underdeveloped, old-fashioned, defeated South. But as Binx shows, in every passage of his involvement with the sophisticated upper middle class in New Orleans, it is the South itself that today makes outsiders of its people, breeds a despair that will never know it is despair.

The Moviegoer was an odd, haunting, unseizable sort of book. It was not "eccentric," did not overplay tone and incident in any current style — it was as decorous as an old-fashioned comedy of manners. But it was evidently and deeply the expression of some inner struggle. The author himself seemed in some fundamentals to feel himself in the wrong, to be an outsider in relation to his society. In *The Moviegoer* Gentilly, New Orleans, the South, had become the representative examples of an

America in which people no longer knew how to *look* at anything, did not know how or what to look for. They lived with only the most distant intimations of their own pain. One man would have to learn to *see* (as if for the first time) with only the minimum chance of saving himself at all. His bride-to-be, Kate, they both know he cannot save.

The author of *The Moviegoer* was a Percy, of the "aristocratic" Mississippi clan that might have stepped out of Faulkner's novels. The Percys were Confederate leaders, Southern planters, lawyers, gentlemen. A Senator Percy was driven out of office by one of those demagogues after whom the Snopeses used to name their even more horrible children. This senator's son, William Alexander Percy, was a lawyer and poet, brought up the orphaned Walker Percy and his brothers, fought the Ku Klux Klan in Greenville, was a friend of Faulkner — and a believer in the traditions of his class. William Alexander Percy romanticized the South in a way that his cousin Walker has never been tempted to do. In his autobiography, *Lanterns on the Levee*, William Alexander Percy said of the old slaveholders, the landed gentry, the governing class: "Though they have gone, they were not sterile; they have their descendants, whose evaluation of life approximates theirs." In 1965, writing on Mississippi as "The Fallen Paradise," Walker Percy wrote:

> *The bravest Mississippians in recent years have not been Confederates or the sons of Confederates, but rather two Negroes, James Meredith and Medgar Evers. . . . No ex-Mississippian is entitled to write of the tragedy which has overtaken his former state with any sense*

of moral superiority. . . . He strongly suspects that he
would not have been counted among the handful . . .
who not only did not keep silent but fought hard. . . .
The Gavin Stevenses have disappeared and the Snopeses
have won. . . . Not even Faulkner foresaw the ironic
denouement of the tragedy: that the Compsons and
Sartorises should not only be defeated by the Snopeses
but that in the end they should join them.

William Alexander Percy, who went to Sewanee and
had the social views of Donald Davidson, Allen Tate,
Andrew Lytle and Robert Penn Warren (before Warren
became a brilliantly sympathetic student of the Negro
movement in the Sixties), wrote that Negroes had "an
obliterating genius for living in the present. . . . [The
Negro] neither remembers nor plans. The white man does
little else; to him the present is the one great unreality."
Walker Percy graduated from the College of Physicians
and Surgeons at Columbia, and as an intern caught
pulmonary tuberculosis from one of the many bodies on
which he performed autopsies. America was just entering
the war. While waiting to be admitted to the famous
Trudeau sanitarium in Saranac Lake, Percy lived in a
boardinghouse, all alone, reading and beginning to write.
He says now, "TB liberated me." His illness, the enforced
absence from his family, the solitariness all seem to have
brought out in him one of those religious personalities
whom William James called the "twice-born." His real life,
his spiritual and intellectual life, his vocation as a writer,
above all his concern with the "sick souls" who haunt his
fiction — all this began when he found himself cut off
from the career he had planned, from the war that was

to be decisive for his generation, from the South that on Percy Street in Greenville he had taken for granted. Typically, it was the religious existentialists Kierkegaard and Dostoevsky, not Faulkner the Southern genius, who influenced him. He became a Catholic. This was one of his many actual "conversions": he underwent an unusually significant personal change, a change of faith within his change of profession. Although he is a natural writer, downright, subtle, mischievous, his novels seem to be essentially the self-determination of a religious personality, of a seeker who after being ejected from the expected and conventional order of things has come to himself as a stranger in the world.

A disposition to look at things in a radically new way is very much what happens in *The Moviegoer, The Last Gentleman, Love in the Ruins*. The violence of Southern history — the violence you can feel in the streets of Greenville today, where stores advertise "Guns and Ammo," where every truck driver seems to have a rifle with him — is in *Love in the Ruins* projected into the future — when the whole country has gone mad with violence. It is not in *The Moviegoer* and a much murkier book, *The Last Gentleman*. But in all three novels the protagonist is someone who feels himself in the grip of a profound disorder, and who as a result cultivates from outside the art of looking. Binx in *The Moviegoer* says that "I am more Jewish than the Jews I know. They are more at home than I am. I accept my exile." Binx is not really in the world he seems to be thriving in. "What are generally considered to be the best of times are for me the worst of times, and that worst of times was one of the best. . . ." The mental refusal, the silent spiritual opposition, the effort to make some countervailing gesture are those of a man who seems to be *here*, with us, but is really out *there*, all by himself.

> *Today is my thirtieth birthday . . . and knowing less than I ever knew before, having learned only to recognize merde when I see it, having inherited no more from father than a good nose for merde, for every species of shit that flies . . .*

This contrast of the here and the there, of the "regular" American world that can never understand the panic it breeds and the self training itself to face despair, to become a microscopist of salvation, gives *The Moviegoer* its special wry charm. Binx does see things in a special light — like the light on a movie screen, the light of hallucination, excessive concentration, obsession, that is given to those who at least turn their faces in the right direction. The Southern writer's secret is still to believe that the world is moral, historical, meaningful.

3

THE DECLINE OF WAR
Mailer to Vonnegut

It is well that war is so terrible — we should grow too fond of it.

> — General Robert E. Lee
> after Fredericksburg

NORMAN MAILER'S *The Naked and the Dead*, published in 1948 with enormous success of every kind, was the first "important" — and is probably still the best — novel about Americans at war, 1941–1945. Mailer at twenty-five was so thoroughly launched by his first book — it was exactly what people brought up on novels and films about the First World War expected of the "new war" novelists — that he was to make many later efforts to disconcert his admirers. But even jealous older novelists — Hemingway called the book "poor cheese, pretentiously wrapped" — understood the book in terms of their own expectations. The moment was still ripe for a novel that would honor war as a test of the literary imagination.

Like everyone else who has written well about war, Mailer was palpably excited by it. The 1941–1945 war, "*the* war" as we used to call it, was a chance to prove his "courage" — always a pressing subject with Mailer — and a chance of getting away from the Brooklyn Jewishness that he found provincial and demeaning. War was a chance to meet head-on the endurance, solidarity, suffering, that have always been the epic stuff of war. "The war was sensational delight posing as pious idealism," said D. H. Lawrence of 1914. Mailer is supposed even to have insisted on being sent to the Pacific because Europe was such old literary territory. He also had a certain vanity about his ability to handle the many technical problems created by war — he had been interested in aeronautics and engineering at Harvard.

All these personal ambitions for war, his unmistakable delight in the dangers and tests of war, his liking for the Texans and rednecks in his outfit, were given shape by Mailer's intellectual fascination with the staggering power that Americans could summon up for war. Mailer was excited by this, but as a radical intellectual with considerable confidence in his own theorizing, deeply suspicious of the overreaching in so much power. His central theme was already, in 1948, American aggressiveness and grittiness in the setting of America the powerhouse, the massive wealth and detailed organization slowly grinding its way over poorer countries. Mailer was to write with excitement about the extreme physical exertion of soldiers, the violence continued on the dead as well as on the living; his political sense of the menace to the world in so much American power was represented by a figure out of the antifascist novels of the Thirties — the sinister, epicene, arrogant General Cummings. The fascist mentality of General Cummings is typical of World War II novels produced soon after the war — Mailer's was a generation that had gone to war recognizing it as part of the same crisis that had produced Hitler. But unlike the "progressive," more simpleminded novelists of the immediate postwar period, Mailer saw the General as also a victim of the military machine that absorbs everything — even generals — into itself. The tormented and tormenting General, a bad man and therefore sexually dubious, is all alone; intellectuals attracted to fascism must be. He hates his wife, he cultivates his professional skills in perfect solitude, and he has no one to communicate his vaguely sinister theories to but his young aide, Lieutenant Hearn, a rich young "progressive" in revolt against his own class. The General sees himself as a prophet of the totalitarian century; in his Nietzschean solitude and his intellectual contempt for the officer class, he has developed a wholly elitist theory of politics against which his outraged aide protests in vain.

In the end, General Cummings's intellectual vanity becomes a joke on him, while Lieutenant Hearn's efforts to display solidarity with the enlisted men under him result in his own death. Sergeant Croft, who hates Hearn for stepping out of place, tricks the lieutenant into exposing himself to Japanese fire; the decisive victory of the American forces on "Anopopei" Island is secured by the clockwork decision of a mediocre staff officer when General Cummings is off the island trying to get naval support for his unconventional strategy. The irony is an important item in Mailer's considered respect for the bludgeoning power of the system, the American military machine that wore down the Japanese as it had worn down the Confederacy with its "meat grinder." Mailer is not sentimental about the depression types who make up his G.I.'s, hard-luck cases who were as pathetic in South Boston, San Antonio and Brooklyn as they are in the army. But though Mailer clearly knows less about generals than he does about Private Gallagher from Boston and Private Goldstein from Brooklyn (General Cummings is an intellectual design for a bad character),* Mailer does not expose the General for the moral pleasure of showing up a fascist. It is the American system in war that interests him, and *The Naked and the Dead* lives up to the old naturalist edict that a novel's form and language should duplicate the social unit it describes. The whole *book* works for Mailer, although many aspects of it are derivative, as a highly organized effort to show war itself as a form of organization. He was moving toward the corollary that has fascinated him ever since: war may be the ultimate purpose of technological society. Though *The Naked and the Dead* owes some of its appeal to the shared experiences that so many readers bring to it, to movies of the war and "biographies" of individual soldiers in the style of Dos Passos — the urgently effective quality of mind behind it is respect for the systematized deployment of skills that Mailer learned as a soldier, respect for the social force brought to war even when generals blunder and enlisted men betray their death wish.

"You and I, Rinaldi," said the Hemingway hero in that far-off war that produced so many exquisite pages of suffering in perfect style. Nobody in novels about World War II "makes" a separate peace. We are very far from the literary detachment of those ambulance volunteers who wrote *In Our Time, 1919, The Enormous Room.* If Mailer's description of war seems "political" and concerned, this is not because he really brings politics to it. He writes as a soldier from the ranks — how he wanted this for his future! — from shrewd observation of the human

* Mailer ten years later might have attempted Douglas MacArthur.

74

capital that was to be won from certain experiences in the field, and after "peace" had broken out, of what World War II did to hammer America into "the world's leading superpower."*

Hemingway, Cummings, even Dos Passos in his "left" days, never saw war as the inevitable extension of American society. Truly a child of the Second World War, Mailer owes his easy handling of the composite sides of war to his social ambition. War gave him his chance to experience what millions of soldiers were going through, to share in the last great mass war that Americans believed in — and to see that contemporary society can be totally organized for anything. The war he describes is entirely one of the cogs in the wheel; there are no free agents, not even any "personalities" except General Cummings and Lieutenant Hearn, because they are intellectuals and have theories — a nice touch. But war as an overriding form of social organization (the Americans were actually better at this than the Nazis) is itself. Mailer's subject, and so makes for that feeling of competence without which one does not write well about war. Mailer is drawn to "modern" war as soon he will be drawn to other displays of social power. War is not politics "by other means," but just war. War has become the decisive form of society, the technical environment inside which we may be said to live. Mailer is often crude in his first novel, but never sentimental. He has social hardening, expertise, acceptance of the situation; there is no dramatization of the novelist himself at war; the values are all

* Robert McNamara in *The Pentagon Papers.*

75

in the play of the material, thus giving him a sense of his professional task that enables him to show with notable precision the different sides of men at war.

American soldiers have to be humiliated into feeling fight. Mailer emphasizes the similarities between his characters in order to demonstrate their dependency. The individual soldiers shown close-up in *The Naked and the Dead* will never recover from the Depression. It is the merciless, savagely disciplined Sergeant Croft who virtually alone in the platoon seems always to know what he is doing and to welcome every test of endurance and skill that comes up. Most of the others are damaged material bitterly resenting every motion they are compelled to make. His fellow officers baiting Lieutenant Hearn are paper pushers who can do no great harm to the military establishment. All these people are humanly limited to a degree that is remarkable even in a "naturalistic" novel. But they are not the product of literary theory; Mailer just has no respect for followers. They are always in friction — pushing, swearing, complaining — and although all this personal violence has not the slightest effect on the course of the war, the atmosphere is proof of General Cummings's dictum that the "natural lot of twentieth-century man is anxiety." What interests Mailer most about soldiers is what follows from the legitimization of violence. He loves not individuals but their psychic extremes, the developing fright of soldiers drunkenly stumbling around Japanese corpses looking for "souvenirs," soldiers pushing themselves unconscious with exhaustion as they obstinately carry a wounded comrade who has died. Fright, fatigue passing into hallucination, and of course killing and being killed become forms of intoxication that get people out of their usual selves, to pass a line — always a prime motive in Mailer. The war of the drafted, miserable G.I. is still the one "big" experience that the common man will have in his life. War frees each man to realize his most personal fantasy before it obliterates him. The sinister General says — "If there is a God, he's just like me." Sergeant Croft "always saw order in death. Whenever a man in the platoon or company had been killed he would feel a quiet and grim satisfaction as though the death was inevitably just." Martinez the "Mex" from Texas knifes a Japanese sentry in order to show that he can scout behind the enemy lines without being heard. But in the end nothing that this platoon does, especially not climbing the great mountain that dominates the island, makes the slightest contribution to victory. The minutely recorded sensations of the men, to which we have been so close through the book, have no relevance to the "victory" gained by the power and multiplication of American resources. This is Mailer's point and in a way his intellectual pride. He has seen beyond the "sensational delight" of war to war as the embodiment of contemporary society.

Mailer's achievement was to turn his relative inexperience into social fact. *The Naked and the Dead* is the product of considerable intelligence. The nearest thing to it for social density and truth, James Jones's *From Here to Eternity* (1951) obviously owes its thorough documentation of the old prewar army to Jones's experience. It is so much a book that has been lived — centering on the army as System and Racket — that the documentation lives on in one's mind with a surly ominous bitterness. Since most of the book takes place before Pearl Harbor (and of course ends with the attack itself), everyone expects America to be at war soon, the officers in particular look forward to war as a way of getting promoted, and so everyone in the book simplemindedly predicts war as a natural, necessary, stimulating activity. This matter-of-factness (as subject) helps to establish the army as a piece of social reality. War still seems entirely "normal," war is what these men know they are in for, war helps men to get along in the world, war is just another part of the natural world.

"Naturalness" is Jones's great theme. His book brilliantly imposes itself on the reader, even when his occasional rhetoric seems as retarded as some of his characters, because he has the strictest, plainest, most functional sense of what his protagonists Warden and Prewitt think of as their "maleness." "Maleness" in Jones's book is need, need is aggressive, sexual, honorable, and indefatigable. Although "maleness" is inevitably described by Jones as tragic (it is the nature of the army — of the world — to frustrate the deepest cravings of a man), we recognize in reading *From Here to Eternity* that Jones sees the tragedy in maleness because there is nothing in his world but "maleness." Prewitt and Warden are doomed not because they seek a freedom which the system denies them, but because the world exists for them only as a way of satisfying this maleness. Of course they can never get their way. They can never see the world itself as anything but a limitation.

This is the fate of soldiers — to feel totally impoverished. But Jones's insistence on needs, his sense of their primitive importance, gives his soldiers a kind of honor, a belief in valor — even when this is only the most embittered obstinacy. Virtually alone among World War II novels, *From Here to Eternity* gives us a view from within of the old regular army, of the "thirty-year man" who enlisted because he was a Harlan County miner's son (Prewitt) who could not find work; a natural leader and organizer (Warden) who could play the game in the army; an old Wobbly (Jack Malloy), or a gutter rat (Maggio) who had nowhere else to go. These tough morsels — even the sadist, Fatso, who happily tortured prisoners in the Stockade — are ultimately a judgment on a society whose men have no real work, whose skills are the real lament of the book. Men are employed by the army, but *they* are not used. Just as their "maleness" is stated by Jones to be always in "excess," is always felt as a burden — so Prewitt's skill as a bugler and fighter, Warden's genuine thoughtfulness, Maggio's antic pride — are all in "excess" of anything they are allowed to have and to do. The regular army before December 7 is shown up as a put-on, a world of simulated busyness, routines which require no intelligence, ferocious strictness whose only purpose is to exact mechanical obedience. These regular soldiers are really boondoggling; this army is just another government work project. The West Pointers riding herd on them equally suffer from this dissimulated idleness and unconscious anomie. But since they are in authority, their fundamental vacuity expresses itself in driving their favorites to gain athletic honors for the regiment and in brutally authoritarian views of America's future role in the world.

Our sense of all this "maleness" not in use, of all this "excess" of a man over his function, is gained without much effort. There is no complexity to most of the characters, no contradiction in anyone's basic nature except the consciousness of being "repressed." When his surrogate voice, Jack Malloy in the stockade, gives us Jones's celebration of the romantic rebel in America, we feel that Jones is interrupting his own documentation; the Wobbly philosopher is as insignificant to the machine as are Prewitt's "views" when compared with Prewitt's sufferings at the hands of the army. But what Jones does capture, harrowingly, is inner desolation so total, regularized and systematized that these soldiers are virtually unconscious of how savage it feels. First Sergeant Milton Anthony Warden, who despises Captain Holmes but also hates this "superior" as a force he cannot do anything about, looks at Holmes walking away after making an empty show of his authority:

> Through the obscuring mist of anger in him, the stark nakedness of the rain drenched earth and muddy grass and the lonely moving figure of Holmes huddled in his topcoat made a picture in his mind of a ghost town street and a strong wind rolling along a tattered scrap of paper in the gutter to some unforeseen and unimportant destination, moaning with the sadness of its duty.

This emptiness is Jones's achievement in *From Here to Eternity*. And just as the characters descend all too smoothly (cogs in the wheel, items in the naturalistic tale) to their various catastrophes, so Jones's own work seems to require no great imaginative effort. It is the old-fashioned product of an old-fashioned war.

World War II turned into a very different war over the twenty-five years in which we have been forced to think of Hiroshima, Auschwitz, Dresden, the thirty million dead, the returning Soviet soldiers imprisoned by their own government for having been captured by the Germans, the threat of universal nuclear destruction. Of *this* war, opposed to the war described in *A Bell for Adano, The Young Lions, The Caine Mutiny, The Gallery* — war as liberal tourism — one can only say what Whitman said of the Civil War — "the real war will never get into the books." No individual experience, as reported in literature, can do justice to it, and the most atrocious common experiences will always seem unreal as we read about them. When the British liberated Belsen on April 15, 1945, they came upon forty thousand sick, starving and dying prisoners, over ten thousand corpses stacked in heaps. Belsen was not the worst Nazi camp, merely the first to be exposed to the world. *The* (London) *Times* correspondent began his dispatch — "It is my duty to describe something beyond the imagination of mankind." This became the only serious and honest view of World War II as, by the Fifties, the liberal intellectual's image of it was demolished by so many uncovered horrors, so many new wars on the horizon, such a continued general ominousness, that "*the* war" soon became War anywhere, anytime — War that has never ended, War as the continued experience of twentieth-century man.

Realism about war, observation from the literary side-lines, even one's own unvarnished experience in a concen-tration camp, could no longer express "War" as they did "*the* war." War as an actuality, bound by space and time, an event that literature "could do justice to," soon yielded to an apocalyptic sense of the possible destruction of man-kind, the boundlessness of its enmities. Above all, we had the sense of a world made totally the same, which it wasn't, and "absurd," that glib term for the rejection of society by those living tolerably in it. Albert Camus in *Le Mythe de Sisyphe* had meant by the absurd no more than what modern writers in the tradition of romantic individualism have always meant: the superiority of man to his naturally limited and frustrating existence. As D. H. Lawrence said, man has his excess always on his hands. It is natural for man to be rebellious against the terms of his life and his death, to be dissatisfied with everything but his own mind, to be an outsider and an overreacher —and thus to feel "absurd" to himself. But now society became "absurd," an untenable term but natural to a period in which the power of the state to make war, to destroy life on the planet, seemed more and more unman-ageable. "War" had come to seem the normal, omnipres-ent condition of daily living, dominating a whole generation by the terror of its weapons and by the visible undoing, in the preparations for war, of those human loyalties and common values in the name of which war used to be fought.

The essence of such novels as Joseph Heller's *Catch-22* and Kurt Vonnegut's *Slaughterhouse-Five, or The Children's Crusade* is that though both are ostensibly about the 1941–1945 war, in which both writers served, they are really about The Next War, and thus about a war which will be without limits and without meaning, a war that will end only when no one is alive to fight it. The theme of *Catch*-22 in particular is the total craziness of war, the craziness of all those who submit to it, and the struggle to survive by the one man, Yossarian, who knows the difference between his sanity and the insanity of the system. But how can one construct fictional meaning, narrative progression, out of a system in which virtually everyone but the hero assents to madness, willingly falls into the role of the madman-who-pretends-to-be-sane? The answer is that *Catch*-22 is about the hypothesis of a totally rejectable world, a difficult subject, perhaps impossible so long as the "world" is undifferentiated, confused with man's angry heart itself — but expressive of the political uselessness many Americans have felt about themselves since World War II. So Heller, who combines the virtuousness of a total pacifist with the mocking pseudo-rationality of traditional Jewish humor, has to fetch up one sight gag after another. "The dead man in Yossarian's tent was simply not easy to live with." "General Dreedle was incensed by General Peckem's recent directive requiring all tents in the Mediterranean theater of operations to be pitched along parallel lines with entrances facing back proudly toward the Washington monument." The book moves by Yossarian's asking sensible, human, logical questions about war to which the answers are madly inconsequent. Heller himself is the straight man on this lunatic stage, Yossarian the one human being in this farcically antihuman setup. The jokes are variations on the classic Yiddish story of the totally innocent recruit who pokes his head over the trench, discovers that everyone is firing away, and cries out in wonder — "One can get killed here!"

Yet the impressive emotion in *Catch-22* is not "black humor," the "totally absurd," those current articles of liberal politics, but horror. Whenever the book veers back to its primal scene, a bombardier's evisceration in a plane being smashed by flak, a scene given us directly and piteously, we recognize what makes *Catch-22* disturbing. The gags are a strained effort to articulate the imminence of *anyone*'s death now by violence, and it is just this that makes it impossible to "describe war" in traditional literary ways. Despite the running gags, the telltale quality of *Catch-22* is that it doesn't move, it can't. The buried-alive feeling of being caught in a plane under attack, of seeing one's partner eviscerated, produces the total impotence of being unable to move, to escape. And this horror-cold immobility is reproduced not in the static, self-conscious distortion of the gags but in the violence of the straight, "serious" passages:

> The forward bombardier would have liked to be a ball turret gunner. That was where he wanted to be if he had to be there at all, instead of hung out there in front like some goddamned cantilevered goldfish bowl while the goddam foul black tiers of flak were bursting and booming and billowing all around and above and below him in a climbing, cracking, staggered, banging, phantasma-gorical, cosmological wickedness that jarred and tossed and shivered, clattered and pierced, and threatened to annihilate them all in one splinter of a second in one vast flash of fire.

84

The urgent emotion in Heller's book is thus every individual's sense today of being directly in the line of fire, of being trapped, of war not as an affair of groups in which *we* may escape, but as my and your nemesis. The psychology in *Catch-22* is that of a man being led to execution, of a gallows humor in which the rope around one's neck feels all too real (and is plainly stamped General Issue). This sense of oneself not as a soldier in a large protective group but as an isolated wretch doomed to die *unaccountably* is more and more a feature of literature about World War II. It haunts all fiction by Jews since the war, even novels which do not deal with the war, like Edward Lewis Wallant's *The Pawnbroker*, Saul Bellow's *Mr. Sammler's Planet*, Mordecai Richler's *St. Urbain's Horseman*. As the Holocaust becomes more and more unreal to every new generation, Jewish writers who were stamped by it turn it into the only Jewish version of Original Sin — evil unredeemed, unexplained, unpunished, even unbelieved by most of mankind. So every account of it by Jewish writers, no matter how dim and remote from 1933–1945 the attempt to pass the story on, turns into one man's account of insupportable and inexplicable evil — into the seeming fantasy of a "world" coming down on the single and often insignificant witness who is telling the story. Just as traditional Christian poetry and epic helped to create a postclassical literature founded on the individual's relation to original sin, so much of contemporary fiction is founded on a struggle with evil "intolerable" because of the inability of liberal politics to explain and of the liberal imagination to represent. There is no politics in our contemporary war novels, for it is impossible to posit any aim to destruction on such a scale as the thirty millions who died in World War II. Destruction was committed at Hiroshima, Nagasaki, Dresden because the weapons for it were available, because these cities were on the timetable.

Kurt Vonnegut's books are haunted by the fact that he was an American prisoner of war in Dresden when the city, in the worst single episode of bombing during the war, was fire-bombed by the American air force. Vonnegut was saved because Allied prisoners were kept in a powerfully built slaughterhouse. Everything Vonnegut has written about his experience is "true" with the same preposterous irony; after the bombing was over, one of the Americans was tried and shot for "stealing" a teapot from the rubble. All this has given *Slaughter-house-Five, or The Children's Crusade* an impishly sentimental humor based on the sheer helplessness, the total ineffectuality, of *anyone* caught up in such a massacre. Vonnegut's introduction to the novel gives his credentials for writing it; he was there. So the novel, an improvisation on the "actual" experience, starts on the breezy but bitterly quiescent note of a man who cannot forget the terror, but at the same time cannot make a great novel out of it — and is not sure that anyone should try. The spirit of competition, once so keen among writers of "war novels" that Mailer knew the Pacific would be more useful to him than old Europe, now turns on which writer *knows* more about the real nature of war.

When I came home from the Second World War twenty-three years ago, I thought it would be easy for me to write about the destruction of Dresden, since all I would have to do would be to report what I had seen. And I thought, too, that it would be a masterpiece or at least make me a lot of money, since the subject was so big. . . .

[The book] . . . is so short and jumbled and jangled . . . because there is nothing . . . to say about a massacre. Everybody is supposed to be dead, to never say anything or want anything ever again. Everything is supposed to be very quiet after a massacre, and it always is, except for the birds.

And what do the birds say? All there is to say about a massacre, things like "Poo-tee-weet"?

The real massacre will never get into the books. But Vonnegut was there. This belittling of war fiction is typical of Vonnegut's way of fading out on his subjects. He enjoys representing the little man who can never do anything about things. Billy Pilgrim, the little businessman from Indianapolis who was another prisoner in Dresden, is a man of entirely unreproachful innocence; he *never* knows what is happening to him, especially when he is taken off by some of Vonnegut's usual visitors from outer space. Yet Billy is a solid good citizen of middle America, able to succeed in business because — the best note in the book — he has suppressed what he never knew. Billy in wartime, a prisoner of war, inspired the German guards to look at him "owlishly," to "coo calmingly. They had never dealt with Americans before, but they surely understood this general sort of freight. They knew it was essentially a liquid which could be induced to flow slowly toward cooing and light."

Vonnegut is always at home with characters who succeed in American business because they still know nothing else. They are not with it in our kind of world. They do not know that it is just one of many worlds: they prosper but they do not think. Thus their freedom from the necessity of explaining anything makes them true Americans, unworldly even when they are extraterrestrial, open to mischief from outer space. Vonnegut's fondness for visitors from other worlds is the drollest expression yet of the Midwestern feeling that the Midwest *is* the Earth and that all other people are different. All that has changed since the West was the country of innocence is Vonnegut's feeling that innocence is dangerous. His use of space fiction is too droll for my taste, a boy's fantasy of creatures more rational than ourselves. Just as there is "nothing to say about a massacre," so there is nothing to explain or protest about earth. The "Tralfamadorian" who takes Billy Pilgrim off condescendingly explains that "Earthlings are the great explainers, explaining why this event is structured as it is, telling how other events may be achieved or avoided. I am a Tralfamadorian, seeing all time as you might see a stretch of the Rocky Mountains. All time is all time. It does not change. It does not lend itself to warnings and explanations. It simply *is*. . . . Only on earth is there any talk of free will." In this spirit Vonnegut deprecates any attempt to see tragedy that day in Dresden. Dresden is simply too much for all of us, whether to remember, record or understand. He likes to say with arch fatalism, citing one horror after another, "So it goes." If someone replies "Auschwitz" when he says "Dresden," he then replies, "I know, I know."

Irrationality is not an uncomfortable support of Vonnegut's fiction. But he is at his best not in *Slaughterhouse-Five* (really a satire on the Great American Novel) but in spoofs of the American scene like *God Bless You, Mr. Rosewater*. There his natural, solid bitterness at the souring of so many American hopes takes on the wildly comic use of inappropriateness, his best weapon. Vonnegut knows how to embarrass and to dislodge the "order" of things. The terrible gets smaller in *Mother Night* without losing its terribleness. An American agent in Nazi Germany is convicted after the war of having been a Nazi, and finds himself in a cell next to Eichmann, who is busily typing his memoirs and asks the American: "Do you know a good literary agent?" In *Slaughterhouse-Five* Vonnegut seems, all too understandably, subdued by his material and plays it dumb. He is funnier when he is ruthless. The book is short, loose and somehow purposefully helpless. But Vonnegut's total horror of war has endeared him to the young, who find it hard to believe that even World War II had a purpose, and who see themselves as belonging to the universe at large rather than to the country which sends them to fight in Asia. Thus Vonnegut, who has no politics, has given a fixed idea to the audience for whom he writes. It is the idea of human vulnerability: we are still too innocent in the face of war to offer any political explanation or protest. Vonnegut's horselaugh of self-deprecation finally becomes his picture of the damned human race. Thus all evil is eliminated from the war which Hitler started but which, as Vonnegut says over and again, certainly made everyone "very tough." By now we are morally perishing of so much toughness; our innocence is proved by opting out of the system. We think longingly of E. E. Cummings's "There's a hell of a better universe next door, let's go."

The gifted, morbid French novelist Louis-Ferdinand Céline was a fascist, served the Vichy regime, and finally fled to Germany with other French fascists and collaborators. In his remarkable account of being cooped up in Germany, *Castle to Castle*, Céline, on the basis of information given him by the Vichy consul in Dresden, tells us more what the Dresden fire-bombing was *like* than does Vonnegut, who was there.

> . . . *the tactic of total squashing and frying in phosphorus . . . American invention! really perfected the last "new look" before the A-bomb. . . . First the suburbs, the periphery, with liquid sulphur and avalanches of torpedoes . . . then general roasting . . . the whole center! Act II . . . churches, parks, museums . . . no survivors wanted. . . .*

Why does the American who was there avoid such strong, plain language? Why symbolically as well as physically did Vonnegut feel out of it? Céline's bluntness, his graphic power (even the dots between the sentences are in his well-known style of red-faced personal fury), incorporate his willingness to take sides, his deep political outrage at the specific American "tactic of total squashing and frying in phosphorus." Vonnegut's evasion of realistic description seems typical of the morally outraged, unpolitical, widespread American sense of futility about our

government's making war in and on Indo-China for almost a decade. The wars now go on forever, and no
writer can be sure which war he is writing about even if
he has been to one. Until Vietnam, Americans did not
fully take in Orwell's prophecy in *1984* that theirs, too,
was a permanent war economy, totally bureaucratized for
war, prepared to make war endlessly. In retrospect even
the fiction of the "separate peace" about the first World
War, based on aristocratic disdain for politicians and
humanist protest against the slaughter of a whole generation, seems more political, more confident of choices, than
those American stories and reports of Vietnam which
made a veteran correspondent there finally say that "the
war — or wars — has become as unreal and macabre as a
bad trip in the East Village."

But of course the Vietnam War is not "a bad trip." Our
disgust with the interminable killing may no longer be a
strong enough emotion to write books with. The disgust
is all too understandable. The Vietnam War has been so
sickeningly "covered" by TV cameramen on the spot, by
dogged journalists still looking for a "fresh angle" on the
war, that the serious novelist trying to describe Vietnam
finds himself outdone by the manic plenitude of American
destructiveness there. A writer looking at his television set
sees American soldiers, from a boat, pouring an unceasing
fire into the forest as if they were spraying insecticide.
The factory methods of Americans making war on Asiatics
have since Hiroshima defeated the most unreconstructed
literary imagination. "We are killing out of spite," said an
American observer. Even so strong and astringent a novel
about Vietnam as William Eastlake's *The Bamboo Bed*

(and there haven't been many novels about Vietnam at
all) finally seems to elude all literary ambition in Eastlake's scorn of every American military "posture." The
Americans fight the natives as Americans once fought the
Indians, but there is no end of Indians. The book is an
indictment of our historic American ferocity, and finally
not about Vietnam but about all of America's wars. As in a
nightmare, the Americans in this endless pageant play of
war* no longer seem to know where they are or whom
they are fighting, and the same war takes place over and
again.

More than anything else, it is the American bad conscience over Vietnam — obviously there *is* no substitute
for "victory"! — that robs *The Bamboo Bed* of every effective quality but scorn. Eastlake is an excellent novelist,
but with such a subject *nobody* comes off right in a novel
— everyone is touched with the same guilt, just as the
Asian forest absorbs and outlasts all the death we pour
into it. The death of Captain Clancy, a brave but too
traditional American warrior, represents nothing but his
own death. A single man's death in Vietnam is a biological
episode important only to the cessation of his sensations.
Nobody cares, for a dead man frightens everyone with the
reality of *his* death. Meanwhile, in the "bamboo bed" itself,
a helicopter on a search-and-rescue operation, a lieutenant and a nurse make love ten thousand feet above the

* Virginia Woolf's last, beautiful novel, *Between the Acts*, a "war
novel" finished on the brink of the war which killed Virginia
Woolf as surely as if she had been hit in one of the bombings she
feared, is a pageant play of English *history* down through the
ages. But the play is conceived by a character in the book, so that
the disturbance of the play answers to the anguish of imagination
that has conceived history as a play that *can* come to an end.

battle. The helicopter is on automatic pilot, swoops and rises merrily through the air like a wild bird released.

The Bamboo Bed is a satire on Hemingway's style and the Hemingway hero. Captain Clancy is an old-fashioned American warrior devoted to the honor of his own maleness. But what to do when *individuals* at war are no longer interesting, when the only real protagonist at war is the nation-state, the war-state, the war-leaders who now think of themselves as being in a "Greek tragedy" because one decision forces another? The contemporary novel, haunted by the power of impersonal structures, still has no practice in employing wholly impersonal characters. General Westmoreland, no doubt in disgust with American troops, anticipates a time when war will be completely automated.

4

PROFESSIONAL OBSERVERS
Cozzens to Updike

Fiction has flourished most successfully in a middle-class world. And it may not be without significance that America, the remaining bastion of an aggressive capitalist spirit which is socially acceptable to all classes, is also the society in which the novel still continues to flourish at an exceptionally high level of performance. . .

— J. H. Plumb, "Lament for the Novel"

I feel a tenderness toward my characters that forbids making violent use of them. In general, the North American continent in this century has been a place where catastrophe has held off. All my novels end with a false death, partial death. If, as may be, the holocausts at the rim of possibility do soon visit us, I am confident my capacities for expression can rise, if I live, to the occasion.

— John Updike, *Paris Review* interview

I N THE PENTAGON during the Second World War, I once
had occasion to interview a general. A subtle-looking
major, sitting off to the side with what looked like
calculated inconspicuousness, distracted me by the inten-
sity with which he studied the very ordinary proceedings
of a writer interviewing a general for a magazine article;
the concentration of interest in that room, on the part of
the major, was so strong that it was audible, and puzzled
me until I came to read his novels. It was James Gould
Cozzens.

When *Guard of Honor* had its success in 1948, suddenly "vindicating" this proud solitary novelist who had
been publishing novels since his college days in the Twenties, I found that despite the "tough" conservative line
that Cozzens had taken on the disturbance of some young
Negro officers at a great air force training and research
base in Florida, I was concentrating on the minuteness
with which Cozzens had "covered" the air force as a
society. He had noticed everything characteristic, he had
stored away every technical name and detail he would
need, and he was now working them all into a long, con-
secutive, three-days' drama of a moral crisis among a few
members of the top brass. It was a drama so "well-made,"
as they used to say of nineteenth-century plays, that the
structure of the book corresponded to a society that was
challenged but would hold.

Major Cozzens had made good use of his proximity to some leading figures in the United States air force. So we see the West Point class ring on Major General Ira Beal's hand as he "drives" the plane in the opening scene, the "not-very-clean khaki shirt, open at the neck, with his stars on the wilted collar," and are then directed to the contrast that the necessary casualness of the youngest major general in the air force piloting his own plane — "a new twin-engine advanced trainer of the type designated AT-7" — makes with the gold crash bracelet hanging loosely on the hotshot young general's *right* wrist* (on his left "was a beautiful Swedish navigator's chronograph the size of a half dollar.") Later in the book, when the head of the air force's own deputy, General "Jo-Jo" Nichols, so cool a customer that he is seen by everyone as vaguely sinister, comes down to the base at Ocanara, Cozzens makes a point of stressing that this disturbingly official man was "perfectly" shaved and almost too well turned out.

All the time I was reading *Guard of Honor*, I was conscious of the closeness with which Cozzens was applying his worked-up knowledge of the air force. With his usual astringency, skepticism, detachment about the human limitations in all ranks created by the social roles that everyone must play, the author was methodically laying out and solving (within limits) the moral problem he had

* "She then replaced the cap on the bottle of lacquer and, standing up, passed her left — the wet — hand back and forth through the air. With her dry hand, she picked up a congested ashtray from the window seat. . . ." [J. D. Salinger, "A Perfect Day for Bananafish."]

Angela undressing "was parting vague obstacles with her hands." [John Updike, *Couples*] laid out by fitting a *structure* together; one could hear him driving in the nails, smoothing out the rough spots. He was working with fine points of air force detail to make a box three days long and confined to a sprawling air force base in Florida. The crucial scenes in the book represent Cozzens's tight, curt devaluation of excessive liberal notions of human possibility; and these depend on Cozzens's expert handling of technical fact, of the self-limiting society that a military base becomes. Far from being merely a "researched" novel, *Guard of Honor* owes its distinction from other novels of *America's* war to Cozens's espousal of the virtue in old-fashioned virtue — principles, ability, self-control, measure. The moral law — not handed down from on high but won by stoic upperclass Protestants through long practice in the values necessary to survival (and by putting down darker, more hysterical races) — was more urgent than any inflamed insistence on equality. *Guard of Honor* disputes the American liberal assumption that Negroes as "victims" of the system usually have the moral advantage — especially in a struggle with professional officers and gentlemen. The book reconstructs the scale of values so that it is not the ill-treated Negro cadets but Colonel Ross, an elderly and altogether too sagacious judge in civil life now attached to the Inspector General's office, whose concern for the system rather than for the Negroes wins our respect in the end. This belief in "society," the country, the air force, is the reason for Cozzens's almost provocative illiberalism, and still reflects the dominating ethical point of view that novels of social rivalry used to take in America. Far from being the kind of hurriedly worked up tourist impressionism of the battlefields brought in by so many war novelists who had one novel to write — *Kilroy Was There* — *Guard of Honor* is a novel about the responsibilities of those professional minds who have been the only upper class in America. The essence of Cozzens's concern with air force ritual and regulations, the top brass and the West Point class ring, the in-group and the great crowd outside, is the fact that for Cozzens, in this book, social ritual was still a show of belief, not of position only. The fine points to which conduct does come down in an elite group like the air force command brought out the humanity-as-responsibility in Judge Ross, if not in immature Major General Ira Beal. Moral leadership is too serious a matter to be left to any major general.

Colonel Ross — always "Judge" to the officers who outrank him — admits to an unexpected amount of strain in the course of the "moral" crisis set off in Ocanara's administrative elite when General Beal's closest friend beats up a young Negro pilot and the handful of Negro officers protest against this and their exclusion (by Florida law) from the white officers' club. The strain is telling. But the "Judge" is the last fairly intact representative of a truly Brahmin priesthood — the doctors, lawyers, clergymen in Cozzens's novels who represent professional intelligence,*

---

* In *Guard of Honor* there is a clear summary of what Cozzens admires as professional intelligence in a young lieutenant of great mathematical gifts who for recreation easily breaks the American cipher. "Here was intelligence in the real sense of the word — not in the misused sense of mere quickness or smartness, or knowing a few things most people had never troubled to learn. This was a strength and clarity of mind so great that it could hold and view simultaneously an infinite number, or any rate hundreds, of bare sequences of digits. . . ."

moral aloofness, detachment from the mere money-
makers and the (mere) masses. Sinclair Lewis, the
doctor's son who also found his favorite protagonists in
modestly competent doctors and lawyers, called them "the
capable" as opposed to the businessman who was now
"Our American Ruler." These disciplined usually unbreakable types have always been the custodians of tradition
in Cozzens's novels. But in *Guard of Honor* Judge Ross
shows signs of doing duty out of habit; he and his wife
have a son overseas who may be killed, and the Rosses
are by no means convinced, looking around them, that it
is still sweet and proper to die for one's country. Things
are breaking down, and it is significant that Judge Ross,
an elderly retread from that more innocent war of 1917–
1918, is astonished by the drunks and incompetents in the
air force management. The air force, with its unheard-of
representation of angry young Black flight officers, has
got beyond him, and so has the great new war which was
going to be just another opportunity for "service." An
elderly man with an elderly wife even more tight-lipped
and superior to the emotional messes of other people, he
can get no comfort from her except the admonishment to
still more tight grim silence. Worried about their son,
attached to a bombing squadron in England, Mrs. Ross
says bitterly — "I blame everything. I worked so long; I
tried so hard — then something comes along, I don't
know what, and just knocks everything over. What is the
use of it?" Colonel Ross agrees: ". . . the longer I live, the
less I know, and the worse I do; and what, indeed, is the
use of it?" The purely ethical traditions of Cozzens's
favorites, the American professional caste, perhaps will

not stand so much questioning. Who and what will teach the teachers of the tribe when the teachers are in dismay? Somehow the great moral tradition of American Protestantism is reduced to the peevishness of the WASP at bay. In fact Judge Ross's real problems come from the technicians, the immaturity and truculence of the "new men" like Colonel Carricker, who sets off the crisis by beating up a Negro pilot, not from the outraged Negroes directly.

No Cozzens protagonist will stand up any longer to the New Disorder. The center will not hold. But possibly a minutely organized, well-made novel may? *Guard of Honor* offers in structure and style the vision of a moral intactness that the chosen few have lost in everything but memory. An old-fashioned solidly worked up novel set up against a bad time and getting worse! But in *By Love Possessed* (1957) the neutral, self-satisfied irony of Cozzens's usual style has been replaced by the effort to contain Cozzens's own disarray before the adulteries by Arthur Winner Jr. and the embezzlements by Noah Tuttle. They were right to look down on Jews, Negroes, Catholics, but have now been shown up as false to the standards they professed.

By Love Possessed was a best seller in the new tradition that few things sell like explicit sex even if the style is too much for the matter. It was a long way in Cozzens's work to these upper-class adulteries on the bare mattress of a summer house. The truth was wrung out of him in pain. There are few texts in contemporary American fiction that more reveal the end of a tradition, the end of a class, the end of "honor," than those passages in which Cozzens savagely yet almost tearfully frames the dereliction with lines from great English lyrics of love and devotion. Cozzens's self-identification with a tradition, a code, a way of life, is the base from which he wrote the novels that he proudly called "illiberal," from which he snapped in *By Love Possessed* at Jews on the rise, Catholics trying to make converts, Negroes "complaining that they are not loved." Cozzens is probably no more of a Tory than is any other writer with his inheritance who regards himself as a "minority." But in the increasingly beleaguered (as it feels to itself) upper-white Protestant class, Cozzens can only blame "emotions" for the loss of control that led Arthur Winner to take his partner's wife and old Noah Tuttle, pride of the local bar, to embezzle trust funds. Another judge, Fred Dealey, expresses Cozzens's archaic psychology of "reason" and "emotion." He has an ideal of "adulthood" by which only the crippled cuckold, Julius Penrose, is satisfactorily "the man of reason." ". . . . The open, illusionless steady gaze, the precise ironic accents, of a Julius Penrose separated, in the rare solitude of an adult mind, from most human beings; with his equipoise of facts envisaged and veracities recognized, ready for whatever might come next." Or as Julius Penrose himself puts it: "Ah, what a mess these possessions by feeling may make of lives!"

Passionlessness as an ideal, an elderly jurist's impartial stance, does not communicate itself to the style of *By Love Possessed*, which is so high-flown that Dwight Macdonald parodied it as *By Cozzens Possessed*. But what really possessed Cozzens in this book — the only surprise in his career — was hardly a desire to please the public.

Cozzens had always made a cult of "the man of reason" and obviously felt himself to be one, perhaps the last one, in American writing, for most of which his contempt is notorious. But it is the fate of a "man of reason" to be utterly surprised, like Arthur Winner Sr., in the face of death. Trying to remain in urbane perfect control, the style of *By Love Possessed* strains itself into a complicatedness that reflects Cozzens's loss of respect for his own class. Cozzens had always been a dry, close, methodical and unpretentious writer. The law was his great love and each novel competently closed in on itself as evidence. Now the style broke down, tried to conceal Cozzens's conflict by unnatural fussiness. A world is supposed to have died. After discovering Noah's peculations, Arthur Winner Jr. says out loud — "I am a man alone." But perhaps that was only Cozzens himself. The "well-made" novel has not survived the shapely class distinctions on which it modeled itself.

After *By Love Possessed* had had its moment, Cozzens was not much liked and regarded. There is something about purely social novelists in America that identifies them too closely with their material, with a particular class, period, extricable attitude. The very closeness, shrewdness, felt superiority of observation that gives American novelists of manners their intense interest also makes them ritual victims of fashion. John O'Hara, who was so outraged when Bernard Malamud won a National Book Award for *The Magic Barrel* that he declared that only solid novelists of their generation like himself and Cozzens should have been considered for the prize was one of the few novelists who now had a good word for

Cozzens. But there is reason to believe that by Cozzens O'Hara really meant O'Hara. He always felt neglected and abused — probably because his burningly acute sense of class and status in America fed on a profound personal sense of injustice. (Hemingway said he was raising a fund to send John O'Hara to Yale.) Even if O'Hara had gone to Princeton, an experience of which he was cheated by his father's death, he would still have felt that he was a Mick from Pottsville, Pa.*

O'Hara nursed his grudges with the acumen of a Balzac hero. The more he published and the richer he became, the more he identified himself with the lonely grandeur of the underrated. He published so many books that he virtually ran out of titles — his short story collections were getting called *Assembly, The O'Hara Generation, — And Other Stories*. By the time he died in the spring of 1970, he had published more than thirty books, over two hundred and fifty short stories, and he was full of riches — his own riches and the lore of the American rich. He now helped them to find names for their racehorses. He was a conspicuous and angry success who in print enumerated the number of cars in his garage with as much passion as he did the number of stories he had written. He even had the square body, totally wary face and somehow

* Jimmy Malloy in *Butterfield 8* to his girl, who has asked him, "Why are you talking about you people, you people, your kind of people, people like you?" "I want to tell you something about myself that will help to explain a lot of things about me," Jimmy replies. "First of all, I am a Mick. I wear Brooks clothes and I don't eat salad with a spoon and I probably could play five-goal polo in two years, but I am a Mick. Still a Mick. . . . James Cagney is a Mick, without any pretense of being anything else, and he is America's ideal gangster. America, being a non-Irish, anti-Catholic country, has its own idea of what a real gangster looks like."

arranged look of propriety that used to be the mark of American managers of industry who had made their way up — seemingly with the force of their faces. But O'Hara in his riches revealed the same inability to tolerate the existence of other American novelists that the Anglos, Irish and Polish had felt about each other in O'Hara's tight and venomous corner of the coal country. So much rancor was now said to be old-fashioned. But O'Hara kept an unrelenting fist on the most trivial signs of social differentiation in an America now much more fluid and hedonistic in the ever-spreading middle class. O'Hara's earliest images of how people succeed in society made up his capital as a writer; he was never able to understand to what extent many younger writers, especially those also writing for *The New Yorker,* took for granted the prodigious enriching of all sorts of uninteresting people in the United States. Least of all was he interested in the churchless individual seeking a "religious" life, as were Salinger and Updike. O'Hara, fantastically overspecialized in the social signs, as fanatical about keeping up the class struggle as a nineteenth-century coal baron, finally the prisoner of his own professional pride,* took the easy way

---

* "If you are an author, and not just a writer, you keep learning all the time. Today, for instance, I was thinking about dialog, listening to dialog of some characters in my mind's ear, and I learned for the first time in my life that almost no woman who has gone beyond the eighth grade ever calls a fifty-cent piece a half-dollar. A male author, writing dialog carelessly, might easily have a female character say 'half-a-dollar' because it sounded vernacularly right to him. But it would be wrong, it would harm his characterization, and he would never know why." [Foreword to *Assembly,* 1961]

Ten years later there were virtually no half-dollars circulating in most parts of the United States.

out of so much social change; he wrote the same kind of story over and over. It was easy because he was concerned with minute social antagonisms; the time remained America's Iron Age.

O'Hara was able to write so much because he finally indulged *himself* in mapping out social roles. For a moment he even became for some critics documentation of *their* heightened concern with social differences.* He once wrote, with his usual bristle, that the emergence of the United States in the first half of the twentieth century was the greatest possible subject for a novelist. But this "emergence" meant, for O'Hara, not a sense of America the superpower at mid-century, but external evidences of the struggle for existence — the struggle between random samples of humanity in America totally preoccupied with their material progress. O'Hara was a novelist of manners crushingly interested *only* in manners, a documentarian whose characters were equivalents for the same social process. But he was never as monotonous as he might have been — he was merely discouraging. He had an old-fashioned avidity for what he never ceased to think of as (especially woman's) Dirty Little Secret.

* Lionel Trilling's "Manners, Morals and the Novel" was an influential defense at this time of status and privilege as necessary to the social novel, as was Mary McCarthy's "America the Beautiful." In his Introduction to the Modern Library edition of O'Hara's stories (the conjunction of their names was significant) Trilling said that "O'Hara's peculiar gift is his brilliant awareness of the differences within the national sameness. . . . The passionate commitment to verisimilitude which is so salient a characteristic of O'Hara's work is a very important trait in a writer. . . ." Trilling compared O'Hara's sense of the hardness of society to that of Kafka. There is reason to believe that to Kafka hardness meant not class distinctions but the State. It was not "society" that murdered Kafka's sisters.

O'Hara's world is one of total ambitiousness (an abstract idea) humanized only by extreme lust. The lust is as predictable as the ambitiousness, but shameful. O'Hara's respect for the American game that produces only winners and losers is so great that the people in his later novels are entirely exchangeable; they seem to get their characters only from their competence in the social process. The lust, the dirty little secret — always treated as one of those sneakinesses that explains the ascendency of certain people — is the most glaring example of the scarcity of motive that dominates O'Hara's mind. O'Hara finds human beings as easy to explain as the profit-and-loss system for which they live; thus they repeat themselves to the point of reproducing themselves from novel to novel as they did from story to story. What does make O'Hara's world exciting is the terror of social displacement never far from the surface. We have reason to identify with that terror; America is a rich country in which many people feel poor. The social soil is still too thin to hold anything of people but their ambition. O'Hara's corner of America seems more "lived in" than most, but it is not human personality that makes it interesting, it is O'Hara's personal excitement, the outsider concentrating on every detail of the world in which he is making his way up. O'Hara's is one old-fashioned class saga in which the *value* of position or great wealth is never doubted. The contention for it is everything. "Society" always comes out on top. Never again, in the work of an American novelist, would there be so much faith in the Establishment.

In February 1968 O'Hara wrote in the preface to *And Other Stories* that although he loved to write short stories

108

and did them easily, ". . . the writing of short stories is becoming an expensive luxury at my age. No one writes them any better than I do, but in energy and time they have become costly because the energy and time come from sources that I must budget for a long novel. . . ." The overgrown novels that O'Hara now published were in fact pointlessly extended biographies of American careers. The only real interest of these absurdly swollen histories was his command of any immediate social situation. The short story was indeed his form, his imaginative model. O'Hara had begun as a reporter probably because he was a natural writer of "pieces." He became a prodigiously expert and expectable writer of stories out of the particular sense of social differences and the pride in his sense of fact that for him were synonymous with the practice of fiction. But he could think of fiction as endless stories, could collect them into book after book because, though this society stirred in O'Hara a fear like Kafka's, O'Hara devoutly believed in the American system itself, never questioned its reality to his characters, and thought of his many casualties as inevitable. As he said, "the development of the United States in the first half of the 20th century is the most important subject for a novelist."

This trust in the circumstances attending one's own riches would have seemed parvenu to Scott Fitzgerald — a writer whose subtle tragedies meant less to O'Hara than Fitzgerald's "glamorous" characters.* To the new virtuosi

---

* Before he became his astonishingly important ghost, the Fitzgerald who died in Hollywood, who had depended in Hollywood on John O'Hara's approbation, seemed a failure and so not calculated to impress O'Hara. Unlike O'Hara, Fitzgerald had a fatalistic despairing love for his own characters (and, of course, constantly

of short stories in *The New Yorker* — Cheever, Salinger, Updike — the next practitioners of an art form that was a way of making points about American society, and that was eventually to disappear from *The New Yorker* as from everywhere else, O'Hara's trust in American capitalism as exclusive reality must have seemed baffling.

John Cheever found in suburbsville almost as many cruel social differences as O'Hara had always known in Gibbsville. But the overwhelming sensation that a reader got from Cheever's special performance of the short story was of a form that no longer spoke for itself. It was not even a "slice of life," as O'Hara's stories were, but had become a demonstration of the amazing sadness, futility and evanescence of life among the settled, moneyed, seemingly altogether domesticated people in Proxmire Manor. As Cheever said in two different pieces of fiction, Why, in this "half-finished civilization, in this most prosperous, equitable and accomplished world, should everyone seem so disappointed?" It is a question that earlier writers of "*The New Yorker* story" would not have asked openly, with so much expectation of being agreed with, and twice. But Cheever's brightly comic, charming, heartbreaking performances always came out as direct points made about "the quality of life in the United States," or "How We Live Now."

---

put himself and his fatal Zelda into his work). Fitzgerald even identified his most appealing characters with the fate of goodness in our kind of world. O'Hara was a social Darwinist of the most extreme kind, more removed from losers than anybody since the first John D. Rockefeller. He created a whole succession of individuals unrelated to anyone. He wrote about people as social information — which shows how carefully, unlike Fitzgerald, he kept himself apart.

Cheever — Salinger and Updike were to be like him in this respect — began and somehow has remained a startlingly precocious, provocatively "youthful" writer. But unlike Salinger and Updike, he was to seem more identifiable with the rest of *The New Yorker*, just as his complaint about American life was more concrete and his fiction more expectable. His stories regularly became a form of social lament — writing never hard to take. What they said, and Cheever openly *said* it, was that America was still a dream, a fantasy; America did not look lived in, Americans were not really settled in. In their own minds they were still on their way to the Promised Land. In story after story Cheever's characters, guiltily, secretly disillusioned and disabused with their famous "way of life" (always something that could be put into words and therefore promised, advertised and demonstrated), suddenly acted out their inner subversion. They became "eccentrics," crazily swimming from pool to pool, good husbands who fell in love with the baby-sitter. Sometimes, like "Aunt Justina," they even died in the living room and could not be moved because of the health laws and restriction by the zoning law on any funeral parlors in the neighborhood.

Acting out one's loneliness, one's death wish — any sudden eccentricity embarrassing everybody in the neighborhood — these make for situation comedy. Life is turning one's "normal" self inside out at a party. The subject of Cheever's stories is regularly a situation that betrays the basic "unreality" of some character's life. It is a trying-out of freedom in the shape of the extreme, the unmentionable. Crossing the social line is one aspect of comedy, and Cheever demonstrates it by giving a social shape to the most insubstantial and private longings. Loneliness is the dirty little secret, a personal drive so urgent and confusing that it comes out a vice. But the pathetic escapade never lasts very long. We are not at home here, says Cheever. But there is no other place for us to feel that we are not at home.

In these terms the short story becomes not the compression of an actual defeat but the anecdote of a temporary crisis. The crisis is the trying-out of sin, escape, the abyss, and is described by Cheever with radiant attention: *there* is the only new world his characters ever reach. ". . . They flew into a white cloud of such density that it reflected the exhaust fires. The color of the cloud darkened to gray, and the plane began to rock. . . . The stewardess announced that they were going to make an emergency landing. All but the children saw in their minds the spreading wings of the Angel of Death. The pilot could be heard singing faintly, 'I've got sixpence, jolly jolly sixpence. I've got sixpence to last me all my life. . . .'" The "country husband" in this most brilliant of Cheever's stories returns home to find that his brush with death is not of the slightest interest to his family, so he falls in love with the baby-sitter. He does not get very far with the baby-sitter, so he goes to a therapist who prescribes woodworking. The story ends derisively on the brainwashed husband who will no longer stray from home. But who cares about this fellow? It is Cheever's clever, showy handling of the husband's "craziness," sentence by sentence, that engages us. Each sentence is a miniature of Cheever's narrative style, and each sentence makes the point that Cheever is mastering his material, and comes back to the mystery of why, in this half-finished civilization, this most prosperous equitable and accomplished world, everyone should seem so disappointed. So there is no mastery in Cheever's story except Cheever's. It is Cheever one watches in the story, Cheever who moves us, literally, by the shape of his effort in every line, by the significance he gives to every inflection, and finally by the cruel lucidity he brings to this most prosperous, equitable and accomplished world as a breaking of the heart.

My deepest feeling about Cheever is that his marvelous brightness is an effort to cheer himself up. His is the only impressive energy in a perhaps too equitable and prosperous suburban world whose subject is internal depression, the Saturday night party, and the post-martini bitterness. Feeling alone is the air his characters breathe. Just as his characters have no feeling of achievement in their work, so they never collide with or have to fight a society which is actually America in allegory. All conflict is in the head. People just disappear, as from a party. Cheever's novels — *The Wapshot Chronicle, The Wapshot Scandal, Bullet Park* — tend to muffle his characters in meaning even more than the short stories do. Cheever is such an accomplished performer of the short story that the foreshortening of effect has become second nature with him. There is the shortest possible bridge between cause and effect. *The New Yorker* column is still the inch of ivory on which he writes. Cheever writes always about "America." He is an intellectual. The Wapshot novels are wholly allegories of place showing the degeneration of the old

New England village, "St. Botolph's," into the symbolic (but spreading) suburb that is "Proxmire Manor."

When last heard from* — in *The New Yorker* for June 19, 1965 — J. D. Salinger gave the impression that he had withdrawn into the godhead of Seymour Glass. In "Hapworth 16, 1924," Seymour Glass is seven years old. But writing to his parents from camp, he displays (to a degree not preposterous only if you already know Seymour Glass) the religious and literary superiority to other people that in 1948, at thirty-one years of age, while on his honeymoon, was to lead him to commit suicide right in front of the sleeping figure of his bride. He had called her "Miss Spiritual Tramp of 1948."

Salinger's evident obsession with Seymour the dead brother, Seymour the artist, saint, spiritual teacher, had taken over his writing ever since "Franny and Zooey." The Glass family had become a chorus ecstatically living in memory of Seymour. It lived by reciting his great deeds of love and perception. Seymour Glass had in fact become, in death, the charisma behind a new religion,† the Glass religion. All Glasses were Seymour's worshippers. Buddy Glass (explicitly J. D. Salinger himself) is the apostle to

---

* Salinger, I am informed by an editor of *The New Yorker*, continues to write but refuses to publish.

† Even the bride, who reports to her mother that Seymour called her "Miss Spiritual Tramp of 1948," is drawn to the man who disapproves of her to the point of (his) death. Only *Salinger's* belief in Seymour's greatness explains his bride's devotion to the man who publicly skipped out of marrying her in "Raise High the Roofbeam, Carpenters," and after she finally eloped with him, scorned her in "A Perfect Day for Bananafish" for not reading Rilke *in German* and punished her for his mistake in marrying him by shooting himself right in front of her.

whom it was left to put the sacred words down. Whether the obsession with Seymour became so extensive that it proved too much for Salinger, or whether Salinger's contempt for the profane non-Glass world became unbearable to himself, is not for the outsider to say. Salinger is outraged by the very act of criticism, wants only readers who are faithful loving friends, like his editors at *The New Yorker* and the armies of young people who gratefully recognized themselves in *The Catcher in the Rye*. He would rather be silent at the moment than see his imaginative world profaned by criticism.

Salinger's extraordinary stories — extraordinary in their residual pain and obsession, extraordinary as fiction — are dominated by the idea of the Glass family as exceptional beings. In a world too plainly made "absurd" by our inability to love it, the Glasses are loved by their relative and creator, J. D. Salinger, on every inexhaustible cherished inch of their lives. His microscopic love for them compels them into our field of vision; we see them though the absoluteness of Salinger's love and grief. And non-Glasses are spiritual trash. One recognizes in Salinger's stories a disturbing death wish, a sympathy with extinction, the final silence tempting to absolutists of feeling. This pertained so long to the unworthy non-Glass world that it may have turned on Salinger himself.

Yet for all this eerie devaluation of everyone outside the Glass family, the whole charm of Salinger's fiction lies in his gift for comedy, his ability to represent society as it is, for telltale gestures and social manners. In what is probably his best story, "Raise High the Roofbeam, Carpenters" — the beautifully spun-out account of what happened among the wedding guests when the bride-groom failed to show up, the meticulous telling of every detail, the light ironic allusions to the contrasts of the shifting social groupings, in the obviously but not ex-plicitly Jewish bourgeoisie, are somehow held together by the intense self-consciousness of brother Buddy Glass the narrator. In the heat of the midsummer afternoon, in a bedraggled uniform, and barely over an attack of pleurisy, he somehow manages to describe completely the external human *performance* of every guest at this fiasco of a wedding.

Salinger's great gift was always comic, Chaplinesque, in his ability to project a world of social types from a fumbling, theatrically awkward observer and narrator, Buddy Glass the English instructor and as yet unpub-lished writer, who is confessedly a failure and somehow ridiculous in his excessive feelings of alienation. Buddy's special thing was to create sympathy for his pratfalls and fumbling, for his own unachieved gestures, that then lighted up other people's gestures and fumbling as a way of life. No American fiction writer in recent memory has given so much value, by way of his hypnotized attention, to the little things that light up character in every social exchange. Salinger has been the great pantomimist in our contemporary fiction. One of his favorite characters is obviously the deaf-mute uncle in "Raise High the Roof-beam, Carpenters," whose mysteriously stiff movements Buddy, as usual, describes with infinite patience and loving curiosity. In "Franny" "the boys who had been keep-ing themselves warm began to come out to meet the train, most of them giving the impression of having at least three lighted cigarettes in each hand. . . . It was a station-platform kiss — spontaneous enough to begin with, but rather inhibited in the follow-through, and with something of a forehead-bumping aspect." In "Raise High the Roofbeam, Carpenters," Buddy reads Seymour's diary in the bathroom (there is no other place to hide):

> I . . . sat for several minutes with the diary under one arm, until I became conscious of a certain discomfort from having sat so long on the side of the bathtub. When I stood up, I found I was perspiring more profusely than I had all day, as though I had just got out of a tub, rather than just sitting on the side of one. I went over to the laundry hamper, raised the lid, and, with an almost vicious wrist movement, literally threw Seymour's diary into some sheets and pillowcases that were on the bottom of the hamper. Then, for want of a better, more constructive idea, I went back and sat down on the side of the bathtub again.

Salinger has a genius for capturing the emotional giveaway. Love is isolating. The fact that his love necessitates so much disdain shows how much social comedy springs from coldness toward the *world*. Salinger gives his hypnotized attention to every "enemy" gesture as well as to Seymour's saintly touch, which leaves stigmata. "I have scars on my hands from touching certain people," Seymour modestly confesses in his diary. This attentiveness, charging the front line of Salinger's fiction, is the beleaguered animal's need to know the ways of the hunter. The whole scheme of values in Salinger's fiction is to give the highest marks to the individual made exceptional by a sensitivity to society that is fear of it. Holden Caulfield endeared himself to the antisocializers of all ages because he went right into the lion's cage — all those phonies! — without liking *anything* of what he relentlessly described.

The same marginality is expressed in the purely contemplative Oriental poetry that usually serves as the scripture of Seymour's sacredness and in the cult of nonaction that places the highest value on a tender, loving, *religious* attentiveness to the littlest things of this world. To notice every seeming triviality (Seymour protests that he loves, loves, loves everything and everyone in his path) is to respect the creation — and gives Salinger's fiction its dense social texture. Extreme importance is given to things made hallucinatory by the Glass family's cherishing. Attention is compulsively fixed, as in a dream, on any item separated from its normal connections — a letter kept in the middle of a manuscript, where the stapling is *tightest.* Yet as each Glass story elongated, as these magical, disrelated, hysterically overstressed gestures, letters, camp memories formed themselves into the cult of Seymour, the reader could not help noticing that all this was founded on an idolatry of certain *persons* altogether unusual in contemporary fiction.

Salinger is an oddity, an obsessive, who commands respect because certain of his characters are so important to him. The Glass stories are not another family chronicle; Salinger's emotions are too selective and even arbitrary. But they do display, to the point of anguish, a sense that *some* people are more important than anything else in the world. So much regard for individual personality (incestuous as the particular case may be) makes Salinger's Holy Family stand out from the great mass of unvalued, unregarded and undescribed individuals in contemporary fiction. *His* people will last.

Salinger, so self-limiting, "special," fanatical, making his American comedy of manners out of desperate love for his own, now makes a deceptively pathetic contrast with John Updike, a virtuoso who seems able to make up stories about anything that interests him intellectually, morally, pictorially. Salinger is of course reporting to someone. His work is pervaded by a filial piety that reminds one of the pilgrim on his knees, with hands uplifted in prayer, who puts himself into a corner of his own painting of Seymour Glass's crucifixion. Even his intellectual loves are those of a worshipper; nothing Oriental and quietist may ever be questioned. Updike writes as if there were no greater pleasure than reconstituting the world by writing — writing is mind exercising itself, rejoicing in its gifts. Reading him one is always conscious of Updike the Gifted, Updike the Stylist, Updike the Concerned Roguish Novelist. Updike is always so much Updike that it is the highest tribute to this gifted and serious writer that the omnipresence of Updike in all his writing finally seems not a hindrance but a trademark, youth's charming flourish of itself. This is a writer confidently personal but not subjective — who indeed pleases his busy imagination, his sense of play, by looking steadily at the contradiction within every human display.

A prime fact about Updike is that he was born in 1932, went to Harvard when there was still a great literary tradition for an undergraduate to join himself to, then felt himself the most fortunate of men when he became part of *The New Yorker* and *its* still debonair literary tradition. Precocious, original, distinctly not a loner, a writer in the postwar suburban style who associated himself with families, townships, churches, citizens' committees, Updike became a novelist of "society" in the Fifties, the age of postwar plenty and unchallenged domesticity for both sexes when many once-poor Americans, moving to the suburbs, felt they were at last coming into their reward.* Domesticity is a dominant subject of Updike's world — and so is the unavailing struggle against it, as in one of his best novels, *Rabbit, Run*. But there is in even the lucid emotions of *Rabbit, Run*, in the filial tenderness of *The Centaur*, a kind of brilliant actionlessness, a wholly mental atmosphere. Updike, thanks not least to the marvelous movement within postwar society and its unprecedented interchange of classes, backgrounds, social information, is an extremely adroit and knowledgeable observer of society and its customs. He likes to put Presidents into his work as a way of showing that President Buchanan (ancient history) and President Kennedy (the Sixties) are the real landmarks.† But such historic moments just serve to date the personal mythology in his characters' minds; they are never forces. There is no

---

* "He thinks we've made a church of each other." [*Couples*]

† INTERVIEWER: Let's turn from myth to history. You have indicated a desire to write about President Buchanan. Yet so far as I can see, American history is normally absent from your work. UPDIKE: Not so; quite the contrary. In each of my novels, a precise year is given and a President reigns; *The Centaur* is distinctly a Truman book, and *Rabbit, Run* an Eisenhower one. *Couples* could have taken place only under Kennedy; the social currents it traces are as specific to those years as flowers in a meadow are to their moment of summer.
[*Paris Review*, interview, winter 1968]

struggle with American society; its character is fixed, though nothing else is.

Updike's characters represent many things to him; he glosses all his own novels. And because Updike fancies them as many-sided and intellectual designs, they are unusually distinct and memorable among characters in contemporary fiction. They always *mean*. Updike's fiction is distinguished by an unusually close interest in every character he writes about. But these characters who represent so much never struggle with anything except the reflections in their minds of a circumscribing reality that seems unalterable. Updike is a novelist of society who sees society entirely as a fable. It stands still for him to paint its picture; *it* never starts anything. On the other hand, it is always there to say "American," now and in the future — Updike's first novel, *The Poorhouse Fair*, started with the future as tyranny, institutions that are there to say that institutions always take over.

The older American novelists of society were not this much used to it. Scott Fitzgerald, who loved its color, its prodigality, profoundly distrusted it and thought it would revenge itself on its critics. Updike, who persistently re-calls Fitzgerald's ability to show society as a dream, has accommodated himself to its dominating possessiveness. Where there are no alternatives, even in one's memory, the proliferating surfaces encourage myths, transferable symbols — a sense of situation, not opposition. Updike is in the best sense of the word an intellectual novelist, a novelist of paradox, tension and complexity who as a col-lege wit in the Fifties learned that we are all symbols and inhabit symbols. His easy mastery of social detail never includes any sense of American society as itself a peculiar institution, itself the dynamo, the aggressor, the maker of other people's lives. Society is just a set of characteristics. Society — our present fate! — shows itself in marvelously shifting mental colors and shapes. Brightness falls from the air, thanks to the God on whose absence we sharpen our minds. But Updike's own bright images of human perception fall along a horizontal line, metaphors of observation that connect only with each other. The world is all metaphor. We are not sure *who* is thinking these brilliant images in *Rabbit, Run*. Need Updike's fine mind be so much in evidence?

> *His day had been bothered by God: Ruth mocking, Eccles blinking — why did they teach you such things if no one believed them? It seems plain, standing here, that if there is this floor there is a ceiling, that the true space in which we live is upward space. Someone is dying. In this great stretch of bridge someone is dying. The thought comes from nowhere: simple percentages. Someone in some house along these streets, if not this minute then the next, dies; and in that suddenly stone chest the heart of this flat prostrate rose seems to him to be. He moves his eyes to find the spot; perhaps he can see a cancer-blackened soul of an old man mount through the blue like a monkey on a spring. . . .*

Updike is indeed a great mental traveler through the many lands of American possibility. Though *The Poorhouse Fair*, *The Olinger Stories*, *The Centaur* and others of his best works deal with the southeasternmost corner of Pennsylvania he comes from, he no more judges the rest of America by it than puts America into it — as O'Hara put everything he knew into his corner of Pennsylvania. Updike has nothing of the primitive attachment to early beginnings that made a whole generation of American realists once describe the big city as a total dislodgement. As a believer in tradition rediscovered, he can weave a surpassingly tender novel about his father, *The Centaur*, into a set of mythological associations and identifications that in other hands would have academicized the novel to death. *The Centaur* is one of his best books. In *Rabbit, Run* he wrote the marriage novel of a period marked by an increasing disbelief in marriage as the foundation of everything. At the end of *Rabbit, Run* the oversize Harry Angstrom ran away from his mopey wife Janice, who while drunk had accidentally drowned their baby, and from the unfathomable insatiable domesticity of the "tranquilized fifties," as Robert Lowell calls them.

Rabbit Redux of course opens on the day in 1969 that saw the first manned American flight to the moon, "leaving the rest of us here." Harry was once too young and is now mysteriously too old. He is now a decaying man in an American city typically running down, is proud to support the Vietnam War when everybody else has seen through it, and in order to provide the reader with a glibly topical symposium, suddenly finds himself sharing his house with Jill, a wild young hippie runaway from her family, and her sometime lover and drug supply Skeeter, a young Black Vietnam veteran who has jumped bail. Yet even an inferior novel, *Couples*, the book of suburban marriage and its now conventional adulteries that shows Updike exercising his gifts and putting up his usual intellectual-religious scaffolding with somewhat too bountiful ease, is *not* a document, for Updike is happily a novelist excited by his characters. And in *Bech* Updike not only takes on the Jew, the Jewish novelist, a subject that has long fascinated and provoked him because "the Jewish novelist" is so much a fact of our times, so important a social category and rival, the most striking sudden success in a society of sudden successes — he even manages to show the comedy in Bech, a failure.

Everything seems possible to Updike; everything *has* been possible. He knows his way around, in every sense, without being superficial about it. His real subject — the dead hand of "society," the fixity of institutions — has gone hand in hand with the only vision of freedom as the *individual's* recognition of God. This is a period when, as Updike says, "God has killed the churches." There is no nemesis: just an empty space between those untouching circles, society and the individual. Updike has managed to be an intellectual without becoming abstract; in an era of boundless personal confusion, he has been a moralist without rejecting the mores. If poise is a gift, Updike is a genius. If to be "cool" is not just a social grace but awareness unlimited, Updike is the best of this cool world. All he lacks is that capacity for making you identify, for summoning up affection in the reader, which Salinger (now "poor Salinger") expressed when in *The Catcher in the Rye* he had Holden Caulfield reserve his praise for authors who make you want to call them up.

5

THE EARTHLY CITY
OF THE JEWS
Bellow to Singer

. . . . It wasn't desolation that this made you feel, but rather a faltering of organization that set free a huge energy, an escaped, unattached, unregulated power from the giant raw place. . . . People were compelled to match it. In their very bodies. He no less than others, he realized. . . . His parents had been servants . . . they had never owed any service like this, which no one visible asked and probably flesh and blood could not even perform. Nor could anyone show why it should be performed; or see what the performance would lead to. That did not mean that he wanted to be released from it, he realized with a grimly pensive face. On the contrary. He had something to do. To be compelled to feel this energy and yet have nothing to do — that was horrible; that was suffering. . . .

— Saul Bellow, "Looking for Mr. Green"

No doubt the world is entirely an imaginary world, but it is only once removed from the true world. At the door of the hovel where I lie, there stands the plank on which the dead are taken away. The gravedigger Jew has his spade ready. . . . When the time comes, I will go joyfully. Whatever may be there, it will be real, without complication, without ridicule, without deception. God be praised; there even Gimpel cannot be deceived.

— Isaac Bashevis Singer,
   "Gimpel the Fool" (translated by Saul Bellow)

Why did I always have to fall among theoreticians!
— Augie March

WHEN JOHN UPDIKE brilliantly conceived Henry Bech, who was in everything he did, and especially in what he couldn't do, "the Jew as contemporary American novelist," Updike was having his fun with that once unlikely but now well-known American product, Bellow-Malamud-Roth. Bellow said that the constant linking of these names reminded him of Hart, Schaffner and Marx. But irritating as it might be to one proudly gifted and much-honored novelist to be linked with other *Jewish* names, Bellow more than any other American novelist of his ability used the modern Jewish experience in his work.

Most of Bellow's characters were Jews, his non-Jewish characters (rare enough) were, like Allbee in *The Victim*, obsessed with Jews or, like Henderson, clamorously produced wittily agonized definitions of human existence remarkably like those of the Jewish protagonists in Bellow's novels — Joseph in *Dangling Man*, Asa Leventhal in *The Victim*, Tommy Wilhelm in *Seize the Day*, Augie March, Herzog, Mr. Sammler. Over and again in Bellow's novels there were the parents who to tyrants in eastern Europe had been nothing but Jews, and in the slums of Montreal and Chicago saw nothing but their own experience reflected back from the neighborhood. There was a natural, enchanted repetition of the Jewish neighborhood, the Jewish family circle, the Jew as college intellectual, radical, dreamer, explorer of lowlife — the Jew discovering worlds new to him. "Look at me going everywhere!" Augie March cries out after pages devoted principally to the emancipation and enlightenment of Augie's senses — "Why, I am a sort of Columbus of those near-at-hand!" More than anyone else, Bellow connected one novel after another with a representative Jew in order to represent Jewish experience itself.

This emphasis on one people's collective idiosyncratic experience, an emphasis so intense that it seems to follow from some deep cut in Bellow's mind, is nevertheless intense in attention rather than partisan. Bellow is positively hypnotized by the part of human life he knows best, as a novelist should be, and he sees everything else in this focus. But without being detached and "impartial" about the long Jewish struggle for survival, he is fascinated and held by the texture of Jewish experience as it becomes, as it can become, the day-to-day life of people one has created. This is very different from writing about people one names as Jews but who, no matter how one feels about them, are just names on the page. Texture is life relived, *life* on the page, beyond praise or blame. In Bellow's first novel, *Dangling Man* (1944), the hero writes of himself: ". . . . To him judgment is second to wonder, to speculation on men, drugged and clear, jealous, ambitious, good, tempted, curious, each in his own time and with his customs and motives, and bearing the imprint of strangeness in the world." To Asa Leventhal in *The Victim*, crossing over to Staten Island,

the towers on the shore rose up in huge blocks,
scorched, smoky gray. . . . The notion brushed Leven-
thal's mind that the light over them and over the water
was akin to the yellow revealed in the eye of a wild
animal, say a lion, something inhuman that didn't care
about anything human and yet was implanted in every
human being too, one speck of it, and formed a part of
him that responded to the heat and the glare . . . even
to freezing, salty things, harsh things, all things difficult
to stand.

In *Seize the Day*, where the West Side of New York is the
most living, throbbing character, Tommy Wilhelm, trying
to make a confident appearance with a hat and a cigar,
feels that the day is getting away from him: ". . . . the
cigar was out and the hat did not defend him . . . the
peculiar burden of his existence lay upon him like an
accretion . . . his entire chest ached . . . as though tightly
tied with ropes. He smelled the salt odor of tears in his
eyes. . . ." In the sunshine of upper Broadway there was
"a false air of gas visible at eye-level as it spurted from the
bursting buses."

This air of having lived, of experiencing the big city in
every pore, of being on the spot, is the great thing about
Bellow's fiction. It is this living acrid style — in the suddenly chastened, too glibly precise, peculiarly assertive
bitterness of postwar American writing, with its hallucinated clarity about details, its oversized sense of our
existence, of too many objects all around (what desolation amidst wonders!) — that made us realize Bellow as
an original. He is a key to something that would emerge in
all the American writing of this period about cities, the

"mass," the common life. This was not the "minority" writing of the poignant, circumscribed novels of the 1930s. Even in the best of them, like Daniel Fuchs's *Low Company, Summer in Williamsburg, Homage to Blenholt,* one had been aware that "Jewish" equals ghetto. Bellow had come out of a ghetto in Montreal, the Napoleon Street that makes one of the deeper sections of *Herzog.* But what made him suddenly vivid, beginning with what was later to seem the put-on of *The Adventures of Augie March* (1953), was his command of a situation peculiarly American, founded on mass experience, that was as far from the metaphysical wit in Kafka as it was from the too conscious pathos of the Depression novels. With Bellow an American of any experience could feel that he was in the midst of the life he knew.

What was perhaps most "American" about it was the fact that despite all the crisis psychology in *The Victim, Seize the Day, Herzog* there was a burning belief in commanding one's own experience, in putting it right by thought. Each of these narratives was a kind of survival kit for a period in which survival became all too real a question for many Americans. The Jewish experience on that subject — and what else had the experience been? — seemed exemplary to Americans, especially when it came armed with jokes. Goodbye to Henry Roth and how many other gifted, stunted, devastated Jewish novelists of the Thirties. In book after book Bellow went about the business of ordering life, seeing it through, working it out. He was intimate with the heights-and-abyss experience of so many intellectual Jews, the alternating experience of humiliation and the paradise of intellectual

130

illumination. And it was this depiction of life as incessant mental struggle, of heaven and hell in the same Jewish head,* that made Bellow's readers recognize a world the reverse of the provincial, a quality of thought somber, tonic, bracing, that was now actual to American experience yet lent itself to Bellow's fascinatedly personal sense of things.

In all of this Bellow became a style-setter for those many writers emerging in the Fifties who found in him a kind of paradigm for taking hold, for getting in there, for being on top of the desperate situation. And indeed no one was more impressed by this angle on life, this sense of command, this ability to be *imaginatively* in charge, than Bellow himself, whose books, one after another, were usually founded on a protagonist who was the nearest possible spokesman for himself. Just as the success story of American Jews "making it" was represented by a bewildering succession of changes in their lives, so Bellow's novels, each registering a different state of awareness but all coming together as successive chapters of the same personal epic, made the nearest and best literary expression of the disbelief behind a Jewish ascent that was also haunted by the Holocaust. Bellow expressed both the American facts and the disbelief.

Here was an American Jewish writer who had a powerful sense of his own experience as imaginative, yet could beat other Jewish intellectuals at putting the universe into a sentence. He was as clever as a businessman

---

* "Up to their necks in dung," an old East European *rebbe* said of his seminarians, "they dream of ancient Assyria, Babylonia, Palestine."

but racked by a sense of responsibility to his "soul." Bellow underwent all these phases in his fiction. But at the center of each narrative was always a hero, a single mind and conscience, adventurous but forever counting the cost of existence. Above all, the Bellow persona was an hallucinated observer of what Sartre called the "hell that is other people" — he brilliantly sized up the strength in other people's arms, lives, faces, seeing what they had to say to the predominating self's vision at the heart of each Bellow novel. The man had been an anthropologist, a traveler, a musician, an editor of the University of Chicago's "great books"; he was a teacher, a lover, a liberated Jewish male and the most watchful of Jewish sons; he had found a way through the thickets of the big-city ghetto, the big-city university, the Depression, the merchant marine during the war; he had been a left radical, a welfare investigator; he was soon to become the sternest of Jewish moralists. And in all this Bellow influenced himself far more than others ever did, which is why book after book added up to what he had experienced and learned. The key belief was that right thinking is virtue and can leave you in charge of the life that is so outrageous to live.

The process of self-teaching thus becomes the heart of Bellow's novels, and the key to their instructiveness for others. One could compile from Bellow's novels a whole commonplace book of wisdom in the crisis era that has been Bellow's subject and opportunity. His novels are successively novels of instruction as well as existential adventure tales. The story as a whole tells, as the best Jewish stories always do, of the unreality of this world as opposed to God's. The hero struggles in a world not his own, a world run by strangers. The Jewish son has indeed lost the paradise that in childhood was within his grasp. In scripture this world is God's world; Jews must be grateful and obedient for being allowed to share it. In Jewish fiction this world is always someone else's world, though it is one in which Jews call themselves Jews and remain Jews. The so-called Jewish novel (there really is one, though only a few Jews have written it, and those who write it are not always Jews) takes place in a world that is unreal, never *our* world. The heart of the world is Jewish (said John Jay Chapman) but in Bellow's novels only one's mother and father have a heart. Bellow is in magnetized relation to the big-city environment, to the vertigo and clamor of New York, to the opulent yet sortable detail. But his is not a world in which a Jew feels at home. The Jew is always in some uneasy relation to "them" — he is a newcomer, parvenu, displaced person whose self-ordering becomes the issue in each book. In his humanist attack on anti-Semitism in France, *Jew and Anti-Semite*, Jean-Paul Sartre defined a Jew as someone whom others regard as a Jew. This understandably provoked Bellow by its lack of knowledge. When even "a prince of European philosophy" knows so little about them, Jews may wonder if this *is* their world. And so the Jew in Bellow's novels is a "stranger" because he really is one — not, like Camus's "*étranger*," because he is free of other people's opinions to the point of total indifference. This representative Jew is involved in a catch-as-catch-can relationship to the world, that famous anchor of the old bourgeois novel, that keeps him lightly suspended just above the earth.*

But the vitality of Bellow's fiction comes from the importance of being a Jewish son, a figure of importance; this may be hidden from everyone but himself. The Bellow hero, though often distraught, has the powerful ego of Joseph relating his dreams to his jealous brothers. This hero is so all-dominating that other males tend to become distinct only if they are intellectuals who personify *wrong ideas*. Nonintellectuals, like the women in the later novels, tend to become "reality instructors," opaque emblems of the distrusted world. The central figure is the only pilgrim who makes any progress. From Joseph in *Dangling Man* to old Mr. Sammler, each of Bellow's heroes represents the same desperate struggle for life — by which he means a more refined consciousness. It is a concentrated example of the age-old Jewish belief that salvation is in thinking well — to go to the root of things, to become a kind of scientist of morals, to seek the ultimate forces that rule us.

Thinking is for Bellow the most accessible form of virtue. The "reality instructors" have become indistinguishable from the worldliness with which they are clotted. Bellow's recurrent hero, by contrast, is so concerned with thinking well that the imbalance between the hero and his fellows becomes an imbalance between the hero's thinking and the mere *activity* of others. Bellow is not a very dramatic novelist, and unexpected actions tend to be dragged into his novels — like Herzog's

* An image in Kafka's parables.

half-hearted attempt to kill his wife's lover — as a way of interrupting the hero's reflections. But evidently Bellow's personae attain their interest for *him* by their ability to express the right opinions. And not surprisingly, the protagonists of Bellow's novels are the voices of his intellectual evolution. A Bellow anthology would take the form of a breviary, an intellectual testament gathered from diaries, letters to public men and famous philosophers that were never mailed, arias to the reader à la Augie March, the thoughts of Artur Sammler that are neural events in the privacy of one's consciousness because they cannot be expressed to others — they are too severe, too disapproving.

Bellow has found fascinating narrative forms for the urgency of his many thoughts. He has been clever in finding a distinct *style* for so much silent thinking — from Joseph's diaries in *Dangling Man* to Herzog's equally incessant meditations and finally old Mr. Sammler's haughty soliloquies, where the style is one of the lightest, featheriest, mental penciling, an intellectual shorthand (here involving brusque images of the city) that answers to the traditional contractedness of Jewish thought. The favorite form for Jewish sages has always been the shortest, and Bellow's best fictions are his shortest. V. S. Pritchett, who admires Bellow for powerful descriptions of city life rare among "intellectual" novelists, thinks that in his long books Bellow "becomes too personal. There is a failure to cut the umbilical cord." Bellow's more lasting fictions will probably be those whose personae are not *exactly* as intelligent as he is — *The Victim* and *Seize the Day*.

In these books the weight of the world's irrationality, which is its injustice, falls heavily upon human beings who win us by their inability to understand all that is happening to them and why it is happening to *them*. Asa Leventhal at the end of *The Victim*, having been persecuted, exploited, terrified by a Gentile who accuses the Jew of having persecuted *him*, ends up innocently saying to his tormentor — "Wait a minute, what's your idea of who runs things?" Tommy Wilhelm in *Seize the Day*, who in one day realizes that he has lost wife, mistress, father, money, God, confronts the depths of his suffering only by identifying with a stranger into whose funeral he has stumbled by accident. These incomprehensions are truly evocative of the "existential situation" in contemporary fiction — that of individuals who are never up to their own suffering, who cannot fully take it in, who have learned only that their suffering has its reasons of which reason knows nothing.

Artur Sammler, on the other hand, is so openly Bellow's mind now, in its most minute qualifications, that one can admire the man's intellectual austerity and yet be amazed that Bellow's hero should be so intelligent about everything except his relation with other human beings. Sammler is an old man, a widower, with only one eye left to him by the Nazis; his wife was shot to death in the same Polish pit from which he managed to escape past so many dead bodies (the fable that haunts Jewish writers). Sammler is old, experienced, intelligent, cultivated. But none of these things accounts for the fact that Artur Sammler disapproves of everything he sees and everyone he knows except a vague kinsman, a doctor who got him to America and supports him. He dislikes all the women especially. The evident fact is that Mr. Sammler is the Jew who, after Hitler, cannot forgive the world, for he recognizes that its exterminations may be more pleasurable to it than its lusts. He has decided, not as the rabbis have decided but as Jewish novelists have decided in this first era of fiction by many Jews, that the "world" is a very bad place indeed. In God's absence human consciousness becomes the world; then the only thing for us, *Mr. Sammler's Planet* ends, is to know and to admit that we know.

The unsatisfactory thing about Mr. Sammler — a "collector" indeed, but of wisdom — is that he is always right while other people are usually wrong — sinfully so. More than most Jewish intellectuals, Artur Sammler is right and has to be right all the time. The Jewish passion for ideological moralism, for ratiocination as the only passion that doesn't wear out (and is supposed not to interfere with the other passions) — that passion has never been "done" in our fiction. There is no precedent for its peculiar self-assertiveness, so different from luxuriating in one's ego as a cultural tradition in the style of Stephen Dedalus. In Bellow's novel, insistently moralistic and world-weary, the hero is totally identified with his own thought. His total rejection of other people because of *their* thought sets up a lack of incident, an invitation to symbolic politics, like the now celebrated scene in which a Negro pickpocket follows old, delicate Mr. Sammler to his apartment house and exposes an intimidating penis, or the corollary scene in which Mr. Sammler's mad Israeli son-in-law — a sculptor carrying a bag of metal pieces — beats the same Negro almost to death near Lincoln Center.

Bellow's intellectual at-homeness with Sammler's thought is so assured that over and again one has the Blakean experience of reading thoughts expressed as sensations. But what is certainly not Blakean are the austere, dismissive jeremiads, the open contempt for the women in the book as crazy fantasists, improvident, gross careless sexpots, "birds of prey." There is a brilliantly immediate, unsparing knowledge of other people's appearance and limitations which in its moral haughtiness becomes as audible to the reader as sniffing, and is indeed that. There is so strong a sense of physical disgust with all one's distended, mad-eyed, pushing neighbors on the West Side that there seems nothing in the book to love but one's opinions.

So much self-assertion is a problem among contemporary American novelists, not least among Jewish writers who have been released into the novel under the comic guise of getting clinically close to their own minds. Jewishness as the novelist's material (which can be quite different from the individual material of Jews writing fiction) is constructed folklore. It is usually comic, or at least humorous; the characters are always ready to tell a joke on themselves. With their bizarre names, their accents, *their* language, they are jokes on themselves. And so they become "Jewish" material, which expresses not the predicament of the individual who knows himself to be an exception, but a piece of the folk, of "Jewishness" as a style of life and a point of view.

This sense of a whole folk to write about is indeed

what Yiddish fiction began with late in the nineteenth century, and folklore remains a style, a manner, an attitude to life among many Jewish entertainers. But the appearance of this subject in the fiction of Bernard Malamud is so arch and clever a transposition into serious literature, a conscious piece of artifice, that one becomes aware of "Jewishness" in Malamud's language and style as the play within the play. The characters are all of a piece and of a tribe; they all speak with vigor the same depressed-sounding dialect, giving a Yiddish cadence to New York English that is pure Malamud and that makes his characters so aware of and dependent on each other that they have become a stock company ready to play any parts so long as they can keep their accents. In "Take Pity," a story that takes place in the next world (and is just as grubby), a recording angel or "census taker, Davidov, sour-faced, flipped through

the closely scrawled pages of his notebook until he found a clean one. He attempted to scratch in a word with his fountain pen but it had run dry, so he fished a pencil stub out of his vest pocket and sharpened it with a cracked razor.

Rosen, a new arrival, tells the story of a refugee whose pitiful little grocery store is failing:

He was talking to me how bitter was his life, and he touched me on the sleeve to say something else, but the next minute his face got small and he fell down dead, the wife screaming, the little girls crying that it made in my heart pain. I am myself a sick man and when I saw him laying on the floor, I said to myself, "Rosen, say goodbye, this guy is finished!" So I said it.

The all-dominating poverty in the Malamud world and of any Malamud character reduces everything to the simplicity of a single tabletop, chair, carrot. No matter where the Malamud characters are — Brooklyn, Rome, or a collapsible hall bedroom in the next world — they are "luftmenschen," so poor that they live on air, in the air, and are certainly not rooted in the earth. In one of the "Fidelman" stories, a young art historian who finally makes his way to Rome encounters and is ultimately defeated by Susskind, a refugee from every country — in Israel he could not stand "the suspense." Poverty as a total human style is so all-dominating an esthetic medium in Malamud, coloring everything with its woebegone utensils, its stubborn immigrant English, its all-circulating despair, that one is not surprised that several of Malamud's characters seem to travel by levitation. They live not only on air but in it, one jump ahead of the B.M.T. All forms of travel and communication are foreshortened, contracted, made picturesque, as it were. Malamud has found a sweetly humorous dialect for the insularity of his characters. The outside world, which for Jews can be "another," does not even reach the consciousness of Malamud's Jews. They exist for each other, depend on each other, suffer each other and from each other with an unawareness of the "world" that *is* the definitive and humorously original element — and for which Malamud has found a narrative language whose tone derives from the characters' unawareness of any world but their own. Turning the tables on those who fear that the son of Yiddish-speaking immigrants might not be "proper" in his English, Malamud adopted a style essentially make-believe and fanciful, a style so patently invented by Malamud in tribute to the vitality of the real thing that the real humor of it is that someone made it up.

Malamud has always been an artificer. Even his first and only "non-Jewish" novel, *The Natural*, is a baseball novel with a deceiving drop in every curve. But from the time that Malamud left his native New York to teach in Oregon, and in what was distinctly a "new life" for him finessed his detachment and whimsicality into an operational set of characters and a terrain distinctly "Jewish," Malamud's own voice became that artfully dissonant irony that says in every turn: Reader, something out of your usual experience is trying to reach you.

Thus Malamud will describe in *The Assistant* Helen Bober reflecting on the life of the utterly spent man, the grocer who is her father: "He was Morris Bober and could be nobody more fortunate. With that name you had no sure sense of property, as if it were in your blood and history not to possess, or if by some miracle to own something, to do so on the verge of loss." The Bobers do not "live": they "eke out an existence." But though they address each other in the same toneless style, as if each word were their last,

    "Why do I cry? I cry for the world. I cry for my life that it went away wasted. I cry for you —"

the truth of this cadence, in its perfect fall of the voice, is so natural yet "made" that it takes us straight to Malamud's own wit behind the voice we hear. Of American Jewish writers, only Clifford Odets, in those plays whose original voice is now unrecognized (probably because it is assumed that all Jews talked this way during the Depression), took the same pleasure in creating this art-language from Yiddish roots. But Malamud is always wry, detached, a straightforward performer, who enjoys spinning some of this speech for the pleasure of seeing whether, with his odd freight, he can make it over to the other side. Gruber the outraged landlord in "The Mourners" says to the old tenant whom he cannot get rid of, "That's a helluva chuzpah. Gimme the keys. . . . Don't monkey with my blood pressure. If you're not out by the fifteenth, I will personally throw you out on your bony ass." Malamud is in fact so much of a "humorist" trying out situations and lines of dialogue for their immediate effect that Bellow once objected to the artifice of the last scene in "The Mourners," where the old tenant says Kaddish for the landlord who has been so cruel to him. "It struck him with a terrible force that the mourner was mourning him; it was he who was dead." Malamud's usual material, however, is so much about the violation of Jews, about actual physical deprivation and suffering, that obviously Malamud has returned the compliment to life, to the repeated violation of Jewish existence, by a kind of literary "violation," a studied contraction, in himself.

Certainly much of Malamud's humor as a writer lies in his conscious attitude of dissonance, his own wry "handling" of situations. What was oppressively pathetic in life becomes surreal, overcolored, picturesque, illustrative of a folk culture in the Chagall style rather than about Jews as fully grown individuals. His characters are all Malamud's children. Yet by the same logic of detachment, Malamud almost absently tends to turn his protagonists into emblems of "Jewish" goodness and sacrifice. In the best of Malamud's novels, *The Assistant*, which in the thoroughness of its workmanship, its fidelity to the lived facts of experience, its lack of smartness and facile allegorizing, is also the most satisfactory single Jewish novel of this period, even Morris Bober apostolically says what no Jew would ever say to a man taunting him, "What do you suffer for, Morris?" "I suffer for you." Morris Bober might live by this without thinking of it one way or the other. He would certainly be too absorbed in the struggle for existence to say grandly to an enemy, "I suffer for you." But *The Assistant* works all the time and all the way, it convinces, because of the tenacity with which Malamud has captured the texture of Morris Bober's grinding slavery to his store, his lack of energy, his lack of money, the terrible hours from six in the morning to late at night. It is the total poverty of the grocer that gives *The Assistant* the rigor of a great argument. (Malamud's stories sometimes tend to be picturesque and highly colored.) In *The Assistant* Malamud's strength is his total intuition of the folk idiosyncrasy involved. The sacrifice of Morris Bober is meaningful because he does not know to what he has been sacrificed.

Malamud's almost automatic identification of suffering with goodness, his old-fashioned affection for Jews as the people of poverty and virtue, is in any event a tribute to *his* past. It does not reflect the world Malamud has lived in since his own rise from the world in which Morris

Bober rose in the dark every winter morning to sell the "Poilesheh" an onion roll for three cents. The hold of the past on Bellow and Malamud — of the immigrant parents, the slum childhood, the Hitler years that inevitably summed up the martyrdom of Jewish history — is in contrast with the experience of the "new" Jewish novelists, whose aggressively satiric star is Philip Roth.

Roth's natural subject is the self-conscious Jew, newly middle-class, the Jew whose "identity," though never in doubt, is a problem to himself, and so makes himself a setup for ridicule, especially to his son. The Jewish son now sees himself not as a favorite but as a buffer state. Far from identifying any of his characters with the legendary virtues and pieties of Jewish tradition, Roth dislikes them as a group for an unconscious submission that takes the form of hysteria. His first work, *Goodbye, Columbus*, builds up from dislikable outward attributes of the we-have-made-it Patimkin family out of Newark, the suburb to which they have escaped, the coarse sentimental father, the shrewish hostile mother, the dumb athletic brother, the brattish kid sister. Even Brenda Patimkin, girl friend to the sensitive narrator, Neil — an assistant in the Newark Public Library who is defined by his lack of status and his friendliness to a little Negro boy out of the slums who regularly visits the library to stare with ignorant wonder at a book of Gauguin reproductions — exists to betray him. Roth is so quick here to define people by their social place, and to reject them, that he does not always grant a personal trait to their intelligence. Brenda Patimkin seems more Sweet Briar than

Radcliffe, just as the narrator Neil Klugman would not necessarily become a Newark Public Librarian just because *he* did not go to Harvard.

Yet what made Roth stand out — there was now a rut of "Jewish novelists" — was his "toughness," the power of decision and the ability to stand moral isolation that is the subject of his story "Defender of the Faith." There was the refusal of a merely sentimental Jewish solidarity. At a time when the wounds inflicted by Hitler made it almost too easy to express feelings one did not have to account for, but when Jews in America were becoming almost entirely middle-class, Roth emphasized all the bourgeois traits that he found. He cast a cold eye on Jews as a group; he insisted, by the conscious briskness of his style and his full inventory of the exaggerated, injurious, sordid, hysterical, that *he* was free. In story after story, in the contrasting voices of his long novels and his short, in his derisions, satires, lampoons, Roth called attention to the self-declared aloofness of his fictional intelligence by the way he worried surprising details and emphasized odd facts in people's behavior. Nathan Zuckerman, the narrator of the story "Courting Disaster," recounts his childhood habit, when given puzzles and arithmetic problems, of dwelling on points different from those he was expected to notice. This "seemingly irrelevant speculation of an imaginary nature" was to become in Roth's own work a stress on his thoughtfulness as an observer. But the marked overstress of oddities was Roth's way of focusing his real subject, social style. The *show* of any extreme, opened to the aroused fine eye of Roth as narrator,* became Roth's way of grasping people fictionally. Harriet in *Goodbye, Columbus*, about to marry into the Patimkin family, "impressed me as a young lady singularly unconscious of a motive in others or herself. All was surfaces, and seemed a perfect match for Ron, and too for the Patimkins. . . . She nodded her head insistently whenever anyone spoke. Sometimes she would even say the last few words of your sentence with you. . . ."

Roth wrote from sharpness as his center, his safety. Yet in a period when many young Jewish writers became almost too fond of "absurdity" as a style, and saw fiction as a series of throwaway lines, Roth — no Lenny Bruce even if he sometimes mimed like one — was notable for his moral lucidity and compactness. He had this ability to figure out a situation stylistically: the style of something was both its comedy and its allegory. Each of the stories in *Goodbye, Columbus* made a point; each defined a social situation without any waste and extended it to evident issues. Even when Roth, in his 1961 lecture "Writing American Fiction," found America "absurd," he insisted on defining the absurdity head-on, made it a problem to be solved, above all established its neatly laid-

* Many of Roth's narratives are in the first person. This may be a necessity for him, since it enables him to change his voice without diminishing the sharp personal effect of "acting" someone like Portnoy. Monologue gives Roth a chance to act out traits, to "become" someone by a different patter.

In "On the Air," the hilarious but finally grotesque story of an intended journey to Princeton by one Lippman, a paranoiac talent scout who hopes to induce Einstein to become an "answer man" on the radio, Roth's delight in the man's spoken style *and* his mania, in the assorted freaks and horrors Lippman runs into at a Howard Johnson, finally makes the reader feel that while Roth will try out any situation, humanity is too mad and vicious to deserve this much attention.

out *comic* reality. Two teen-age sisters in Chicago, Pattie and Babs Grimes, had disappeared, were rumored dead. It turned out that they had been living with two tramps in a flophouse. The mother gave interviews to the Chicago press and basked in her sudden fame. Roth found in this episode the kind of scandalousness, disorder all around, which he was always to take with the greatest possible seriousness, even when he mockingly imitated it:

> *The American writer in the middle of the 20th century has his hands full in trying to describe, and then to make* credible, *much of the American reality. It stupefies, it sickens, it infuriates, and finally it is even a kind of embarrassment to one's own meager imagination. The actuality is continually outdoing our talents, and the culture tosses up figures almost daily that are the envy of any novelist. Who, for example, could have invented Charles Van Doren? Roy Cohn and David Schine? Sherman Adams and Bernard Goldfine? Dwight David Eisenhower?*

Roth seemed willing to meet the problem. But though the 1960s closed on more public disorder than Roth could have dreamed of, he did not become the novelist of this disorder, or even the journalist of it, as Mailer did. Roth significantly scored his first popular success with *Portnoy's Complaint*, which succeeded as a comic monologue with baleful overtones, very much in the style of a stand-up Jewish comic. The exactitude and fury of memory, the omnivorous detail going back to the most infantile rejections and resentments, captured perfectly a generation psyche which was more anchored on family, and more resentful of it, than any other. Now its

147

novelists found the analyst's couch, the confession, the psychoanalytical recital, the litany of complaint, its most serviceable literary form.

In Portnoy the Jewish son had his revenge, as in Bellow's novels the Jewish son had his apotheosis. A whole middle class of sons and daughters, turning and turning within the gyre of the nuclear Jewish family — nucleus indeed of the Jewish experience and the first scenario of the psychoanalytic drama — found in Portnoy its own fascination with the details of childhood. It was this emphasis on the unmentionable, Roth's gift for zanily working out usually inaccessible details to the most improbable climax, like Portnoy masturbating into a piece of liver, that was the farce element so necessary to Roth's anger. There was the calculated profanation of mother, father, the most intimate offices of the body — a profanation by now altogether healthy to those therapeutized members of the professional middle class to whom everything about the body had become, like the possibility of universal destruction through the Bomb, small talk at the dinner table. Portnoy's howls of rage, love and anguish were so concentrated that this made them funny. Some of the incidents were so improbable that this alone made them necessary. Ronald Nimkin, the young pianist, hanged himself in the bathtub. Portnoy reminisces:

> *My favorite detail from the Ronald Nimkin suicide: even as he is swinging from the shower head, there is a note pinned to the dead young pianist's short-sleeved shirt: — "Mrs. Blumenthal called. Please bring your mah-jongg rules to the game tonight. Ronald."*

In any event, the Jewish mother had by now become such a piece of American folklore — I'll make fun of my ethnic if you'll make fun of yours — that *Portnoy's* success may be attributed to the fact that Roth was the first writer so obsessed with the Jewish family as to remove all the mystery from the Jewish experience. Roth secularized it all to the last micrometer of stained underwear, yet gave it his own "hard," fanatically enumerative quality. Whom do *you* suffer for, Alex Portnoy? I suffer for me. To be Jewish is to resent. What made Roth interesting in all this was that, with all his comic animosity, he was still glued to the Jewish family romance and depended on an "emancipated" Jewish audience as much as he depended on Jews for his best material. "Your book has so many readers!" I once heard an admirer say to Roth. "Why," she continued enthusiastically, "you must have at least six million readers!"

The "Jewish" identity of Norman Mailer lay precisely in the fact, as he said in *The Armies of the Night*, that to be a nice Jewish boy was the one role unacceptable to him. By this Mailer meant a rejection not of Jewishness — that would have been bourgeois and out of date — but of the sweetness, the conscious propriety that would have limited his social curiosity, social omnivorousness, his proven ability to play as many parts as possible in his books and through his books. More than any other novelist of this period (he was said to have "sacrificed" his career as a novelist to this) Mailer projected Mailer into the variousness of American life. He became not a famous novelist like Hemingway but, like another Mailer hero, Jack Kennedy, so much a personification of the ambitious American male that Mailer willingly offered himself up on the public stage as both a model and a hazard.

Mailer became recklessly and extravagantly a piece of American life because he was willing to prolong *his* individuality, *his* Jewish defiance, to the limit. He, for one, would find out in every nook and cranny of his psychic existence what it was like to be the most unassimilable Jew in American society. What was "Jewish" in this was his conscious exceeding of the group, and of other writers; he would be champ. As Disraeli said on becoming prime minister, "I have climbed to the top of the greasy pole." In a period when some Jews took pride in not being nice — "priests and Jews are civically timid," thought Kant — Mailer insisted on upsetting all expectations. He would play bad. But what was creative in this "role" was Mailer's belief in the validity of his most private thoughts. He made his fantasies interesting to many Americans. He would write as if, yes, he believed in the Devil. The Mailer who became such a laughable, publicizable part of the American consciousness was always there because he had somehow turned his most intimate wishes and fears into public symbols. Mailer accomplished what so few novelists were still able to do — he made his mind public. He was definitely not one of that minority group which will always feel excluded from the great American reality. He was inside this reality and on every side of it, willing to shift for a better view at a moment's notice. The voraciousness of American life, its power in human affairs, its fury of transformation, had found in Mailer a writer who would always find any and all of it "credible," who would never regard America as "a kind of embarrassment to one's own meager imagination."

Mailer began, in *The Naked and the Dead*, as a novelist traditional but forceful. Through the inevitable ups and downs of being a novelist — the second book, *Barbary Shore*, read like the deliberately offbeat book that will follow a best seller — Mailer wrote mysteriously about a Long Novel in the making that something equally important kept him from accomplishing to his satisfaction (his first sign of turning himself into a Cause). He wrote advertisements not for himself but for this Long Novel. There was as yet nothing he so much wanted to do as to beat Hemingway (his idol, personal and literary) at Hemingway's own game. The intense but speculative interest in politics again showed itself in *Barbary Shore* — a novel of conspiracy, a deliberate exercise in political paranoia about a radical in a Brooklyn Heights rooming house who is really a government agent. This plot, like many of Mailer's future intuitions about the amount of plot in American life, turned out to be an inspired guess. Many ex-radicals were now government agents and CIA money had been secretly channeled through cultural foundations to impress them with the importance of the right anticommunist line. But the depressed and windy monologue of the confessedly "sick" narrator, a war casualty, also signaled a moodiness of Mailer's, psychic, intellectual, political, that would never choose silence when it could box the universe with words. Mailer's many words would always depend on his psychic intuition into the staggeringly involved experience of our time. He was indeed an "existential" seeker of the truth the uncovering of which was the real value of any situation. Himself as the only oracle and prophet needed to grab the golden ring of truth as he spun round and round the carousel. "Truth" as the shifting existential fact. Prophecy as disclosure of the mysterious hidden will behind human behavior. The frantic joy of seizing the hidden "connections" of things. There was beauty, there was truth, with Mailer as the only discoverer you needed to know. These had obviously become more important to Mailer than the literary ideals that had prompted him to give out so many advance warnings, Joyce-like, of a great work in progress.

Mailer was not going to write his "long novel." This intended a tribute to an age that was already behind him — the age of the single masterpiece, the "perfect" work of art, to which a Joyce or Proust dedicated his life. But Mailer was going to turn his diagnostic skills, his personal verve, his instinct for all that could be taking place simultaneously in America, into a heady demonstration of personal insight. He would become a cultural force — that is, operating like a nineteenth-century man of letters — even as he insisted on himself as a threat to all those timid folk who would not follow him on his personal trek through the unconventional. Thanks partly to the influence of Wilhelm Reich's emphasis on sexual openness as the key to self-liberation in everything, Mailer now began *his* public confession and defiance. In *The Deer Park* he used ideological sex as a counterweapon to the Hollywood terrorized in the Fifties by the blacklist. As always with Mailer, "politics" as an arena of conflict was equal to sexuality, and had the same issue: never be a

loser! Charles Eitel — I tell — the Hollywood director
and ex-communist pushed out of the industry because he
wouldn't tell — finally yields to pressure from the pro-
ducers. He is down to his last resources in Desert D'Or,
Palm Springs. But since Eitel finally gives in, what is he
doing as a propagandist of sexuality as "knowledge" —
and why does he fascinate us? Mailer's confidence in his
ability to write a novel without caring any longer about
The Novel was as striking in *The Deer Park* as his distrac-
tion. Eitel, supposedly the political refugee from both
Stalinism and McCarthyism, and therefore a model
American radical of our time, finally shows himself an
alchemist. He is trying to change sex into pure spirit by
way of his mistress, a wretchedly untalented nightclub
performer who in fact excites him because in her own
utter lack of confidence she is entirely at his mercy.
Eitel the dominator (in bed) might or might not have
had something to learn from the weakness of his mistress.
But he had nothing to teach his alter ego, Norman
Mailer, for whom sexual sensations communicated themselves as psychic events, Faustian claims to knowledge.
Eitel and Elena settling into the routine of lovemaking:

> *And Eitel felt changes in his body race beyond the*
> *changes in his mind, as though all those nerves and*
> *organs which he had tired almost to death were coming*
> *back to life, carrying his mind in their path, as if Elena*
> *were not only his woman but his balm. . . . They would*
> *explore a little further, he would come back with more.*

Eitel in crisis "would gamble for knowledge . . . like a
cave wanderer he would be able to wander into himself."

This claim to knowledge from within, romanticism as propaganda, based on the sacred intuitions of Mailer himself, was now to give Mailer's polemical imagination a fury of dissemination all over the American land that went beyond what anyone might have predicted of the dutiful naturalist behind *The Naked and the Dead* and the gloomy radical behind *Barbary Shore*. Even before he published *The Deer Park* Mailer had shown this ability to make his imagination public. One somehow knew not Mailer himself — that would always be too much for him and everyone else — but Mailer's fetishes, his drive, his necessary plunge into events, his ability to make connections between his psyche and American life. So insistent was this intuition, with Mailer's ability to spread every particle of as news to the outside world, that it imposed itself through *The Deer Park*, *An American Dream*, *Why Are We in Vietnam?*, not because these books communicated themselves as novels, but because they didn't.

Mailer's fantasies and ideas broke into the texture of every fiction he now wrote — and one remembered these books. Mailer succeeded in imposing his personal sense of things, as he did not his novels; his characteristic sense of imbalance, of different orders of reality to be *willed* together, did in fact reflect the imbalance between everyone's inner life and the constant world of public threat. This was the way the liberal imagination did in fact think of its problems. As a series of circles, not interlocking but fascinating each other; personality was a theater, politics another. Mailer's "new journalism" was to dramatize this split consciousness with radical gestures.

The Marxist view of the world as a consistent piece of
reality economic, social, cultural, could not have been
less real at this time. Still, there was no escaping the violent eruptions created by the pressure on everything in
sight of American power, wealth, the seeming unlimitedness of national and personal ambition. But whatever
Mailer's fantasies of cultural authority in this situation,
his several powerful insights were too scattered and spas-
modic to make his *ideas* influential. As he said of *An
American Dream*, "it might prove for some to be my most
substantial attack on the problem of writing a novel of
manners."* What made these novels, even the deliber-

* *An American Dream* is in fact a novel of ambition, a snob document, which is why it is often unintentionally funny in its postur-
ing. Barney Kelly on top of the Waldorf Towers describes himself
as a "grand (not good) Catholic." "Once you're located where I
am, there's nothing left but to agitate the web. At my worst, I'm
a spider. Have strings in everywhere from the Muslims to the
New York Times."
It is amusing to note how few Jews interrupt Mailer's recent
communings with power. A noteworthy exception and a self-
proving narrative is "The Time of Her Time," which was described
in *Advertisements for Myself* as part of a "Long Novel." It puts the
would-be-Irish hero, Sergius O'Shaugnessy, to grips with the ungiving Jewish girl, Denise Gondelman. He tries to conquer her in
the contemporary style — to force her to satisfaction. But though
he succeeds technically he has nothing else of her. And at the end
she has a sexual insult for him.
A Denise Gondelman is indeed rare in Mailer's later fiction. He
much prefers a devil figure like Deborah Caughlin Mangaravidi
Kelly who is as socially important as she is wicked. Her husband
says after he kills her, "She smelled like a bank."
Mailer's mythology of personal power works as episode in scene
after scene of *An American Dream*. His fantasies are irrepressible,
as in the descriptions of sex with Deborah's "Nazi" maid Ruta, on
whom Rojack performs, mythically. As always in reading Mailer's
descriptions of intercourse, one is impressed by how much of a
war novelist he has remained.
In "The Time of Her Time" he is really inside the psychic "cave"
the Mailer hero is always talking about. And the experience — the

155

ately scatological farce *Why Are We in Vietnam?*, so effective as messages to the age (in between messages on the antiwar demonstration before the Pentagon, national political conventions, the heavyweight championship, the flight to the moon, women's lib) was the fact that in fiction, fortunately, Mailer could not incessantly be on top of all his material. He was traveling too fast, and despite every effort to show himself in control, looked more like the eye of the hurricane. He was always on the spot, a witness to his participation.

What was striking about Mailer's adventurist fiction was the sense of risk that for him pervaded everything in America. The American Faust was rushing to meet God or the Devil. Despite the bullying effect of his overwriting, Mailer's typical fantasy in *Why Are We in Vietnam?*, of a transistor planted in the body through the rectum that may "contact" the mind of God, did express the fright at the heart of contemporary consciousness. Since the Devil was assuredly loose again, man had desperately to reach the God whose hidden will was behind the force of things. This despair, Mailer's own frantic will despite his personal cockiness — this was to make the experience of reading him equal to a plunge into the age. We were at its mercy.

Bellow's Jewishness had increased over the years to the point where old Mr. Sammler's control, sobriety,

---

genuine internality described — is of a man's *sensations*, comparatively rare in other writers' unilluminating descriptions of sex as performance. And since sex as sex is comedy, not mythology, "The Time of Her Time" amuses the reader instead of instructing him.

wisdom had become the only protection against the age. Jewishness Mailer disliked because it limited and intellectualized. The world was too open, the disorder too flagrant, to permit oneself any identity but this possibility of total receptivity through oneself.

With his contempt for knowledge-as-control, his desire to leave all those centuries of Jewish tradition (and of Jewish losers) behind him, Mailer represents the unresting effort and overreaching of the individual Jewish writer who seeks to be nothing but an individual (and if possible, a hero). By contrast, Isaac Bashevis Singer represents the transformation of all Jewish history into fiction, fable, story. He accepts it for his own purposes. He is a skeptic who is hypnotized by the world he grew up in. No one else in modern Jewish writing stems so completely from the orthodox and even mystical East European tradition. No one else has turned *"the* tradition" into the freedom of fiction, the subtlety and mischievousness and truthfulness of storytelling. Singer, totally a fiction writer but summing up the East European Yiddish tradition in his detached, fatalistic, plainspoken way, represents a peculiar effortlessness in the writing of "Jewish fiction," when compared with the storminess of Bellow and Mailer. That is because Singer shares the orthodox point of view without its belief, and he meticulously describes, without sentimentalizing any Jew whatever, a way of life which was murdered with the millions who lived it. The demons and spirits so prominent in Singer's East European narratives have in his "American" ones become necessary to the survivors. "It is chilling," V. S. Pritchett noticed, "to know that he is describing ghosts who cannot even haunt because their habitat has been wiped out."

The occult presences in Singer's work represent that belief in another world which Singer grew up with, but which no longer necessarily represents "God's" world. There may very well be a God, since we are in the grip of forces so clearly beyond our power to understand and change them. But His, Its, inscrutability is the only attribute. Singer has transposed the terms without abandoning them.

There was a great religious tradition among Jews in eastern Europe. Orthodoxy was deeply habitual for millions, ritualized to the point where a pious existence was *interrupted* by one's outer existence. The inwardness of this "true" existence seems to have moved into Singer's work as a mental body, pages and pages. What is extraordinary in Singer's work is the conversion of the Jews — into storytelling. Singer was the son of an ultraorthodox Warsaw rabbi. He was brought up to follow the letter of the law that is all letter, punctilio, observance — the magnification in every possible instance of God's will, God's concern, God's observance of His creatures. There was a horror of the "unclean" — that is, the world itself. In his memoir, *In My Father's Court*, Singer describes his father firmly closing the windows of his study on the screams of a woman being raped in a Warsaw street. But his son the storyteller, though still in the orthodox costume of gabardine and wide-brimmed velvet hat, showed his independence by finally, one day, going out on the balcony to look at the life of Warsaw. He was to write about everything he knew in this unholy world, to sit apart from the tradition in order to describe the human experience of it. But some deep spirit of acceptance, still, not of God but of fact, enabled him to write and write with astounding ease — and without the tension so marked in his gifted brother Israel Joshua Singer (author of *Yoshe Kalb* and *The Brothers Ashkenazi*), who had a more painful struggle with tradition and family and was concerned with heresy and "immorality" as dramatic situations.

Isaac Bashevis Singer, who came to America in the 1930s and wrote for the Yiddish press, was after the war to become, through English versions of his work, the most widely accepted of all modern Yiddish writers. Living and writing in America, he somehow seemed the survivor and novelist of a whole tradition that had been destroyed by the Nazis and Communists, and that tormented its descendants in America because they had no access to it, perhaps had never had any — and so had no way of explaining why so many Jews had gone to their deaths.

Singer, who would not have presumed to offer an explanation, provided through his fiction the only one needed: the Jewish tradition. In English "translation" that was often adaptation, writing to Jews and non-Jews alike who could not read Yiddish, Singer became the fictional historian of the whole Jewish experience in eastern Europe because his extraordinary intelligence and detached point of view turned the heart of the tradition — acceptance of God's law, God's will, even God's slaughter of His own — into story, legend, fantasy. And Singer himself believed in acceptance: of human nature, the world's wickedness, God's total mysteriousness, the peculiarity of Jews themselves. The audience that read him week after week in the Yiddish newspaper was too close to view it as the last word, and many of these readers missed Singer's sophistication, artfulness and cunning use of the tradition in his work. Indeed, Singer was so cool in both senses of that American word that his gifts were not readily appreciated by other Yiddish writers. There is a brilliant and funny story by Cynthia Ozick, "Yiddish in America," about an unsuccessful Yiddish writer who cannot understand the fame of "Ostrover" and is convinced that it is all a matter of finding the right translator. But of course it was Singer's own lightness, ease and resourcefulness that convinced so many readers that, for all they knew, the tradition now lived only in the pages of Isaac Bashevis Singer. As Singer delightedly said, "I call myself a bilingual writer and say that English has become my 'second original!' "

Through this "second" language Singer reached American Jews often dominated unconsciously by the customs of their ancestors, but for whom the customs had disappeared with the ancestors. This gave Singer his unforeseen, ironic, much-enjoyed status as an American writer. He was the only American Jewish writer who knew the tradition so thoroughly that it was *in* him, and so he could simulate the credulity, the innocence, the timorousness, above all the unworldliness. Was it possible that in the twentieth century whole masses of people should have believed that *whatever* happened was God's will? Singer the storyteller had his own version of this: the wickedness of the world is never an "historical" accident, and what is happening has always happened.

Things are as they are. The evidence of this world is to be accepted. Singer could thus make his characters real as Jews: they were the people of acceptance.

With such characters there would seem to be missing the decisive element in modern fiction — the indetermination of one's own existence to oneself, freedom as one's only heaven and hell. Unlike the many Jewish personae in modern American fiction, for whom a wholly willed, insistent claim on existence is the very theme of their striving and suffering, Singer's characters live in relation to God as the Power in and behind everything. They lived, the East European Jews were as a matter of fact the last generation to live, wholly in the eye of God — they lived to be responsive to God alone.

This mysterious fidelity, total obligation, meant that not individual characters but their way of life is the real matter of a Singer story. What the reader sees is never the individual's effort to determine his own life, but the fact that he is constantly being acted on — like the poor cuckold and unconscious saint in Singer's best story, "Gimpel The Fool" — by the whole force of his culture. There the dead wife appears to the husband she had cheated in every possible sense in order to keep Gimpel from blaspheming the tradition.

Of course Singer's characters include sinners like Yasha in *The Magician of Lublin* and those many demons, imps, sprites who move in and out of Singer's world as naturally as Jewish relatives — which they are. And in his bitter American novel, *Enemies: A Love Story*, he shows how irreparably the survivors of Hitler's and Stalin's camps had been crazed by the condemnation of

Jews. But what Singer's many damaged and insatiable characters in America feel as the real force in their lives is still the Jewish tradition — because they cannot come to terms with it. The world is twice wicked because they cannot understand it. It has done everything to them, and still they do not live *in* it. They live in their imagination, as they did when they were believers.

6

CASSANDRAS
Porter to Oates

I feel like a very efficient tool or weapon, used and in demand from moment to moment.

— Sylvia Plath

WHEN KATHERINE ANNE PORTER published *Ship of Fools* in 1962, ending one of the longest suspense stories in twentieth-century American literature, the feeling that Miss Porter had "done it at last," had brought out her "big" novel that was a summing up of all her skills in the shorter form, was really a tribute to her much-read, much-taught short stories. These stories were commonly cited, especially in English departments, as "simply the best stories ever written in America," and under the scriptural eye of the New Criticism in the Forties and Fifties were contentedly analyzed as the last word in form, style and moral tone. Miss Porter's long battle to complete her novel was certainly sustained, in great part, by her admirers. To write "perfect" or "almost perfect" short stories was to be identified with a total irreproachability that some of the world's greatest novelists would not have understood, but which for a time in America was identified with the right balance, reserve, irony — the discretion of persons who knew that literature makes nothing happen, a balance supposedly feminine.

Writers expert and specialized in the short story — in situations without all their visible consequences — somehow attract more attention to their expertness, professionalism and skill than do the authors of long novels. Just as plays are usually written to be produced, short stories are usually written with an eye on the magazines that created the modern short story in America.* As Cyril Connolly said of magazine pieces, they are paid on the head and praised on the head. Writers seemingly limited to the short story, like Frank O'Connor, have been defensive about not producing a novel — O'Connor wrote a book about the short story, *The Lonely Voice*, to prove that the Irish as a society were unable to produce novels; he defined the short story as "the art form that deals with the individual when there is no longer a society to absorb him, and when he is compelled to exist, as it were, by his own inner light." But in the literary America of just before our day, the short story, though increasingly difficult to market, was peculiarly identified (especially by magazine editors who had no other standard for short stories) with Perfection. A short story was the "perfect" work of literature, though clearly not the perfect commodity. This "perfection," the absence of visible faults, was somehow a moral virtue as well. It bespoke detachment, balance, wisdom; above all, the seemingly flawless surface. As Frank O'Connor said: "A man can be a very great novelist as I believe Trollope was, and yet be a very inferior writer. . . . I cannot think of a great storyteller who was also an inferior writer. . . ."

The "perfect" or "almost perfect" short story as nofault literature — she herself said that "there are almost

* And by the 1970s seem to have abandoned it.

perfect stories in Eudora Welty's *A Curtain of Green*" —
spurred, drove and tormented Katherine Anne Porter on
for several decades to achieve a novel that would be as
achieved as her short stories, but that would also display
over a large canvas her sense of the age. Unlike so many
perfect and near-perfect writers, Katherine Anne Porter
was driven by an idea of history, a point of view almost
too definable that would give her no rest. She had, as she
said, no problems as a writer of short stories. A famous
dependability made her turn out some of her best stories
at a single sitting. This surely rested in theme, in sensibility, in the honest lucidity of her style, on the recurrent
theme of her heroine's vulnerability in a bad bad world.
Endurance was her only triumph, and came through a
wholly personal style in life of discipline and survival.
Miss Porter's stories were romantically tragic stories written around the fate of a mildly idealized heroine. They
succeeded as cyclical descriptions of a woman's whole
life, and expressed the necessary discord, as the author
saw it, between a woman and the stoniness of nature in
Mexico, between a woman and her ferocious society, between a woman and the senselessness of her hopes.

A whole generation of Americans in college formed
their idea of fiction on these always "faultless" stories
which in their balance-seeking prose, their laconic irony,
express perfectly indeed the necessary contrast between
the inner beauty of her heroines and their contracted
destiny. In Miss Porter's stories the key figure of the
heroine still stands for the eager life-force that the world
does defeat — for the artist in life who, as in the Willa

Cather she admired, sums up the moral elegance in the tragedy of conflict that *must* ensue between a woman and what Henry James called "life at its stupid work." The nineteenth-century novelist's attempt to raise at least his heroine above the materialist muck* is perpetuated in Katherine Anne Porter's stories. Woman becomes a work of art in a world stupid with violence. *She* is the "perfection" within the perfectly constructed story — whose passionate aim is to establish the existential reality of a woman's life against the destructiveness practiced by nature, poverty, revolution. Life is a cheat. The world is senseless. But the heroine, the receiving center of sensibility in all these stories, remained the human center

* Henry James saw in her "a certain habitual assurance which is only a grace the more. She combines . . . all that is possible in the way of modesty with all that is delightful in the way of facility." He said of her in *The Ambassadors*: "By a turn of the hand she had somehow made their encounter a relation. And the relation profited by a mass of things that were not strictly in it or of it. . . ." George Eliot called her the frail vessel that carries the inestimable treasure of the world's affection. Flaubert, in a lyrical passage that characteristically violates his determination to show life as banal, cannot help noticing that Emma's "parasol, of silk colored like a pigeon's breast and pierced by the sunlight, lit up with shifting reflections the white skin of her face." Tolstoy described her as a round smiling woman whose very way of walking created a bond between people looking at her. Dostoevsky has her trying to take all the anguish of a murderer's soul into her own. Dreiser has her say to the man who has been keeping her for years: "He said that if you married me you would only get ten thousand a year. That if you didn't and still lived with me you would get nothing at all. If you would leave me, or if I would leave you, you would get all of a million and a half. Don't you think you had better leave me now?"

As Henry James said, "she" *makes* the "picture." Especially in American fiction, where there have been so many men without women, so many whales, bears, misogynists, mad sea captains and solitary cowboys, the distinct need of women as a civilizing agent turned the heroine into a cultural ideal like the furnishings.

within the mechanical circle of "fate." The most eloquent symbol of this fate was the landscape of Mexico.

Ship of Fools was the mechanically extended performance of a writer whose sensitiveness to shock had naturally expressed itself in short forms and urbane irony. But it was important for Miss Porter to write this Grand Hotel of a novel based on the long voyage from Vera Cruz to Hamburg which she had taken in the early 1930s on the eve of Hitler. Over the years her increasingly alarmed sensibility had turned into a totally dismissive view of history. Twentieth-century war, revolution and counterrevolution had always been the special background of her work. But more and more a favorite image became that of falling. She could actually speak in an essay of "that falling world between 1850 and 1950. We have been falling for a century or more, and Ezra Pound came along at just the right time to see what was happening."

In *Ship of Fools* Miss Porter wanted to put this bad news all together. She wanted to make a declaration, with the largest number of human illustrations, about the disintegration of what a Southerner liked to call "the established order." She would show all human relationships corrupted in — possibly by — a general human badness typified by Germans even in 1931, all things and peoples slowly drowning in a sea of hatred and distrust that would leave nothing to believe in. What was there to believe in except the organization of many characters from different nations into that supreme effort artistically and morally — A Novel? Frank O'Connor's definition of the short story was too applicable to *Ship of Fools* — "the art form that deals with the individual when there is no longer a society to absorb him, when he is compelled to exist, as it were, by his own inner light." Miss Porter seemed to be saying what so many Southern literary men have known as a matter of course — the world has been "falling" since 1850. (As Cleanth Brooks once said, Emerson was responsible for Hitler.) She was too sophisticated in the pioneer modernism of her generation to pretend to the reactionary would-be Christianity of those Southern critics who admired her most. But she had an esthetic sense of form as perfection, of a Big Novel as the ultimate esthetic seal put on human affairs. And she thought of politics in symbols of cultural disintegration that were to seem causes.

The novel that was conceived in the Thirties and begun in the Forties as *No Safe Harbor* turned over the years into *Ship of Fools*. The world was now a shipload of fools rather than of the homeless modern souls who had been suggested in her original title. To accept tragedy in a secular age had always been a positive contribution with her, an affirmation of stoicism like Thomas Hardy's that she had upheld against the willed belief of T. S. Eliot. The indignation Katherine Anne Porter had felt about individual Germans in the early Thirties, even before Hitler, swelled over the years into a vision of Nazism as the center of a world sickness. But the "big" novel that would become the representative voyage *into* the dissolution of Western society now existed to sum up one woman's bitterness. The many years in which Miss Porter worked to assemble her many scenes into one novel themselves became the subject of her novel. The older

Miss Porter got in the writing of it, the more she fell into the thought that life is a voyage to nowhere, and that time makes monkeys, dwarfs, dupes of us all.

In *Ship of Fools* the treacherousness of virtually all the characters reflects a total literary negation of actual life: an ingenuous attempt to fix the character of Our Time by consistently repulsive, undifferentiated *racial* types — the untrustworthy Spanish Gypsy, the low cunning Jew, the race-proud Teuton. Character after character is meant to represent a national type, but these indexes to History reflect a personal dislike, a total suspicion, that expresses itself in generalization. Herr Lowenthal, a German Jew who is a salesman of Catholic religious objects, is not permitted to eat with the other Germans. He "retired into the dark and airless ghetto of his soul and lamented with all the grieving wailing company he found there; for he was never alone in that place . . . then feeling soothed, the inspired core of his being began to search for its ancient justification and its means of revenge. But it should be slow and secret." Dr. Schumann, the decent ship's doctor, tears into pieces some malicious notices put up by Spanish students. "He looked into the half-circle of staring, hard persons with an impression that he was gazing into eyes that had got misplaced; they belonged to some species of fierce beast peering out of a cave or ready to leap in a jungle, prowling and sniffing for blood; the same expression, only older and more intensely aware and ready, that had dismayed him in the eyes of Ric and Rac . . . who stood huddled together shoulder to shoulder, facing out like wild cattle in danger. His look was a mixture of repulsion and incredulity — surely these creatures could not really exist."

Everything in *Ship of Fools* is premonitory after the fact, symbolic of a future that has already happened — and is essentially causeless, timeless, undifferentiated from other periods. Human nature is simply not to be trusted, and this certainly puts a burden on the untrustworthy souls, not actions, Miss Porter seeks to portray. Since virtually all the Germans on board the ship in 1931 are already Nazis, and the men and women are so much alike, it would seem that Miss Porter is attempting to create an allegory of the most daemonic political event of our time on the basis of her dislike of the human species. Dr. Schumann, the Catholic ship's doctor who falls in love with the revolutionary Spanish countess, finds in himself

> *a confusion so dark he could no longer tell the difference between the invader and the invaded, the violator and the violated, the betrayer and the betrayed, and the one who hated or who jeered or was indifferent. The whole great structure built upon the twin pillars of justice and love, which reached from the earth into eternity, by which the human soul rose step by step from the most rudimentary concepts of good and evil . . . this tower was now crumbling and falling around him. . . .*

Rarely has a novel of such pretended scope, with so many characters, been at the mercy of so few ideas. The leaning tower, the collapse of tradition! These seem to take place not in the social world, as action and its consequences, but as protection against the disbelief in everything that has turned even the young lovers — the only characters in the book to whom life offers any hope — into continually quarrelsome, frustrated people.

Ship of Fools was designed as an epic, but is really a harsh personal statement. It has a point of view — something I do not find in the artfully written, beautifully constructed, uninvolving novels of Eudora Welty. It showed a sentimentally total rejection of existence in our time that brought home to me the imbalance in a literary sensibility so purely defensive — as opposed to other writing by women, like Flannery O'Connor's, that erases our too-easy view of the world. Someone who knows Flannery O'Connor's life well says that her point of view was based on unadmissible rage against her physical limitations. Certainly her often frighteningly deep stories were also marked by an exceptional sense of public performance, by a thorough lucidity of style, by instinctive literary tact and form. It is hard to think of modern women writers who write as "carelessly" as Balzac and Dostoevsky. But Flannery O'Connor did not start from the "heroine" as a passive, silently enraged victim of her position. Although she, too, was so naturally a short story writer that her novels seem to be extended from their origin as short stories, what distinguishes her stories is the inevitable incident, accident, catastrophe, that follows from the meticulously rendered limitations of someone's human nature. Her characters express themselves in the mistakes that have become their natures. They are complete in the smallest gesture, in the moment's involuntary action that can decide a life forever. People in her stories are the synapse between what they unknowingly are and what, as the point of each story, they do. And these flashes of connection are immediate, convincing, irreversible; a particular feature of O'Connor's style is that a sentence is exact not showily, as is the nature of a fine "performance," but physically, the way different parts of a body fit each other. Words become facts in her dramatic world — action, gesture, death. *There* was completeness of a kind so often lacking in "perfect" short stories, a lack of self-consciousness, that put the full weight of what it had to say into story after story.

"Woman's fiction" exists not as writing by women but as inordinate defensiveness against a society conceived as the special enemy of the sensitive. The most extreme example is Shirley Jackson's "The Lottery," the shocker about a woman who is chosen by lot to be stoned to death by all the inhabitants of a contemporary American village. The story no doubt was intended to represent our panic during the McCarthy period and its ritual destructions. But the rest of us are in this story only if we see ourselves there. "The Lottery" cast a more calculatedly horrible version of the assault, deception, betrayal which occurs in so many Shirley Jackson stories where a woman as victim is the main figure and where her defenselessness is the story.

The fiction of sensitiveness is usually distinguished by its too conscious style. It offers an illusion of control. In some writers the style is a leading character, as in Jean Stafford's elaborately written *Boston Adventure* and those brilliantly ungiving stories whose tightness of structure is at such variance with the usual theme of a young woman's inability to sustain relationships. The novel of sensitiveness, *about* sensitiveness, probably found its ultimate justification in Salinger's *The Catcher in the Rye* — in the image of a totally unlovable world created by an adolescent boy who is orphaned by the death of his brother. Salinger's book became *the* book of migrant anti-Establishment youth in its time: it became a spiritual home away from home for a whole generation because Salinger's genius has been to turn the preoccupation with style into a character's spoken style, to convey representative emotion. The sensitiveness of Holden Caulfield — whose charm is that he is not an adult male and hates most adult males as phonies — is turned into a useful and comic condemnation of the "world" because it knows its sensitiveness to be so specialized. Its distortions are *right*.

For many women writers in our day, the old novel of sensitiveness invites parody and counterstatement. And it is in this context that one can understand the strange, funny, perverse, calculatedly unacceptable fictions of Jane Bowles. In her (one) novel, *Two Serious Ladies*, the two heroines are unaccountably innocent passersby through a totally depraved world. They are so closed off from the rest of us by being so strange, offbeat and untouchably innocent that they turn even the few male characters attending them — it is essentially a novel of women and of their journeying into places beyond their ken — into versions of singularity as strange as themselves.

In Jane Bowles all women characters become parallels to each other. Everything is dialogue, but nothing advances by dialogue, there is no natural exchange of experiences, only a mystified scratching by the characters themselves on the impenetrable surface of each other's personalities. This inability to get below the surface is a mark of the cartoon-like queerness of the women as central characters. They live in the world by not understanding it. And the unwillingness to dig for any "deeper" reality is the mark of Jane Bowles herself, who always worked with dialogue as if she were a Restoration dramatist fascinated not by the "hardness" of her characters but by their naturally closed-off state.

She, too, was a dramatized oddity; her one novel, her one play *In a Summer House*, her stories, all appeared in 1966 in one volume as *The Collected Works of Jane Bowles*, as if she were not going to write again. She had had it? Now we had the finished-off phenomenon of Jane Bowles, described by her friend Truman Capote in his introduction to *The Collected Works* as

> *that Jane, with her dahlia-head of cropped curly hair, her tilted nose and mischief-shiny, just a trifle mad eyes, her very original voice (a husky soprano), her boyish clothes and schoolgirl's figure and slightly limping walk . . . the eternal urchin, appealing as the most appealing of non-adults, yet with some substance cooler than blood invading her veins, and with a wit, an eccentric wisdom no child, not the strangest wunderkind, ever possessed. . . .*

The surfaces that her characters present to each other — they remind me of the wild collection of faces in the cartoons of George Price — are somehow summed up by

Jane Bowles in the deliberately, comically deadpan surface of her work. Her characters are made original by
characters that cannot open or communicate; they are
total separates. Their gracious innocence in depraved
joints in Panama is Jane Bowles's joke, but it is not a
joke on *them*; they become fond of whores and pimps
and obvious confidence men without knowing what these
strangers do. Their "innocence" is indeed what interests
Jane Bowles in her characters — their incommunicable
queerness.

These *are* serious ladies, perhaps because the world is
so plainly not serious that only the unconscious virtue of
certain women can give it dignity. They are first and last
untouched souls, oddities, privacies, as the women in
Gertrude Stein's *Three Lives* are nothing but "characters." Although Jane Bowles's women are closer to
women than to men, they do not identify with anybody
at all. They are like all remarkable children in literature:
provisional guests in this world. Things happen to them
without modifying them — that is the comedy of *Two
Serious Ladies*. They just pass through the world. And
such is the form of their "seriousness," their unbreakable
singularity, their sweet dim inexpressiveness, their obviously privileged position, that they turn the "world" into
an inconsequential background to themselves, a series of
farcically tenuous stage sets — islands, country estates,
tropic bordellos. These are cities not on any map, streets
that do not lead into each other, islands that are *unaccountable*. The prevailing strangeness and unconnected-
ness of these women makes each of them a presence that
just bulks over everything else. As there is no real trans-

action between them, so there is no action. The absurdity and intractability of being nothing but an unresisting yet untouched single "character" is all:

> *"I've always been a body-worshipper," said Mrs. Copperfield, "but that doesn't mean that I fall in love with people who have beautiful bodies. Some of the bodies I've liked have been awful. Come, let's go over to Mr. Toby."*
>
> *The girl had the bright eyes of an insatiable nymphomaniac. She wore a ridiculous little watch on a black ribbon around her wrist.*
>
> *Away in the back of the room a man was bowling up a small alley all by himself; Miss Goering listened to the rumble of the balls as they rolled along the wooden runway, and she wished that she were able to see him so that she could be at peace for the evening with the certainty that there was no one who could be considered a menace present in the room.*

Mrs. Bowles conceived of her fiction as an ironic extension of the old insistence, in women's fiction, that woman is the heart of a heartless world. The world in her altogether dry, vaguely jeering pages becomes even more heartless than one could have imagined it. It is literally deaf, dumb, uncomprehending, made up of characters and situations which do not flow together in the slightest, which never interact. It is a world composed somehow of silence. Since women are the point of it, it dramatizes the heroine as farcically a force, the woman who to her own mind is so original that her personality is the only weight in the story, its dominating indecipherable presence. Woman is the idiosyncrasy around which this bizarre existence is composed.

This detached consciousness of self becomes, in the work of Susan Sontag, an intellectualized fancy, a series of improvisations on what the mind can work out. This seems related to the delusive sovereignty of the novelist's gift, which more and more gives writers who are speculative intellectuals in the novel, like Robbe-Grillet and Sontag, the itch to turn a novel into nothing but a new theory of the novel. Ideas run rampant. The function of the novel is to show that "the novel" is finished, and that the fanciful individual performance has liberated us from the old bonds of narrative.

Brigid Brophy has said, commenting on her comic novel about a woman's mind in totally operative confusion, *In Transit*:

> *Baroque is the juxtaposition and interpenetration of death themes and life themes — as it were, black marble and white marble. The aim of the design is to bring the reader suddenly around a corner to confront an incongruity — which may be comic or ironic and is always in Bad Taste. . . .*
>
> *People who proclaim the novel dead are mistaken. The mistake is to think there's any such thing as "the novel." What they have in mind is the nineteenth-century novel. Novels live splendidly on.*
>
> *The nineteenth-century novel had to fill-in and anesthetize the boredom of nineteenth-century life, for which reason it was the slave of its narrative. Nowadays this function is performed by thrillers. The rest of fiction has been set free.*
>
> *. . . It was slavery to narrative which made novels read-once-and-throw-away consumer goods. Twentieth-century prose fiction can be, as poetry has always been, re-readable. It is free to be as serious as serious music.*

Brophy is a natural novelist whose many pronouncements evidently flow from the mischievousness of her
imagination. One does not mind her blowing her own
horn, since she so much delights in making music. There
is always a charge of new energy, though one is stimulated only in the abstract, as by revolutionary theory.
Susan Sontag is a grimmer figure, for the idea of alternatives in every possible situation always replaces the bread
of life. In her novels as in her essays, she is concerned
with producing a startling esthetic which her words prolong. She is interested in advancing new positions to the
point of making her clever, surprisingly sustained novels
experiments in the trying-out of an idea. One respects
these books, even their total intellectual solemnity, because they are entirely manifestations of Sontag's personal will over esthetic situations defined as those in
which originality functions by asserting itself. The problem, she wrote in *Styles of Radical Will*, is really: How is
art — even radical art —

*useful for individual survival in an era of permanent
apocalypse? Good and bad have become useless concepts — the most valid forms — in art — in philosophy
— are those which accommodate the greatest ambiguity;
they are profoundly disturbing but are psychologically
appropriate to our condition. Bergman's* Persona *and
the films of Godard are exemplary esthetic models. . . .*

*Art must tend toward anti-art; the elimination of the
"subject" . . . the substitution of chance for intention,
and the pursuit of silence. . . . Art is unmasked as gratuitous, and the very concreteness of the artist's tools
. . . appears as a trap. Practised in a world furnished*

with second-hand perceptions, and specifically con-
founded by the treachery of words, the artist's activity
is cursed. . . . Art becomes the enemy of the artist, for
it denies him the realization — the transcendence — he
desires. Therefore, art comes to be considered something
to be overthrown.

These mettlesome remarks in summary of too much are, like many of Sontags irreconcilable sentences, challenges and defiances, provocations no doubt to herself above all. The "new" is for her never a tradition, a common resource she shares with anyone else. Above all the "new" is never natural, something to live with; it is an assertion, a voice, a self, in a world so determinedly construed from the outset as totally without foundation, "permanent apocalypse," that the "new" is expressive by reason of being different from moment to moment, not because of its human resonance or its durability.

Yet what makes Sontag's novels more than curiosities is her belief that fiction is a trying-out, an hypothesis which you carry out, not prove. The "world" is entirely plastic. Today we improvise, and tonight we shall improvise something else. Her books are films in the sense that there are shots of one idea after another. And they "work," they operate within their context (if hardly on our emotions), because Sontag is one of those provocative writers, like William Gass trained first in philosophy, for whom a narrative is a situation one "supposes" as philosophers do, in *illustration* of an argument — now just suppose that this table . . . — rather than a story the writer himself is the first to believe.

The philosopher Hans Vaihinger formulated a philosophy of "as if." We cannot truly know what is real, and so we construct systems of thought to satisfy our mental need, then assume that actuality agrees with our constructions. We act "as if" the real were what we assume it to be. Sontag's two novels advance constructions of reality by the protagonists that *then* they try to live up to. In *The Benefactor* a nondescript young Frenchman, Hippolyte, has bizarre dreams and then tries to reproduce them in his life. The "dreams" are really scenarios, not dreams; Hippolyte's actual experiences are intellectually worked out footnotes to the dreams, and without the slightest touch of comedy. Surely a man trying to live by his dreams is naturally comic? But Sontag has no humor, for that would involve her in something like Kafka's whimsical identifications with "K." She is proud, but her hero is a ninny, a straw man. *"Now let us just imagine that this ninny, Hippolyte. . . ."*

But what is striking about *The Benefactor* especially is the fact that the author can sustain her hypothesis, her *fancy*, through a novel that takes place not in Paris, where the characters are living, but in Susan Sontag's will to keep this up. At one point she says in behalf of her Hippolyte: "Thus every gesture in the dream gained the status of a ritual." Jean-Jacques, a writer, tells Hippolyte: "You can't write, you are a born specialist, the sort of person who can do only one thing." Of Jean-Jacques himself the author explains: "Because he was absolutely committed to his work, writing, he could afford to be unreliable in every other way — and to ornament his life with games, strategies, and artifacts."

After Hippolyte kills — Hippolyte *thinks* he has killed his mistress Frau Anders by setting fire to her house — we read: "Imagine to yourself, reader, that you are a murderer." No wonder that Hippolyte can finally say to Jean-Jacques — "Your life is a museum of counter-banalities. But what's so wrong with banality? . . . Do you grant me that art doesn't consist primarily in creation but in destruction?"

These propositions, which may sound like the rootless cultural baggage of our time satirized by Donald Barthelme, are improbable out of context, but plausible in the altogether theorizing world that Susan Sontag has created for her characters. *The Benefactor* works because its author really sees the world as a series of propositions *about* the world. Her theoreticalness consists of a loyalty not to certain ideas but to life as the improvisation of ideas. She is positive only about moving on from these ideas, and this makes her an interesting fantasist about a world conceived as nothing but someone thinking up new angles to it. Sontag writes about situations, is always figuring out alternatives to her existing ideas about them and thus works at situations in the way that a movie director works something out for an induced effect. But she is always in the book, visibly parallel to the scene she is writing. A book is a screen, as she is a mind visibly "projecting" her notion of things onto it. Screen and mind are separated by Sontag's refusal to tell a story for its own sake.

Death-Kit — which improbably relates the effort of one "Diddy" to discover whether he did or did-he not commit a murder — also has a dummy for hero. His supposed plight is just an occasion for the author's ambitious critical intelligence to think ahead of the reader. Although Sontag admires the "new wave" French writers and movie directors, what excites her is not their hatred of all conventionality but a desire to astonish, to replace someone else's way of *looking* at things. The total abstractness of even the American setting in *Death-Kit* is striking. The book is a series of variations on the theme of perception, and just as Diddy is a pun on his need to find out whether he did or didn't kill a workman in a train tunnel, so the tunnel is obviously symbolic, as is the fact that Diddy writes advertising copy for a manufacturer of microscopes and that his girl Hester is blind. Exploring all sorts of interesting considerations about "sight," like exploring the fantasy gimmick of a man trying to make his life conform to his dreams, certainly keeps Sontag more interesting than her characters. Abstractness gives her total authority, and it would seem to be this total control that interests her in the writing of a book, and that interests us in the reading of it. We do not experience a novel; we experience her readiness to see what she can think of next.

How to survive is just an experimental theme in Susan Sontag's novels, not a burning issue. In Sylvia Plath, who became a heroine of the death school so close to the surface in our time, we now have a case rather than a writer. Gifted as she was, it cannot be denied that she always wrote of herself as a case. But the real function of her posthumous fame has been to celebrate so thoroughgoing a coldness, so elegantly but murderously phrased a rejection of the world. Sylvia Plath's problem was put perfectly by the psychiatrist in "Hannah Green's" *I Never Promised You a Rose Garden* — "The sick are all so afraid of their own uncontrollable power! Somehow they cannot believe that they are only people, holding only a human-sized anger." Sylvia Plath's despair at being nothing but this self, a self able to describe itself "perfectly" but unable to describe the death it longed for, could willfully attach itself to any of the many names in our time for political horror. In *Ariel* the long-dead father, who had been a professor of biology in Boston, was hysterically if not altogether sincerely condemned as *you bastard, you Nazi you.*

Sylvia Plath's own power was intense, shocking, disconnected. Her professionalism could express any selective state of emotion, but not grief. As she complained, "I feel like a very efficient tool or weapon, used and in demand from moment to moment." By the same token all outward facts are scornfully devaluated in her brilliantly cutting poetry, made to seem just murderous. The electrocution of the Rosenbergs is mentioned early and almost jauntily in *The Bell Jar* just to remind you what year it was when "Esther Greenwood" got to New York by winning a woman's magazine college contest. So in the novel which Sylvia Plath herself disliked, and which she had written with her usual facile use of every bit of her experience, there is no connection between the girl's world and the surrender of herself to the bell jar which *we* now know was moving down on her with the force of gravity.

Sylvia Plath's talent was fluent, practiced, totally "professional" even when she was in college. So that the astonishing precisely memorable thing about her work is its total lovelessness toward the "world" — it could not even distract her from her fixation on her fate — and her practiced literary use of it for effect. It was as if she robbed an orchard of its most colorful fruit without eating any. The world existed just to be written about.

Nevertheless, the sense of *mankind's* vulnerability in this age gives a special resonance to all personal testimony by gifted women writers. By the act of writing well, by their acute sense of performance, they somehow put themselves on the line and thus right in the path of the disturbance that was settling and subject to all contemporary writing, and made it move. This was certainly different from that bourgeois commodity — that type not so much of social fiction as of the object-cluttered bourgeois world — that has been known as "women's fiction." "Women's fiction" is marked by its uneasy concern with the bourgeois property world and its determination that the "second sex" become the first sex in the American family. By contrast with so much of the new fiction created by women in the age of protest directed against a system based on the illusion of unlimited power, "women's fiction" is a document in the form of satire, and based on the dissatisfied wife.

In the novels of Alison Lurie, for example, the chief figure is always that of a wife whose husband is an organization man of one kind or another — at a New England college, an insurance company, a research and development corporation. Her rebellion against *his* ties takes the form of an affair with an artist or composer or psychoanalyst. The resolution is not love for either husband or lover but the inability to satisfy her "true nature"; the rejection of the convention forced on her by her husband's employment leads her to lovers who are equally part of the system. She is always a dependent. No wonder that Alison Lurie's novels are earnest, smooth satires of the New England college, the Los Angeles research and development corporation, the hippie scene, the writer's colony. They are written up like research projects, are full of information, insistent on surface detail in the style of women writers who have felt like spies when allowed into the husband's office. Their theme is still a woman's inability to live her own life, which makes her quite passive when the woman is outside the organization where all the interesting fights are taking place. The men and women in her novels belong by occupation to different species, which makes the exchange of vital information impossible and sex necessary. Indeed, bed is the only place where her men and women can meet. So the differences between them must never be resolved.

Maybe this will be more and more a significant theme in "women's fiction" — sexuality as the expression of the necessary *misunderstanding* between the sexes. But what follows for the heroine of Alison Lurie's novels is obviously old-fashioned rivalry, the ironic sense of detail with which one woman makes fun of another woman's dress after a dinner party — the nagging attention to small details fundamental in a consumer society that *is* the status society. This cult of "observation" is already archaic, for the writer who makes so much of marginal detail is a girl who has not enough to do. In Alison Lurie's first novel, *Love and Friendship*, the wife complains when her lover after making love out of doors goes to meet a class: "But it's only ten practically. What'll I do the rest of the morning?" In *Real People* the wife of an insurance executive, free to write at an artist's colony, complains bitterly:

> *Really, I want to write all the stories I've thought of and then discarded because they might shock or hurt someone. . . . Only of course I can't. . . . Gerry said I had a patron, as writers did in the seventeenth and eighteenth centuries. . . . It's true. Clark and all the rest of them are my patrons just as much as those English lords were Dryden's or Pope's. There is the same avoidance of all topics which might annoy them; the same gross or subtle glorification of their way of life: the same praise of their virtues (reliability, good taste, justice, moderation) and blindness to their faults.*
> *Hopeless. The whole thing is hopeless.*

And judging by the sterile maliciousness of *Real People*, obviously so much dependency is. The famous acidulousness of Mary McCarthy's fiction is something else, for she is essentially a brilliant culture critic, with the critic's irritable sense of mental independence, who stolidly taught herself to write fiction as a way of putting into relief one woman's unassimilability. There is always one theme in Mary McCarthy's fictions: none of these awful people is going to catch *me*. The heroine is always distinctly right, and gives herself all possible marks for taste, integrity and indomitability. Other people are somehow material to be written up. This heroine began in the Forties as the bohemian girl in a world of men she would do anything with except respect; she went on with undeviating sharpness to discuss academic types in *The Groves of Academe*, old radicals and ex-utopians in "The Oasis," Cape Cod residents in *A Charmed Life*, college girls of the Thirties in *The Group*, America and Americans at large in *Birds of America*.

This most recent book is less in the form of a novel than Mary McCarthy's other books, for the protagonist is for the most part a young American student in Paris, Peter Levi, rather than his celebrated musician mother, Rosamund Brown, and we are steadily told what Peter thinks. His mother, though she soon disappears from the book, is more directly active a figure in her few scenes, and what *she* thinks is that America has gone to hell in the form of frozen foods. Rosamund Brown is a lovely sweet artist woman who wants to cook in her New England kitchen with the same access to real food that her mother had in Marietta, Ohio. The theme is that Nature Is Dead. What is interesting about this, and more than a little touching, is that though the evidence as a novel given for this is paltry, and everybody in the book except mother and son is, as usual, contemptible, Mary McCarthy as a polemicist at last rises to a point beyond the heroine's intense self-approval. Nature *is* dead now for most Americans, and it is interesting that so stark a traditionalist should have appeared in Mary McCarthy to say so.

"I come from California, come from a family, or a congeries of families, that has always been in the Sacramento Valley." Some native Californians think that Joan Didion is sentimental about that "always" bit, that the place was never as much "Eden" — as she likes to describe it — before the aerospace industries and the supermarkets came in. But Joan Didion's professional sense of style in all things — she has several times done a perfect piece around the fear of a nervous breakdown, and not had one — gives a smooth literary fervor to the constant theme of decline and fall. The story between the lines of *Slouching Towards Bethlehem* is surely not so much "California" as it is her ability to make us share her passionate sense of it. And her own reportorial voice carried very clearly indeed even at a time when "the article as art" was being more noisily promulgated by Norman Mailer and Tom Wolfe. *Slouching Towards Bethlehem* established itself extraordinarily well for a collection of "pieces"; her novel *Play It as It Lays*, though it definitely made its mark as a picture of a woman's despair within the total *nada* of the Hollywood scene, seemed to one of her old editors "depressing" and less valuable than her reportage.

Living in Malibu, overlooking the Pacific Ocean, Joan Didion has described how, when the Malibu hills were on fire, the young surfers in the water would look up at the fires raging overhead and go on with their surfing. Obviously only a very gifted writer with a particular eye for the harsh, inhuman, even antihuman extremes that surround our still fragile settlement on this continent would have brought into conversation the typical Joan Didion picture — Hell as Sunny California — the hills on fire in Malibu and the surfers joyfully sporting below. But Joan Didion constantly presents such moral symbols in her work with a sense of style that is both brilliant and inert, as befits a very vulnerable, defensive young novelist whose style in all things is somehow to keep the world off, to keep it from eating her up, and who describes southern California in terms of fire, rattlesnakes, cave-ins, earthquakes, the indifference to other people's disasters, and the terrible wind called the Santa Ana. With that inescapable sense of style that seems to cry "Danger!" she writes in "Los Angeles Notebook":

> *The city burning is Los Angeles's deepest image of itself: Nathanael West perceived that, in* The Day of the Locust; *and at the time of the 1965 Watts riots what struck the imagination most indelibly were the fires. For days one could drive the Harbor Freeway and see the city on fire, just as we had always known it would be in the end. Los Angeles weather is the weather of catastrophe, of apocalypse . . . the violence and the unpredictability of the Santa Ana affect the entire quality of life in Los Angeles, accentuate its impermanence, its unreliability. The wind shows us how close to the edge we are.*

Everything Joan Didion writes seems attuned to some physical anxiety surrounding her in the atmosphere of southern California. She is so responsive to the insecure surface of California that the inescapably alarmed fragility of the woman helps to explain the impending sense of catastrophe that informs so much of her work, the smartly written but brooding sense of nemesis that is the insistent theme of *Play It as It Lays*. One woman reviewer said that the book was not merely *about* nothingness, but that there was a "nothing" to the book's heroine, a movie actress who sees doom, falsehood, and violence everywhere in the Sunny West. Maria Wyeth gives herself at request to several moneyed Hollywood hoodlums, but seems to take no pleasure in her body.

Silence as a form and fear of imminent breakdown is a significant element in both Joan Didion's reportage and fiction. There are also a good many silences between her written sentences, which have a look of getting freshly loaded before they hit you. She refers often to her fragility in *Slouching Towards Bethlehem*, and she writes about her panics with a deliberation that is not merely disarming but that always makes a point, in perfect style, about something other than herself.

> *I went to San Francisco because I had not been able to work in some months, had been paralyzed by the conviction that writing was an irrelevant act, that the world as I had understood it no longer existed. If I was to work again at all, it would be necessary for me to come to terms with disorder. . . .*

The most striking feature of her spare, tight, histrionically desolate one-line sentences in *Play It as It Lays* is that, as in her reportage, all personal damage reflects cultural sickness. What Rough Beast Does Slouch Towards Bethlehem? When a visitor asked her to define the "evil" she sees on every hand, she replied: "The absence of seriousness." The lady is a moralist in an old-fashioned tradition. She feels "intellectually," she lays it all out, and somehow it is all so mod, empty, American, that you feel for *her*. Children in Haight-Ashbury on drugs. Abortions. Children with brain damage. An actor making love to Maria in Vegas who suddenly breaks open a popper of amyl nitrate to intensify his orgasm.

Hell now exists, as real as you and me; but in Joan Didion's fiction, as in her articles, it always has a name, a location, weather, the California specific to itself — "oil scum on the sand, a red tide on the flaccid surf and mounds of kelp at the waterline. The kelp hummed with flies." In *Play It as It Lays* Maria unbelievably opens the novel with: " 'What makes Iago evil?' some people ask. I never ask." The novel gives us inner devastation matched by fire in the California hills, husbands and wives who cannot feel anything, former lovers who return only to inflict pain, a homosexual who persuades Maria to hold his hand as he commits suicide. All this despair positively insists on saying, in the ready phrase of the homosexual's wife, "Everything is shit" and describes itself as a feature of the local life as well known as the casting couch.

Hannah Arendt once remarked that she had never seen in Europe such unexplained personal suffering as she saw here. In Joan Didion's work the names given to physical threats and devastation, the brilliantly ominous details to present life in California, are meant to explain this suffering, but they don't. The young woman who went about everywhere as a reporter with "a pervasive sense of loss" was to give this to *all* her heroines, including Joan Didion. But the vague, haunted Lily McClellan in *Run River* — my favorite among the three Didion books — makes us feel that her sleeping with various men she does not care for is the expression of a deep personal fright, and not a judgment on her husband Everett McClellan's futile belief that "order" must be kept up at all costs. "The easiest lay in the room, I can always spot them, something scared in their eyes," a drunk at a party says about Lily. Sometimes female "fright" says more about despair than what happened to Sacramento.

In *Play It as It Lays* Maria Wyeth, a movie star separated and soon casually divorced from a husband who once directed her in a gang-bang picture, comes from Silver Wells, Nevada. There she had a solid sort of old-fashioned gambler for a father, a perfect straight shooter of a mother. It is all gone now — the real Old West is gone, and Maria is numb, utterly numb, with a sense of the "nothing" all around her. After a felt but entirely furtive affair with a married man, she has an abortion. The go-between on the drive to the abortionist's:

> *You may have noticed, I drive a Cadillac. Eldorado. Eats gas but I like it, like the feel of it. . . . If I decided to get rid of the Cad, I might pick myself up a little Camaro. Maybe that sounds like a step down, a Cad to a Camaro, but I've got my eye on this particular Camaro, exact model of the pace car in the Indianapolis 500.*

This is typically brilliant, but all is symbol, every character is a *statement* that evil reigns, as real as sunshine. The center is not holding. Everyone in the book except Maria acts the pimp, the stud, the call girl, the pervert, the decadent hairdresser, the orgiast, the suicide. It is all shit, evil as what Joan Didion calls a "deprivation of seriousness," all money, sex, private terror. The assignations are as coldly calculated as tax deals.

What made *Play It as It Lays* unusually interesting,

gave it an attention few new novels get nowadays, is the graphic readability it makes of our "condition." The book proceeds by a succession of rapid closeups, scenes often just a short chapter, a tattoo of one-line exchanges that does everything to wing its message to the reader. There are intense descriptive scenes of Maria wildly driving the frightening California freeways to show that she can manage them, at Hoover Dam registering the throb of the turbines in her body. The book is a film that gets its rhythm from the most relentless cutting, and the silence between the curt scenes is calculated, disturbing. The book is so cunning in its rapid-fire rhythm that all sorts of questions about the characters get overlooked under the spell of its intimacy with dread.

Joan Didion is too much in control throughout the book, literally the director-*auteur*, as they now say in cinema circles. Maria would hardly ask "Why should a coral snake need two glands of neurotoxic poison to survive while a king snake, *so similarly marked*, needs none. Where is the Darwinian logic there. . . ." Joan Didion is so professional a moralist that the message emerges, hypnotic but unbelievable: nothingness is the medium in which we live. She is almost too skillful a demonstrator of the widespread lack of confidence among middle-class Americans that makes them shocking to themselves. Her real subject is the individual woman who is mysteriously a torment to herself, and it is her loyalty to this subject rather than her nostalgia for some mythical past California that makes her understand the American smartness and knowingness from which no writer so smoothly professional and acceptable is free.

What interests me most in her writing is what, from her woman's point of view renders the world incommunicable. *Run River*, a first book much less smart than her next two but evocative of Lily Knight McClellan's mysteriousness to herself, has an emotional depth that I much prefer to the brilliant journalism of *Slouching Towards Bethlehem* or the evasive sentimentality behind the rapid-fire technique of *Play It as It Lays*. Lily McClellan is one of the few women left in contemporary American fiction who *don't* know what life is all about, who move through their days with the full gravity of being alive. Lily's moral and physical fragility, her *not* knowing, her *not* being on top of things, her almost accidental love affairs, give her an authenticity, all around, missing in Maria Wyeth. In the midst of all that California light and space, we get the existential feeling of what it was like to be alive in the Great Valley:

> The afternoon heat could bleach those towns so clean that the houses and the buildings seemed always on the verge of dematerializing; there was a sense that to close one's eyes on a Valley town was to risk opening them a moment later on dry fields, the sun bleaching out the last traces of habitation, a flowered straw hat, a neon advertisement which had blinked a moment before from a wall no longer visible. . . .
>
> It was a great comfort, watching the towns come and go through the tinted window of the Greyhound bus. The heat drained the distinctions from things — marriage and divorce and new curtains and over-drafts at the bank, all the same — and Lily could not at the moment imagine any preoccupation strong enough to withstand the summer.

Lily's husband, Everett McClellan, is somewhat dim and unreal, as the men in Joan Didion's two novels generally tend to be. Perhaps this is because, as his sister Martha says about Everett to his wife Lily: "All Everett wants is a little order."

> "I guess that's what everybody wants."
> Martha lay down again. "Maybe everybody wants it. But most people don't want it more than anything else in the world. The way Everett does. You might want it, I might want it. But when the opportunity to have it practically hits us over the head, we just knock ourselves out getting out of the way." She paused. "Take you for example."

I am sure that in Joan Didion's deliberate mind, *Run River* is a novel about decline and fall in the Sacramento River Valley, and that the "pervasive sense of loss" she remembers from earliest childhood has been steadily translated into the many symbols — the disaster of the McClellans' marriage, Lily McClellan as a lost lady, the decline of a "certain pride" — that have made her almost too professional a writer about our moral condition. But the involuntary unacknowledged strength of her sensibility, the really arresting thing, is seen not in the clear cold eye, the writer's famous detachment, the "perfect" sentences, the amusing social cattiness about arrivistes and kept women and the huddled mob life of New York — but in the sense of fright, of something deeply wrong. No, the center is not holding. But the center is not the proprietary middle class that was in Sacramento, or the Establishment that tells us where the bodies have been buried after more powerful people have disposed of them. The "center" is that inner space, that moral realm, where, as Mark Schorer said in his review of *Play It as It Lays*, the question that keeps nagging is: "What makes us hurt so much? You have to be more than merely skillful with the little knives and so on to get away with it."

> So the days pass, and I ask myself whether one is not hypnotised, as a child by a silver globe, by life; and whether this is living.
> — Virginia Woolf
> *Diary*, 28 November 1928

A "sense of fright, of something deeply wrong." In Joyce Carol Oates's most notable novel, *them*, this seemed to express itself as a particular sensitivity to individual lives helplessly flying off the wheel of American gigantism. While writing *them* (a novel which ends with the 1967 eruption of Detroit's Blacks) she said that Detroit was "all melodrama." There a man can get shot by the brother of the woman he is lying next to in bed, and the body will be disposed of by a friendly policeman. The brother himself pops up later in the sister's life not as a "murderer," but as a genially obtuse and merely wistful fellow. Nothing of this is satirized or moralized as once it would have been. It is what happens every day now; there are too many people for murders to count. There are too many murderers about for the murderer to take murder that seriously.

Joyce Carol Oates seemed, more than most women writers, entirely open to *social* turmoil, to the frighteningly undirected and misapplied force of the American power-house. She plainly had an instinct for the social menace packed up in Detroit, waiting to explode, that at the end of the nineteenth century Dreiser felt about Chicago and Stephen Crane about New York. The sheer rich chaos of American life, to say nothing of its staggering armies of poor, outraged, by no means peaceful people, pressed upon her. It is rare to find a woman writer so externally unconcerned with form. After teaching at the University of Detroit from 1962 to 1967, she remarked that Detroit is a city "so transparent, you can hear it ticking." What one woman critic, in a general attack on Oates, called "Violence in the Head," could also be taken as her inability to blink social violence as the language in which a great many "lower-class" Americans naturally deal with each other.

Joyce Carol Oates is however, a "social novelist" of a peculiar kind. She is concerned not with demonstrating power relationships, but with the struggle of people now-adays to express their fate in terms that are cruelly changeable. Reading her, one sees the real tragedy of so many Americans today, unable to find a language for what is happening to them. The drama of society was once seen by American social novelists as the shifting line between the individual and the mass into which he was helplessly falling. It has now become the free-floating mythology about "them" which each person carries around with him, an idea of causation unconnected to cause. There is no longer a fixed point within people's thinking. In the American social novels earlier in the century, the novelist was a pathfinder and the characters were betrayed as blind helpless victims of their fate, like Hurstwood in *Sister Carrie* or virtually everybody in Dos Passos's *U.S.A.* Joyce Carol Oates is not particularly ahead of the people she writes about. Since her prime concern is to see people in the terms they present to themselves, she is able to present consciousness as a person, a crazily unaccountable thing. The human mind, as she says in the title of a recent novel, is simply "wonderland." And the significance of that "wonderland" to the social melodrama that is America today is that they collide but do not connect.

Praising Harriette Arnow's strong, little-known novel about Southern mountain folk, *The Dollmaker*, Joyce Oates said:

> *It seems to me that the greatest works of literature deal with the human soul caught in the stampede of time, unable to gauge the profundity of what passes over it, like the characters of Yeats who live through terrifying events but who cannot understand them; in this way history passes over most of us. Society is caught in a convulsion, whether of growth or of death, and ordinary people are destroyed. They do not, however, understand that they are "destroyed."*

This view of literature as silent tragedy is a central description of what interests Joyce Oates in the writing of fiction. Her own characters move through a world that seems to be wholly physical and even full of global eruption, yet the violence, as Elizabeth Dalton said, is in their own heads — and is no less real for that. They touch us by frightening us, like disembodied souls calling to us from the other world. They live through terrifying events but cannot understand them. This is what makes Oates a new element in our fiction, involuntarily disturbing.

She does not understand why she is disturbing. She takes the convulsion of society for granted, and so a writer born in 1938 regularly "returns" to the 1930s in her work. *A Garden of Earthly Delights* begins with the birth on the highway of a migrant worker's child after the truck transporting the workers has been in a collision. Obviously she is unlike many women writers in her feeling for the pressure, mass, density of violence in American experience not always shared by the professional middle class. "The greatest realities," she has said, "are physical and economic; all the subtleties of life come afterward." Yet the central thing in her work is the teeming private consciousness, a "wonderland" that to her is reality in action — but without definition and without boundary.

Joyce Oates is peculiarly and painfully open to other minds, so possessed by them that in an author's note to *them* she says of the student who became the "Maureen Wendall" of the novel, "Her various problems and complexities overwhelmed me. . . . My initial feeling about her life was, 'This must be fiction, this can't be real!' My more permanent feeling was, 'This is the only kind of fiction that is real.'" Her ability to get occupied by another consciousness makes even *them*, her best novel to date, a sometimes impenetrably voluminous history of emotions, emotions, emotions. You feel that you are turning thousands of pages, that her world is as harshly overpopulated as a sleepless mind, that you cannot make out the individual features of anyone within this clamor of everyone's existence.

This is obviously related to the ease with which Joyce Oates transfers the many situations in her head straight onto paper. I sense an extraordinary and tumultuous amount of purely mental existence locked up behind her schoolgirl's face. She once told an interviewer that she is always writing about "love . . . and it takes many different forms, many different social levels. . . . I think I write about love in an unconscious way. I look back upon the novels I've written, and I say, yes, this was my subject. But at the time I'm writing I'm not really conscious of that. I'm writing about a certain person who does this and that and comes to a certain end." She herself is the most unyielding lover in her books, as witness the force with which she follows so many people through every trace of their feeling, thinking, moving. She is obsessive in her patience with the sheer factuality of contemporary existence. This evident love for the scene we Americans make, for the incredible profusion of life in America, also troubles Joyce Carol Oates. Every writer knows himself to be a little crazy, but her feeling of her own absurdity is probably intensified by the dreamlike ease with which her works are produced. It must indeed trouble her that this looks like glibness, when in point of fact her dogged feeling that she writes out of love is based on the fact that she is utterly hypnotized, positively drugged, by other people's experiences. The social violence so marked in her work is like the sheer density of detail — this and this and this is what is happening to people. She is attached to life by well-founded apprehension that nothing lasts, nothing is safe, nothing is all around us. In *them* Maureen Wendall thinks:

> *Maybe the book with her money in it, and the money so greedily saved, and the idea of the money, maybe these things weren't real either. What would happen if everything broke into pieces? It was queer how you felt, instinctively, that a certain space of time was real and not a dream, and you gave your life to it, all your energy and faith, believing it to be real. But how could you tell what would last and what wouldn't? Marriages ended. Love ended. Money could be stolen, found out and taken . . . or it might disappear by itself, like that secretary's notebook. Objects disappeared, slipped through cracks, devoured, kicked aside, knocked under the bed or into the trash, lost. Her clearest memory of the men she'd been with was their moving away from her. They were all body then, completed.*

The details in Oates's fiction follow each other with a humble truthfulness that make you wonder where she is taking you, that is sometimes disorienting, for she is all attention to the unconscious reactions of her characters. She needs a lot of space, which is why her short stories tend to read like scenarios for novels. The amount of *listening* this involves is certainly singular. My deepest feeling about her is that her mind is unbelievably crowded with psychic existences, with such a mass of stories that she lives by being wholly submissive to "them." She is too attentive to their mysterious clamor to *want* to be an artist, to make the right and well-fitting structure. Much of her fiction seems written to relieve her mind of the people who haunt it, not to create something that will live.

So many inroads on the suddenly frightening American situation is indeed a problem in our fiction just now; the age of high and proud art has yielded to the climate of crisis. Joyce Oates's many stories resemble a card index of situations; they are not the deeply plotted stories that we return to as perfect little dramas; her novels, though they involve the reader through the author's intense connection with her material, tend as incident to fade out of our minds. Too much happens. Indeed, hers are altogether strange books, haunting rather than "successful," because the mind behind them is primarily concerned with a kind of Darwinian struggle for existence between minds, with the truth of some limitless human struggle. We miss the perfectly suggestive shapes that modern art and fiction have taught us to venerate. Oates is another Cassandra bewitched by her private oracle. But it is not disaster that is most on her mind; it is the recognition of each person as the center of the coming disturbance. And this disturbance, as Pascal said of his God, has its center everywhere and its circumference nowhere.

So her characters are opaque, ungiving, uncharming; they have the taciturn qualities that come with the kind of people they are — heavy, hallucinated, outside the chatty middle class. Society speaks in them, but *they* are not articulate. They do not yet feel themselves to be emancipated persons. They are caught up in the social convulsion and move unheedingly, compulsively, blindly, through the paces assigned to them by the power god.

That is exactly what Oates's work expresses just now:

a sense that American life is taking some of us by the throat. "Too much" is happening; many will disappear. Above all, and most ominously, hers is a world in which our own people, and not just peasants in Vietnam, get "wasted." There is a constant sense of drift, deterioration, the end of things, that contrasts violently with the era of "high art" and the once-fond belief in immortality through art. Oates is someone plainly caught up in this "avalanche" of time.

7

THE IMAGINATION OF FACT
Capote to Mailer

Population is easily our biggest problem, our nastiest and messiest. I've been working on a novel which concerns what I regard as the only possible solution — birth control medications in food. A novel is a piddling sort of contribution, but it may get people interested.

> — Dr. Michael Crichton

. . . a shallow horror sensation that cold springs of personal fear swiftly deepened.

> — Truman Capote,
> *In Cold Blood*

WHEN TRUMAN CAPOTE EXPLAINED, on the publication in 1965 of *In Cold Blood: The True Account of a Multiple Murder and Its Consequences*, that the book was really a "nonfiction novel," it was natural to take his praise of his meticulously factual and extraordinarily industrious record of research as the alibi of a novelist whose last novel, *Breakfast at Tiffany's*, had been slight, and who was evidently between novels. Capote clearly hungered to remain in the big league of novelists, so many of whom are unprofitable to everyone, even if he was now the author of a bestselling true thriller whose success was being arranged through every possible "medium" of American publicity. Capote is a novelist, novelists tend to be discouraged by the many current discourtesies to fiction. Clearly Capote wanted to keep his novelist's prestige but to rise above the novelist's struggle for survival. *In Cold Blood*, before one read it, promised by the nature of the American literary market to be another wow, a trick, a slick transposition from one realm to another, like the inevitable musical to be made out of the Sacco-Vanzetti case.

What struck me most in Capote's labeling his book a "nonfiction novel" was his honoring the profession of novelist. Novels seem more expendable these days than ever, but *novelist* is still any writer's notion of original talent. What interested me most about *In Cold Blood* after two readings — first in *The New Yorker* and then as a book — was that though it *was* journalism and soon gave away all its secrets, it had the ingenuity of fiction and it was fiction except for its ambition to be documentary. *In Cold Blood* brought to focus for me the problem of "fact writing" and its "treatment." There is a lot of "treatment" behind the vast amount of social fact that we get in a time of perpetual crisis. These books dramatize and add to the crisis, and we turn to them because they give a theme to the pervasive social anxiety, the concrete human instance that makes "literature."

In Cold Blood is an extremely stylized book that has a palpable design on our emotions. It works on us as a merely factual account never had to. It is so shapely and its revelations are so well timed that it becomes a "novel" in the form of fact. But how many great novels of crime and punishment are expressly based on fact without lapsing into "history"! *The Possessed* is based on the Nechayev case, *An American Tragedy* on the Chester Gillette case. What makes *In Cold Blood* formally a work of record rather than of invention? Because formally, at least, it is a documentary; based on six years of research and six thousand pages of notes, it retains this research in the text. Victims, murderers, witnesses and law officials appear under their own names and as their attested identities, in an actual or, as we say now, "real" Kansas town.

Why, then, did Capote honor himself by calling the

book in any sense a "novel"? Why bring up the word at all? Because Capote depended on the record, was proud of his prodigious research, but was not content to make a work of record. After all, most readers of *In Cold Blood* know nothing about the case except what Capote tells us. Capote wanted his "truthful account" to become "a work of art," and he knew he could accomplish this, quite apart from the literary expertness behind the book, through a certain intimacy between himself and "his" characters. Capote wanted, ultimately, to turn the perpetually defeated, negative Eros that is behind *Other Voices, Other Rooms* into an emblematic situation for our time. As Norman Mailer said when running for Mayor, "Until you see what your ideas lead to, you know nothing." Through his feeling for the Clutter family *and* its murderers, Capote was able to relate them — a thought that would have occurred to no one else.

Fiction as the most intensely selective creation of mood, tone, atmosphere, has always been Capote's natural aim as a writer. In *In Cold Blood* he practices this as a union of Art and Sympathy. His book, like so many "nonfiction" novels of our day, is saturated in sexual emotion. But unlike Mailer's reportage, Capote's "truthful account" is sympathetic to everyone, transparent in its affections to a degree — abstractly loving to Nancy Clutter, that all-American girl; respectfully amazed by Mr. Clutter, the prototype of what Middle America would like to be; helplessly sorry for Mrs. Clutter, a victim of the "square" morality directed at her without her knowing it. None of these people Capote knew — but he thought he did. Capote became extremely involved with the murderers,

Perry Smith and Dick Hickock, whom he interviewed in prison endlessly for his book and came to know as we know people who fascinate us. He unconsciously made himself *seem* responsible for them. Kenneth Tynan drew blood when, with the glibness which knows that "society" is always to blame, Tynan entered into the spirit of the book completely enough to denounce Capote for not doing everything possible to save his friends Perry and Dick.

This fascinated sympathy with characters whom Capote visited sixty times in jail, whom he interviewed within an inch of their lives, up to the scaffold, is one of many powerful emotions on Capote's part that keeps the book "true" even when it most becomes a "novel." Capote shows himself deeply related to Alvin Dewey of the Kansas Bureau of Investigation, who more than any other agent on the case brought the murderers in. And as a result of *In Cold Blood* Capote, who had so successfully advertised his appearance on the jacket of *Other Voices, Other Rooms* in 1948, had by 1969 become an authority on crime and punishment and an adviser to law-and-order men like Governor Reagan. Capote was a natural celebrity from the moment he published his first book. *In Cold Blood* gave him the chance to instruct his countrymen on the depths of American disorder.

Yet with all these effects of *In Cold Blood* on Capote, the book itself goes back to the strains behind all Capote's work: a home and family destroyed within a context of hidden corruption, alienation and loneliness. Reading *In Cold Blood* one remembers the gypsy children left hungry and homeless in *The Grass Harp*, the orphans in *A Tree of Night, The Thanksgiving Visitor* and *A Christmas*

Memory, the wild gropings of Holly Golightly in *Breakfast at Tiffany's* toward the "pastures of the sky." One remembers Capote himself in his personal pieces and stories in *Local Color* searching for a home in New Orleans, Brooklyn, Hollywood, Haiti, Paris, Tangier and Spain — then returning to Brooklyn again in "A House on the Heights":

> *twenty yards ahead, then ten, five, then none, the yellow house on Willow Street. Home! And happy to be.*

The victims in *In Cold Blood* were originally the Clutters, but by the time the crime is traced to the killers and they are imprisoned, all seem equally victims. As in any novel, innocent and guilty require the same mental consideration from the author. In any event, innocence in our America is always tragic and in some sense to blame, as Mr. Clutter is, for incarnating a stability that now seems an "act." Capote is always sympathetic to Nancy Clutter, who laid out her best dress for the morrow just before she got murdered, and Nancy is the fragile incarnation of some distant feminine goodness, of all that might have been, who gets our automatic sympathy. But despite Capote's novelistic interest in building up Mr. Clutter as the archetypal square and Mrs. Clutter as a victim of the rigid life-style surrounding her, Capote's more urgent relationship is of course with "Perry and Dick." Almost to the end one feels that they might have been saved and their souls repaired.

This felt interest in "Perry and Dick" as persons whom Capote knew makes the book too personal for fiction but establishes it as a casebook for our time. The background of the tale is entirely one of damaged persons who wreak worse damage on others, but the surface couldn't be more banal. Perry is the "natural killer" selected by Dick for the job, and Dick's father can say to Agent Nye of the Kansas Bureau of Investigation:

> "Was nothing wrong with my boy, Mr. Nye, . . . an outstanding athlete, always on the first team at school. Basketball! Basketball! Dick was always the star player. A pretty good student, too . . ."

Terror can break out anywhere. The world is beyond reason but the imagination of fact, the particular detail, alone establishes credibility. It all happened, and it happened only this way. The emotion pervading the book is our helpless fascinated horror; there is a factuality with nothing beyond it in Perry's dwarfish legs, the similar imbalance in Dick's outwardly normal masculinity and his actual destructiveness. On what morsels of unexpected fact, summoned out of seeming nowhere by the author's digging alone, is *our* terror founded! On the way to rob the Clutters, Dick says:

> "Let's count on eight, or even twelve. The only sure thing is every one of them has got to go. Ain't that what I promised you, honey — plenty of hair on them-those walls?"

The Clutters are stabbed, shot, strangled, between mawkish first-name American "friendliness" and bouncy identification with one another's weaknesses. Nancy couldn't be sweeter to her killers, Perry worries that Dick may rape her, Kenyon asks Perry not to harm his new chest by putting the knife on it. All this "understanding" between "insecure" people makes the crime all the more terrifying. It is the psychic weakness that removes so many people, taking their "weakness" for themselves, from any sense of justice. So much fluency of self-centered emotion makes crime central to our fear of each other today.

We may all have passing dreams of killing. But here are two who killed perversely, wantonly, pointlessly, yet with a horrid self-reference in the pitiful comforts they offered their victims that establishes their cringing viciousness. And the crime, like the greatest crimes of our time, is on record but remains enigmatic, "purposeless," self-defeating. The will to destroy is founded on what we insist are personal weaknesses, but which we cannot relate to what has been done. Even before the Hitler war was over, there were Nazis who said, "At least we have made others suffer." The fascination of Capote's book, the seeming truthfulness of it all, is that it brings us close, very close, to the victims, to the murderers, to the crime itself, as psychic evidence. Killing becomes the primal scene of our "feelings" that with all the timing of a clever novelist and all the emphatic detail brought in from thousands of interview hours by a prodigious listener, Capote presents to us as a case study of "truth" we can hold, study, understand.

As a novelist, dramatist, travel writer, memoirist, Capote had always been rather a specialist in internal mood, tone, "feeling"; now an action, the most terrible, was the center around which everything in his "truthful account" moved. He was ahead of his usual literary self, and the artfulness of the book is that it gets everyone to realize, possess and dominate this murder as a case of the seemingly psychological malignity behind so many crimes in our day. The book aims to give us this mental control over the frightening example of what is most uncontrolled in human nature.

Technically, this is accomplished by the four-part structure that takes us from the apparently pointless murder of four people to the hanging of the killers in the corner of a warehouse. The book is designed as a suspense story — why did Perry and Dick ever seek out the Clutters at all? — to which the author alone holds the answer. This comes only in Part III, when the book is more than half over. Each of the four sections is divided into cinematically visual scenes. There are eighty-six in the book as a whole; some are "shots" only a few lines long. Each of these scenes is a focusing, movie fashion, designed to put us visually as close as possible now to the Clutters, now to Perry and Dick, until the unexplained juncture between them is explained in Part III. Until then, we are shifted to many different times and places in which we see Perry and Dick suspended, as it were, in a world without meaning, for we are not yet up to the explanation that Capote has reserved in order to keep up novelistic interest. Yet this explanation — in jail a pal had put the future killers on to the Clutters and the supposed wealth in the house — is actually, when it comes, meant to anchor the book all the more firmly in the world of "fact" — of the public world expressed as documented conflict between symbolic individuals. It was the unbelievable squareness of the Clutters as a

family that aroused and fascinated the murderers. The
book opens on Kansas as home and family, ends on
Alvin Dewey at the family graveside,

> *Then, starting home, he walked toward the trees,
> and under them leaving behind him the big sky, the
> whisper of wind voices in the wind-bent wheat.*

The circle of illusory stability (which we have *seen* destroyed) has closed in on itself again.

Capote's book raises many questions about its pre-
sumption as a whole, for many of the "fact" scenes in it
are as vivid as single shots in a movie can be — and
that make us wonder about the meaning of so much easy
expert coverage by the writer-as-camera. ("A movie
pours into us," John Updike has said. "It fills us like milk
being poured into a glass.") One of the best bits is when
the jurors, looking at photographs of the torn bodies and
tortured faces of the Clutters, for the first time come into
possession of the horror, find themselves focusing on it in
the very courtroom where the boyishness and diffidence
of the defendants and the boringly circular protocol of a
trial have kept up the jurors' distance from the crime.

There is a continuing unreality about the murder of
the four Clutters that Capote all through his book labored
to eliminate by touch after touch of precious fact. He is
our only guide through this sweetly smiling massacre. He
is proud of every harrowing or grotesque detail he can
dredge up — Perry unbelievably tries to buy for a face
mask black stockings from a nun, remembers that after
the attack on Mr. Clutter he handed a knife to Dick and

said, "Finish him. You'll feel better." The labor after so
many facts emphasizes the world of conflict, social bitterness, freakishness, the "criminal" world, the underworld for which Capote asks compassion in the epigraph
from Villon's "Ballade des pendus":

> *Frères humains, qui après nous vivez,*
> *N'ayez les cueurs contre nous endurcis,*
> *Car, si pitié de nous povres avez,*
> *Dieu en aura plus tost de vous mercis.*

— But now, "real" or "unreal," this murder is public.
Closeness is the key. The hope of the book is to get us
close, closer, to what occurred in the heart of Middle
America and occurs every day now. There is in us, as
well as in the Clutters' neighbors, "a shallow horror sensation that cold springs of personal fear swiftly deepened."

The horror is now in the nature of the "fact" material.
What can be reconstructed as fact from actual events
may take the form of a cinematic "treatment" and easily
use many shifts of time and place. But it makes our participation in the story more narrow and helpless than a
real novel does. The attempt at closeness is all through
Capote's work; he attempts to induce it here by identifying us with "real" people we may think we know better
than we do — victims and murderers both.

The reason for the "nonfiction novel" (and documentary plays, movies, art works) is that it reproduces events
that cannot be discharged through one artist's imagination. Tragedy exists in order to be assimilated by us as
individual fate, for we can identify with another's death.
Death in round numbers is by definition the death of

strangers, and that is one of the outrages to the human imagination in the killing after killing which we "know all about," and to which we cannot respond. Capote worked so long on this case — "his" case — because to the "fact writer" reporting is a way of showing that *he knows*. The killing of the Clutter family was not "personal," as even Gatsby could have admitted about *his* murderer's mistake in killing him. History is more and more an example of "accident." The Clutters were there just for their killers to kill them.

"The event" is fascinatingly inscrutable though it is in the public light — just one of many killings in our time by people who did not know their victims. As with so many mass murders, many witnesses and documents are needed to reconstruct the true history of the crime. But irony more than truth is the motif of such fact books, for the point made is that there is no "sense" to the crime. This is what relieves the liberal imagination of responsibility and keeps it as spectator. In a "real" novel — one that changes our minds — a single Raskolnikov or Clyde Griffiths commits a singular crime (and is usually pursued by a single law-enforcer who has no other crime to uncover). The resolution of the crime — murder is the primal fault — gave the moral scheme back to us. But as Joan Didion said when she decided not to do a "fact" book around the taped memories by Linda Casabian of living in the Charles Manson "family," there was nothing she could *learn* by writing such a book.

In the many gratuitous murders that have soundlessly bounced off the imagination of our time, murderers and victims remain in every retrospect forever strange to each other. Apart from "war crimes" like Auschwitz, Hiroshima, Dresden, Mylai, the dropping of Viet Cong prisoners on villages from American helicopters, the torture, confessions and executions of whole masses of people as "enemies of the state," there are the murders by Detroit policemen (described by John Hersey in *The Algiers Motel Incident*) of three Negroes just because they have been found in a motel with white women, the killing of parents and children on a Kansas farm by two not abnormally rootless American boys of whom we know enough to know (even if they do talk of killing as "scoring") that we don't know them, the murder of eight-months-pregnant Sharon Tate and six other people by members of the Charles Manson "family."

These are now public events, matters of record, horrors taking place in the well-publicized arena that is now the domain of "reality." The news of these things is so instantly and widely disseminated that the sense of being left behind can frustrate the writer brought up on the necessary consistency of art, the significance of even a murderer's motive, and Chekhov's belief that if a gun is mentioned in Act One it must go off in Act Three. What we are dealing with here is not the pressure of "reality" on fiction, but the shape that so many public crimes and happenings are taking in a middle-class culture that for the first time is dividing on a wide scale, and where the profoundest disaffection is often felt exactly among these dutiful thinkers who are most conscious of literature itself as a tradition. One sees on every hand how many cherished personal images of literature are being destroyed by the fury of public events and technological change.

But if white middle-class writers who have always thought of literature as theirs are struggling to find a form and language for this "crisis of literature," so-called minority writers brought up on collective experiences of oppression –– who have all too sufficiently been named as Negro, coolie, Black, African, peasant — have always thought of themselves as creatures of history, and have often created works of literature without thinking of themselves as more than powerful speakers, as Malcolm X did in the extraordinary recital of his life to the editor friend who then wrote it.

James Baldwin cares desperately for literary distinction. He has achieved it not through his novels, which after *Go Tell It on the Mountain* seem heavy expositions of a complicated sexual travail, but through his ability to turn every recital of his own life into the most urgent symbol of American crisis. In *Notes of a Native Son* he describes himself on August 3, 1943, a fanatical Harlem preacher's emotionally alienated son,* following his father's coffin to the cemetery through Harlem streets that were "a wilderness of smashed plate glass" after a wartime race riot. The day of his father's funeral was Baldwin's nineteenth birthday; the day of his father's death had seen the birth of a posthumous child.

Only Baldwin, with his genius for finding the widest

---

* In an interview in E. W. E. Bigby's *The Black American Writer* (Penguin), Baldwin says: "I've hated a few people, but actually I've hated only one person, and that was my father. He didn't like me. But he'd had a terrible time too. And of course, I was not his son. I was a bastard."

possible application for his personal fury, could put his disturbed emotions into this trinity of death, the heaped-up glass in the Harlem streets, the birth of a posthumous son. In this aria, Baldwin shows himself an extraordinary spellbinder. Rage, grief, loneliness are his literary capital, and he works on his own poignancy and American guilt with the same fervor. Now that militant Black nationalism has dismissed him (along with so many other talented writers) as superfluous, one can agree that Baldwin joined the cause rather late and has never been a natural militant.*

As a writer Baldwin is as obsessed by sex and family as Strindberg was, but instead of using situations for their dramatic value, Baldwin likes to pile up all possible emotional conflicts as assertions. But for the same reason that in *Giovanni's Room* Baldwin made everybody white just to show that he could, and in *Tell Me How Long the Train's Been Gone* transferred the son-father quarrel to a quarrel with a brother, so one feels about *Another Country* that Baldwin writes fiction in order to use up his private difficulties; even his fiction piles up the atmosphere of raw emotion that is his literary standby. Why does so powerful a writer as Baldwin make himself look simpleminded by merely asserting an inconsequential succession of emotions?

---

* Baldwin up to the 1960s was a markedly esthetic and even precious writer whose essay attacking *Uncle Tom's Cabin* (and not just Mrs. Stowe), "Everybody's Protest Novel," was more expressive of his literary sophistication than his later attempts at militancy. In conversation, during his expatriate days in Paris, Baldwin once said memorably that a perfect article for a Jewish magazine would be "A Negro Looks at Henry James."

They encountered the big world when they went out into the Sunday streets. It stared unsympathetically out at them from the eyes of the passing people; and Rufus realized that he had not thought at all about this world and its power to hate and destroy.

"They out there, scuffling, making that change, they think it's going to last forever. Sometimes I lie here and listen, listen for a bomb, man, to fall on this city and make all that noise stop. I listen to hear them moan, I want them to bleed and choke, I want to hear them crying."

The college boys, gleaming with ignorance and mad with chastity, made terrified efforts to attract the feminine attention, but succeeded only in attracting each other.

But in *Notes of a Native Son, Nobody Knows My Name, The Fire Next Time*, Baldwin dropped the complicated code for love difficulties he uses in his novels and simplified himself into an "angry Black" very powerfully indeed — and this just before Black nationalists were to turn on writers like him. The character who calls himself "James Baldwin" in *his* nonfiction novel is more professionally enraged, more doubtfully an evangelist for his people, than the actual James Baldwin, a very literary mind indeed. But there is in *Notes of a Native Son* a genius for bringing many symbols together, an instinctive association with the 1943 Harlem riot, the streets of smashed plate glass, that stems from the all too understandable fascination of the Negro with the public sources of his fate. The emphasis is on heat, fire, anger, the sense of being hemmed in and suffocated; the words are tensed into images that lacerate and burn. Reading

Baldwin's essays, we are suddenly past the discordancy that has plagued his fiction — a literal problem of conflict, for Baldwin's fiction shows him trying to transpose facts into fiction without sacrificing the emotional capital that has been his life.

This discordancy has been a problem in Black writing, as in most minority writing that deals with experiences that may in fact be too deep, too painful, and so inexpressible. Nor does the claim to literature work for those, like Eldridge Cleaver, who mythologize rape into a form of social protest — *Soul on Ice* is propaganda. To turn the facts into literature, and literature into whatever will "change our minds," is a special problem for radicals. The heroic Soviet writer Andrey Sinyavasky said in his great polemic against "socialist realism" that a work of literature can spring from anything but must not be eclectic. A peculiar directness, an unconscious return to scriptural models, a lack of all literary pretense, saved Malcolm X as a writer. He cared desperately about salvation, not literature, and made his Autobiography the searing personal document it is by never saying "my book."

It is safe to say that Malcolm never thought of his life as a novel. In East Lansing, Michigan, where Malcolm Little grew up, Negroes weren't allowed into town after dark. When Malcolm was four, the family's home was set afire by two white men; white policemen and firemen stood watching as the house burned down to the ground. Malcolm's father, a free-lance Baptist preacher and a follower of Marcus Garvey's Back to Africa movement, was murdered by white men; his mother broke down and spent the next twenty-six years in the state asylum.

Malcolm and the other younger children became wards of the state.

He eventually went to a suburb of Boston to live with a tough older sister; as a crude country kid he excitedly entered into the big-city world of jazz, drugs and hustling that he observed as a shoeshine boy at Roseland State Ballroom in Boston. He helped to rob a jeweler, was sent to prison, learned to read and write, was converted by his brother to the Black Muslim movement. There he found for the first time expression of his strong natural devoutness in what he thought of as a liberating universal religion of all the dark and oppressed peoples. But he was forced out of the movement by the leader's jealousy and was murdered while speaking to his followers from the stage of the Audubon Ballroom in Harlem.

In Malcolm's literal recital of his life to Alex Haley — he was a naturally gifted speaker as well as a religious agitator too busy to write — the freedom he displays comes from his austere sense of fact and his ability to read other people's souls. The book is an example of straight autobiography in a time of novelized autobiographies* — of autobiography as a religious pilgrimage, of a man seeking his way up from his personal darkness to some personal light. Everything is rooted in the Negro's tie to history through his oppression. All love relationships are sparse, treated as gifts, but are not elaborated. There is not much room in Malcolm's book

---

* Hortense Calisher describes these as "veiled autobiography posing as novel — currently a novelist's straight path to being lovable."

for love. He found himself only as a leader, and he expected to become a sacrifice.

No doubt someone will make a novel of Malcolm's life, as William Styron has made a novel of Nat Turner's insurrection. Turner lived as a slave, was hanged as the murdering leader of a slave revolt, and left twenty pages of "confession," taken down by the court-appointed counsel who hated him. Styron is an elegantly accomplished novelist who in a book entitled *The Confessions of Nat Turner* still wanted to be a novelist, a Virginian who felt himself intensely involved with the Negro struggle and wanted to write a historical novel that would reflect the present crisis and above all bring white and black together. Surely this much relevance would not violate the integrity of fiction! Indeed Styron's strong feelings as a liberal Southerner did not override his novel, which far from being declamatory in the evangelical style of Harriet Beecher Stowe (who also wrote a novel about Nat Turner) turns Nat Turner into an extraordinarily sensitive and dreamy autodidact who once petted with another slave boy but died a virgin, who organized an insurrection but could kill no one but the white woman he loved, whom he could possess only by standing guard over her corpse with a sword.

Styron's book is full of sensitive landscapes that could apply to any Southern boy's growing up. They do not make the connection between slavery and insurrection that must have existed in Nat Turner's mind for him to organize the "only effective, sustained," the only significant slave revolt in American history. Styron wanted to dispel the strangeness of the "Negro" — especially in

bondage, where even the most concerned Southern defender cannot now imagine his individual *feelings* — by
showing him to be as complicated as oneself. But though
many Southern white writers were deeply moved by Nat
Turner, the book was violently attacked by Black nationalists. Styron's Turner was too sensitive for them. Harriet
Beecher Stowe had answered the angry Southern critics
of *Uncle Tom's Cabin* by providing documentation for
every horror she described in her novel. But Mrs. Stowe
was worried not about "fiction" but about the violation of
Christianity in a slave society. Styron was relevant to too
many things at once: to the art of the novel, to the original twenty-page confession, and above all, to his contemporary belief that our psychology can illuminate the
mind and heart of a Negro slave in 1831. Entering into
Nat Turner's "dreams" as confidently as we do, we recognize that what our contemporary, William Styron,
wanted most to do in this book was to become a Negro
mind, to get past the everlasting barrier, to make
"human" and "clear" what makes us afraid in the shadows we still occupy.

That ambition is natural to our Freudianism and our
liberalism. Othello will always be strange to the Vene-
tians, but what a Southern writer of Styron's liberal
urgency wanted above all, in 1967, was to dispel the
strangeness by dramatizing Turner's "feelings," which
would show that Negro and white are kin. Styron has
always been a novelist of feelings — elegiac in *Lie Down
in Darkness*, histrionically "wild" in *Set This House on
Fire*. Nat Turner waiting for death talks so much to us
about his dreams that he becomes our alter ego — an-

other Southerner Styron wants and needs to understand for the sake of justice and civic peace. But the narrative is so dreamlike that we cannot really believe this man has been a slave and the organizer of so many killings. The violence that is the background to the imaginative literature of fact, the violence that in literature still has the power to surprise and to transform us, to reveal us to ourselves when we are caught in the *act* — this is missing in Styron's book. Though it finally describes the insurrection, Nat Turner's 1967 introspectiveness does not prepare us for it. The link between a tortured self and a violent self, such as novelists describing a killing must show in a killer, is not present in *The Confessions of Nat Turner*. Styron himself called his book "a meditation on history," and it is more that than it is a dramatic novel. But of course Nat Turner was a "real person." So there is no end to the many meditations on history we can weave around him.

Our relationship to things of public record is never as sharp and finished as it can be to a wholly invented character or deed. What is invented in one mind can remain a fable for the reader. What has actually happened and been recorded — this has already been participated in and glossed by so many people that we are confronted with rival myths, partisan fragments of fact in many minds at once. Nat Turner existed, so we shall never agree on what he was "really" like. Norman Mailer's version of the 1967 march on the Pentagon, *The Armies of the Night*, is scornfully rejected by people who marched with him. Eichmann the organizer of the gas chambers, on trial in Jerusalem, provoked so many different versions of his character and responsibility that even many who suffered together at his hands came into conflict over the truth of events that they had lived through side by side.

But this is natural. What is artificial is the interposition of so much "art" into journalism as a way of making "literature." Why should any pretense to literature be brought to the agonizing facts of our time except as a way of glorifying the individual journalist suddenly interested in being "creative"? Great history has usually been narrative history, but the narratives have been shaped by a point of view, a philosophy of history and of human motives. History is what the unifying passion of the historian brings to the scattered facts. It is not an ironic and derisory style daubed on the facts like theater makeup.*

---

* "The new journalism" is a technological product, like the drawn-out dramatization of the day's news on television by reporters who, being on camera, have naturally come to think of themselves as actors. There is so much "news" today, and so much submission to it by a vast audience that submits to every fresh shock as cavemen submitted to thunderstorms, that the reporter-as-actor can get away with anything, especially getting the facts wrong, so long as he hypnotizes the audience.

Henry Luce encouraged his staff to think of an article rewritten from the *New York Times* as a "story." Then, especially on failing newspapers like the *New York Herald Tribune*, writers were given their head in the hope of titillating an audience surfeited with mere "news." Tom Wolfe, who was trained as a scholar in American studies but understandably went further as a dramatizer of celebrities in a pixie hah-hah style designed to make you think of *him* as an original, has written many amusing profiles of American leaders like Hugh Hefner, Leonard Bernstein, but has become altogether too conscious of mere personality, especially his own. So much of contemporary magazine and even book review journalism now deals in personal gossip about the Ameri-

229

Art and outrage have no necessary connection with each other. This is another horror for us who for thirty years have tried to make Hitlerism accountable to our humane culture. The horror is that so many frivolous, hysterical, ignorant, *trivial* people could have captured the hearts of so many Germans and have killed human beings for reasons no more "significant" and "historical" than their own murderous vanity and rage. One is now supposed to honor Napoleon for the millions of deaths he caused because he was the vehicle of historical progress. In the case of Hitler and his gang, no delusion is possible. Like the boy who stabbed an enemy in a gang war and as he took the knife out, said to the corpse, "Thanks very much!," Hitler operated on the weakness of his victims and the fear he inspired in the outlookers. He had no serious historical ideas, no tenable hopes. All those millions died to the frenzy of murdering gangsters. They died *meaninglessly*. And how do you make art out of what is inherently meaningless, was never a contest?

---

can great that the only justification for a "fact piece" is usually forgotten in Wolfe's *ad hominem* writing.

In any event, such writing depends on a most credulous audience. When Michael J. Arlen described the frivolity of the "New Journalism" one reader replied in the June 1972 issue of *The Atlantic*, "The most insulting accusation Arlen made was that the New Journalism is non-factual. . . . Wolfe never suggests any lack of truth or any sacrifice of reality. Instead, he insists, and rightly so, that the New Journalism adds to the depth of reality and truth, that literary devices such as symbolism, dialogue, experimentation in narration, imagination in development, etc. complement the facts by adding new dimensions of reality, providing the reader with an entry into the situation being recounted."

Inevitably, Wolfe has come to think that "the new journalism" makes novels unnecessary. Journalists take themselves too seriously. First they describe facts, then they see "trends," and finally, they see themselves as a trend.

Nowhere has totalitarianism as a climate, or totalitarianism as a subject, been able to produce a work of art. What it does provoke, from the many ground down in our time by the Moloch of "History" or "Race," is occasional personal testimony. The victims alone can testify to the power of these murderous abstractions. Their own existence is the moral authenticity they have saved from what André Malraux properly defined as the only purpose of the concentration camps. "The supreme objective was that the prisoners, in their own eyes, should lose their identity as human beings."

In any event, experience does not necessarily take the form of "literature" to those who in the modern Hell, the degradation of whole classes and races of people, have known the lowest abyss of suffering. Even Tolstoy, whose shame in the face of other people's destitution was only "moral" suffering, could say nothing more than: "One cannot live so! One cannot live so!" The "structuring," to use a more mod word than "fictionalizing," may come later in the victim's life. Usually it does not come from the victim at all, but from concerned intellectuals. The anthropologist Oscar Lewis wrote a whole series of books — *The Children of Sánchez* and *La Vida* are the best known — in which, having taped the detailed monologues of those usually illiterate people who live below the level of anything *we* know as poverty, he transcribed this testimony, translated it, obviously selected from it, inevitably heightened it.

Lewis had a conscious rivalry with belles-lettres. He often stated his belief that the real "culture of poverty" was his specialty and that such poverty was beyond the ken of even the grimmest naturalistic novels. (Although James Agee similarly wished to confront his middle-class readers with the lives of powerless tenant farmers, the moving force behind *Let Us Now Praise Famous Men* was a poet's discovery of documentary as a form.) Lewis thought of himself as a transformer of his bourgeois readers. He could have echoed Whitman: *Through me, many long dumb voices,/Voices of the interminable generations of prisoners and slaves,/Voices of the diseas'd and despairing . . .* Should an anthropologist so openly put the emphasis on "me"? Lewis insisted that *his* material was not to be duplicated elsewhere, that he was working out a wholly new literary domain. The transmutation of research into "a new kind of book" inevitably inflates the writer's idea of himself.

This sense of oneself as a "pioneer" is very important to the writing of the "nonfiction novel." Norman Mailer would not have attempted his literary march on the Pentagon, would not have re-examined the astronauts, if he had thought any other writer capable of this. Mailer will always be the dominating voice in every book of reportage he writes — he has to feel that he is writing history as a form of action. Then, energetically moving against history's own actions, he feels himself in complete control of materials that have been opened up by his literary curiosity. The raw material in all such cases is a fact of human experience so extreme that the writer is excited by his literary intimacy with it. This suggests an influence on the audience proper to the shocking novelty of the material. Oscar Lewis was driven not so much by the anthropology that he had learned as a practiced field worker in Haiti, Cuba, Mexico, Puerto Rico, as by literary abilities set in motion by his need to use material that would liberate, agitate, revolutionize. So Mailer has been saying for years that the really repressed material is in our social thinking, not in the private psyche — that the struggle in America (and America is the persona behind all his nonfiction tracts) is whether this fat overgrown self-indulgent society, unable to master "progress," will be able to confront its secret fears and festering injustices. Capote in his murder book is saying, less directly, that murderers are loose all over the place. Notice the attention he gives to the bodies and most intimate physical habits of all "his" characters. There is the connection between Mr. Clutter, who disdained evil and complexity, and the outsider, vagabond, pervert, who said to his pal, "Finish him off. You'll feel better."

Oscar Lewis's "characters" in *La Vida* describe sexual sensations that have never been reported by women in our middle-class fiction for the reason that these women have much more to live for. The lack of money among Lewis's people is nothing compared with their lack of general satisfaction. At the same time the absolute domination by the family seems to fill up the vacuum created by emotional scarcity. We have here something like the bondage we have seen in Malcolm X and James Baldwin. But in Lewis's transparently literary creations these wretched of the earth are supposed to be real people talking into a tape recorder. This verisimilitude was Lewis's pride as a social liberator whose polemic took the form of getting people to tell their life stories. We are involved with whole families whom *we* never see in Mexico. And if our middle-class souls protest that we never seem to get out of these low dark rooms and alleyways, Lewis would respond that ours is an era marked by the return of the repressed, the painful, the unacceptable, the frightful.

Revolution or therapy? For purposes of the imagination of fact, the horrible is like Artaud's prescription for "the theater of cruelty": we put into the play what we are most afraid of. But do *we* as readers of the nonfiction novel, as mere spectators of the television horror show, act anything out? Do we ever do anything more than have "feelings"? Before the great screen of fact created by the information and communications revolution of our time, we remain viewers, and it is truly amazing how much crisis and shock we can take in without giving up anything or having the smallest of our habits changed in the least. The Eichmann trial in Jerusalem was, as Harold Rosenberg said, a necessary purging of emotion — for the survivors and intended victims! But perhaps the S.S. man in Russia quoted in Hannah Arendt's *Eichmann in Jerusalem* was just a thunderstruck tourist when he reported that "there was, gushing from the earth, a spring of blood like a fountain. Such a thing I had never seen before."

In the often apocalyptic personal remembrance of Hitler's hell, the survivor's natural feeling of guilt is also a pervasive horror of human nature that has filled the air since the war. Often enough in this new literature of exposure the truly horrible fact comes in as a judgment on oneself. In Elie Wiesel's *Night*, his memoir of Auschwitz, a child being hanged proves too light for the rope and strangles so slowly that Wiesel, a former Chassid, cries out with the other prisoners that God himself is hanging on the gallows. In *Counting My Steps*, Jakov Lind's memory of his adventures under the Nazi occupation, he describes the police driving Jews out of their houses in Amsterdam while he scurries for safety to the apartment of a married woman, also a refugee.

> *A few minutes after the last shouting had died away, afraid of special punishment, all of them went, one by one. . . . We had been eating silently for nearly fifteen minutes when from outside came the sounds of pots and pans being dragged over the cobblestones, the crying of a child, the barking of a dog, the shouting of a loud-speaker, march music, and the tenor of a high-flying bomber. . . . We sat and ate our lunch. . . . I went to her bed, she opened her gown, my fly. [He makes love for the first time in his life.] A key turned in the door. . . . Gunther kissed his wife, said, "They will soon be here. Let's go." I had passed the test and survived. All that was left now was to beat the police to it as well.*

We say about a book like Jerzy Kosinski's *The Painted Bird*, the stupefying itinerary of cruelties inflicted by Polish peasants during the war on a homeless boy, "What a writer!" And to ourselves we add, "With experiences like that, how can you miss?" It is the writer himself who seems to get turned on in these shattering memoirs, to rise above our helpless nonparticipation. Such books seem to be made out of a hardness that has burned away everything but the ability to write with this concentrated purity of feeling. Literary power is still our ideal, and we are jealous of the power that discovers itself in extreme experiences. We locate imaginative authority in the minority man, the battered refugee, the kook, the deviant, the mad poet, the suicide, the criminal. Genius, says Sartre in his book on Genet, is not a gift but a way out one invents in desperate cases. (This is obviously Sartre's hope for the downtrodden masses.)

Subject — the "situation," the accident, the raid, the murder — is so primary in these novelized special cases that the only force apparently able to do justice to extreme experiences is the writer's myth of himself as an agent for change. The world and the battered author, the revolutionary demonstration and the ego, the crime and the reporter, the moon and me!

These are the now chilling polarities in Norman Mailer's brilliantly literary but evanescent descriptions of the 1967 march on the Pentagon, the 1960 and 1968 national conventions, the first landing of American know-how on the moon. They move us out of the inherent consistency and exhaustive human relationships of the novel onto the great TV screen of contemporary history, and Mailer's illusion is that he is somehow helping to change history. Mailer is the greatest historical actor in his own books, but they do not convey any action of his own. They are efforts to rise above the Americanness that he loves to profane, but which fascinates him into brilliance. The nonfiction novel exists in order *not* to change the American situation that makes possible so much literary aggression against it.

Mailer's tracts are histrionic blows against the system. They are fascinating in their torrential orchestration of so many personal impulses. Everything goes into it on the same level. So they end up as Mailer's special urgency, that quest for salvation through demonstration of the writer's intelligence, realism, courage, that is to be effected by making oneself a gladiator in the center of the ring, a moviemaker breathing his dreams into the camera.

Yet the theme of Mailer's reportage is the unprecedented world now, rushing off to its mad rendezvous with the outermost spaces of blind progress. Mailer's reportage responds excitedly to great public demonstrations, conventions, crowds, coordinations of technological skill. He has carried over from his fiction many sensory equivalents for the sound and weight of crowds, for physical tension, anxiety, conflict, for the many different kinds of happenings that his mind can register as he watches Jack Kennedy arriving in Los Angeles in 1960, senses the Florida cracker's feeling that *he* has made it as the Saturn booster goes up from its Florida pad in 1969. Mailer has both lived and written his life with the greatest possible appetite for the power and satisfaction open to successful Americans since 1945; but his reportage has become steadily more baleful and apocalyptic — not least because his subjects soon lose their interest for everybody but himself.

One aim of his highly colored style has been to find new images for energy, for savoring the last possible tingle of orgasm, for life among the managers, for the sexual power and thrust (sex as thought, thought as sex) inseparable from the experience of self-representative American males. But a new reason for so much style is to keep the zing in his subjects. Mailer has been the hungriest child at the American feast, directly in the line of those realistic novelists for whom John O'Hara spoke when he said that the development of the United States during the first half of the twentieth century was the greatest possible subject for a novelist.

But clearly Mailer's reportage represents his dilemma as an artist forced back on too many "ideas" — a superbly gifted writer too good for this genre. *Of a Fire on the Moon* is a book of such brilliance, and of such sadness in trying to keep different things together, that like a rocket indeed it has been set off by forces that at every moment threaten to explode it. Proust says somewhere that notes are fantasies. But in Mailer it is precisely with his fantasies, the greatest of which is that he can bring to some portentous world-historical consummation the battle in himself between so many loves and so many Spenglerian despairs, that he has written his moon book. It is not *exactly* a book about the journey of the Apollo 11, not exactly a book about the "WASP" types who fascinate him by their bureaucratized steadiness, all those dumb other reporters, the computer age. . . . It is a book about a novelist trying to write instant history.

Of course we all have a sense these days of being ridden down by history, and want to do something about it. Never has there been such a concerted consciousness, in the name of history, of how little history is leaving our minds and our souls. Never have there been so many techniques for circulating facts and dramatizing them.

Real history, partisan history, and commercial history are so thick a part of contemporary writing that it is as if History had come back to revenge itself on its upstart rival, Fiction. But not without Fiction's own techniques, as one can see nowhere better than in Mailer's allegory of *himself* as history. The effort sprouts more coils around Mailer himself than the serpents did around Laocoön and his sons. With one breath he must say yes! serpents are of the essence and *I* can take anything! with the next make a mighty heave to get the damned things off him, two Americans to the moon, and the book to the publisher.

Such ambition, such imagination, such wrath, such sadness, such cleverness, so many ideas! The flames licking Saturn-Apollo on its way up had nothing on this. It is as if Mailer were sketching the possibilities of one brilliant novel after another. The dreaming, longing, simulating — of masterpieces — give the reader the sense that Mailer was really dreaming of other books all the time he was writing this one. The giveaway at crucial passages of philosophizing — and that was another reason for taking on the assignment; it was like asking Hamlet to give a lecture on Monarchs I Have Known — is that with the whole universe to travel up and down on his typewriter, Mailer cannot help fudging the world-historical bit; he is not always clear to himself, and damn well knows it. Rather than dramatize the American contradictions that are eating him up, he tries to keep them all in eloquent bursts that stagger you with ideas, but that leave you uneasy. The performance is not of the moon but of the effort to talk about it.

Journalism will no more diminish than will the "communications industry," but the new art-journalism, journalism as a private form, has already had its day. It went through a whole cycle in the Sixties, and no longer astonishes. Issues die on it as fast as last week's issue of *Time*, and while the professional reporter can still depend on a bored downgrading of human nature, Mailer depended for his best "pieces," like *The Prisoner of Sex*, on challenges to his manhood that not even the Kate Milletts will always provide. Mailer identified creative vitality in his best tract, *The Armies of the Night: History as a Novel: The Novel as History* with his revolutionary élan. But America has worn out the revolutionary in Mailer; the historical blues are more a problem to the novelist-as-reporter than to the novelist or reporter as such. Mailer in *Of a Fire on the Moon* describes the lifting of the Saturn-Apollo in language born in the envy of *Moby-Dick* and manifest destiny — language that somehow suggests there may yet be political hope in so much mechanical energy. Some transformation of minds may yet take place in outer space!

But the possibility of doom is just as strong in Mailer's own moon trip as in his enthusiasm for a technical wizardry of which, in the end, he knows less than he does about doom. With so many agonies of contradiction in himself, not the brilliant novelist's lesser rhetoric will do — that just passes out symbols like party hats to *surprise* — but the patience and depth of fiction itself, dramatic imagination, the world reconstructed in that personal sense of time about which space centers, sex movements and all other plurals know nothing, but which is a writer's secret treasure. Despite all our rapture about them now, the great nineteenth-century novels were not and certainly are not the "world." The world is a world, dumb as nature, not a novel. The world as our common experience is one that only the journalist feels entirely able to set down. It is a confidence that those who stick to fiction do not feel, for if the "world" is not an experience in common, still less is it a concept on which all can agree. It is not even as close as we think. As Patrick White, the Australian novelist, says in one of his books — "Why is the world which seems so near so hard to get hold of?"

8

THE ABSURD AS A CONTEMPORARY STYLE
Ellison to Pynchon

What could I dream of that had the barest
possibility of coming true? I could think of
nothing. And, slowly, it was upon exactly
that nothingness that my mind began to
dwell.

> — Richard Wright,
>   "The Man Who Went to Chicago"

Alas, what is terrible is not the skeletons,
but the fact that I am no longer terrified
by them.

> — Chekhov, *Notebooks*

Why is everybody such a swinger all of a
sudden?

> — Philip Roth, in conversation

RALPH ELLISON's *Invisible Man*, published in 1952, has proved the most believable of the many current novels of the embattled self's journey through an American reality defined as inherently "absurd." Certainly more than any other Black writer Ellison achieved as dramatic fact, as a rounded whole, beyond dreamy soliloquy or angry assertion, a demonstration of the lunatic hatred that America can offer, on every face of its society, to a Black man. This irrationality is more real, more solidly grounded to Blacks writing out of actual oppression than is the *idea* of an irrational society to white writers dislocated in the country they used to take for granted and who now find so much of America "meaningless."

The hatred that society shows to an actual victim of racist hatred is not the same thing as "meaninglessness," which is a middle-class state of mind, a temporary fatigue, that represents the sometimes frolicsome despondency of intellectuals who see no great place for their moral influence — for changing things — in a future laid out in advance by technology. "Meaninglessness" is an intellectual conceit in all senses of the word; it is not something that one lives, as the nameless and somehow generic "hero" of *Invisible Man* must live the absurdity of a life that is constant contradiction to his words. He has a gift for "eloquence," for beautifully saying the expected, and is constantly promised a greater share of life by the white (and Black) authorities over him while he is actually a nigger who is kept running.

Ellison's book is about the art of survival, a subject that has made tragic comedians out of many ordinary blokes in the literature of our time. And it turns on the self-deceptions of eloquence — a problem among all oppressed people, a special resource of Blacks, and a problem-theme in all Ellison's work: "God's trombone" is the phrase for a masterful Negro preacher in a published fragment from his work-in-progress. But eloquence is the seat of all contradiction, the gift that is the hero's only chance for life but that also works against itself in the life of Ellison's "Invisible Man." And this complex use of eloquence comes out of a tradition of monologue — American, nineteenth-century, frontier-revivalist, musical — that reflects Ellison's passion for the trumpet as much as it does the famous "single voice" in Melville, Mark Twain, Faulkner, that gave Ellison the courage to discover an Oklahoma Black's affinity with them.

Monologue, as it happens, has become the favorite free form for comic fiction about the world's irrationality. The clownish single voice heard in so many contemporary American novels may be the natural vehicle of those many writers who see man near the end of the twentieth century as a hilariously futile creature, trying by repeated rituals to save himself in a world that majestically ignores him. The schlemiel hero, the nonhero, the antihero, are all easy riders of despair; in their fluently disenchanted Romantic prose they mark the end of the Romantic faith that perception will yet unite man with a world that once waited for him to give it meaning. The function of the contemporary hero is to cancel the affirmations but to keep the setting of what once made him feel like a god.

Ellison's *Invisible Man* does not use the monologue form lightly or capriciously in the interests of personal fantasy. It is an old-fashioned storytelling device that owes to Ishmael and Huck Finn and Faulkner's unstoppable voice in *The Bear* the ability to get people into view through rumination. Whenever the hero-narrator of *Invisible Man* tries to report dreamlike material and the headiness of pure association under the influence of pot, he is less interesting than when he is simply *there* to bring in the succession of characters who "keep this nigger running." The voice is in that specific tradition of anecdote, rhapsody, sermonizing, yarn-spilling, that Ellison learned to recognize as his tradition from reading Constance Rourke's beautiful book, *American Humor*, which demonstrated the primacy of the monologuist's art in American writing. "I was to dream of a prose," said Ellison, "which was flexible, and swift as American change is swift."

Constance Rourke was one influence on Ellison by way of the critic Stanley Edgar Hyman, who was strong on myth and folklore; Hyman also led Ellison to Lord Raglan's *The Hero*, which taught him that a myth is always "a narrative linked with a rite, and that it celebrates a god's death, travels through the underworld, and eventual rebirth." But *Invisible Man* is founded essentially on eloquence as redemption through art and as a snare to the ambushed minority man — who in this case finally flees a Harlem mob and the New York cops into a man-hole, and then takes up residence in the Harlem cellar from which he addresses us and recites his life.

To talk "well," to "make an impression" on the audience, to talk so well that finally one talks only to invigorate oneself — this is indeed to be a clown who cannot respect his role nor get out of it. This is the literal absurdity of the artist who even at his peak must doubt that his performance refers to anything more than himself. The hero begins by being a "good boy" who can say all the expected right things to the Negro college president and to the white businessmen, doctors, preachers. He is so good and dutiful that he is less an individual than the service Negro putting off all feelings of his own in order to get approved. He is the nobody, the nothing man who believes all the slogans sold him by the Establishment. His gift for mouthing these in public with the requisite "sincerity" inevitably makes him the creature of the Negro college's president, Bledsoe. Bledsoe, having no reason to suspect him of anything, has him drive the white, spare, thin-blooded New England trustee, Norton, around the countryside. Norton is a parody of Emerson, and reflects a special aim on the part of a writer who shares Melville's distrust of Emerson and who is named Ralph Waldo Ellison.

Our hero ignorantly drives Norton to the old slave quarters, where a shabby old Negro tenant farmer named Trueblood, in one of the great comic episodes in American fiction, relates the story of how he got his daughter as well as his wife with child. They were all bundled up against the cold in the same bed, and Trueblood was a powerful dreamer. "But once a man gits hisself in a tight spot like that there ain't much he can do. It ain't up to him no longer. There I was, tryin' to git away with all my might, yet having to move *without* movin'."

Norton collapses on hearing the full story, and in an effort to get medical aid, the hero inevitably tangles Norton up with some mad Negro war veterans. He has a totally unconscious gift for putting himself in the wrong with everyone in the book. This is his real craftiness, his "authenticity," the negation of his famous innocence. In the early nightmarish scenes in which he is blindfolded and led into a prize ring before the boozed up white Establishment of the town to battle with other blindfolded Black boys, he finds that the "coins" tossed into the ring give off an electric shock. But "ignoring the shock by laughing, as I brushed the coins off quickly, I discovered that I could contain the electricity — a contradiction, but it works."

Ellison was working consciously with so many literary symbols and rituals in the book that he clearly thought less about making the hero's character complex than he did about putting into his book his lessons in the symbol-hunting fashionable literary criticism of the time. He has explained that "each section begins with a sheet of paper; each piece of paper is exchanged for another and contains a definition of his identity, or the social role he is to play as defined for him." Similarly, the prize of a brief-case, presented to him early in the book by the whites in town after he has made his first ridiculously self-demeaning speech, accompanies him everywhere, like the piece of an old slave manacle given him by his secretly antiwhite grandfather. But the hero's innocence is so amazingly overdone that his delightful mistakes — like speaking to the assembled whites of social "equality" when he means to say "responsibilities," or his driving Norton to hear Trueblood's helpless tale of a winter night, or his getting the colors mixed up in a paint factory — are of course the best thing about him. He is shown as a man of unwitting guile and finally of profound gifts of self-protection in his flight from all opinion not his own. Yet Ellison felt that *he* could manipulate his nonhero into a devastating example of the absurdity, the self-contradiction, that a man always in trouble must feel about his existence when he remembers his goodness, helplessness, innocence.

Whatever else Ellison's nonhero or antihero may be, he is not a complex, rounded, subtle figure. He is not flexible in the least. That seems to be a condition of all "novels of the absurd." Although Ellison's tale is told in monologue and emphasizes the rhetorical variety possible to the single voice, the protagonist is audibly manipulated by a novelist who is fascinated by "eloquence." Ellison, when interviewed by Robert Penn Warren for a book of individual testimony called *Who Speaks for the Negro?*, said:

> *One of the advantages of being a Negro is that we have always had the freedom to choose or to select and to affirm those traits, those values, those cultural forms, which we have taken from any and everybody. . . . We*

probably have more freedom than anyone; we only need to become more conscious of it and use it to protect ourselves from some of the more tawdry American values.

This is a freedom to choose roles, to borrow personalities — a point that has often been made by whites, whether compassionately or contemptuously, about the Negro's lack of roots. Ellison's protagonist is "free" in his imagination only at the end of his tale, when he is ready to begin writing it. But the very point of *Invisible Man* is that while Ralph Ellison may now be "free" as writers are, his unhero certainly isn't. This lack of self-direction in his life makes the book tragicomic, as true comedy must be. He *always* looks for what is not there. He approves of his feelings, and recognizes nothing else.

This sense of society as grindingly, continuously, *totally* against us is something new in fiction, for those who have experienced total rejection by a "master race" have just begun to describe it. But Ellison escapes the trumped-up farcical tone of so many would-be comic novels about the horrors of being an American — as he escapes the confines of his symbolism — by his natural sense of event. His protagonist gets stretched out on every possible betrayal, humiliation and pratfall. We get from *Invisible Man* a sense of real experience, real suffering, the mad repetitions of the outsider's efforts to get a foothold and the resonances of his failure. Talking to us from the coal cellar to which he has just escaped ahead of the police and everyone else, he exists by and in his voice — a voice that at the beginning and at the end of his journey finds its true analogy in Louis Armstrong's

251

uplifted horn and the quavery sound "What did I do/To be so Black and Blue?" By contrast, the teller of this tale sees all around him in Harlem

> *birds of passage who were too obscure for learned classification, too silent for the most ambiguous words, and too distinct from the centers of historical decision to sign or even to applaud the signers of historical documents. We who write no novels, histories, or other books.*

The vibration of this voice has been lasting. It is a voice powerfully urgent but not aggressive; full of the wistful seeking to be more than one's feelings and of the contradictions inherent in anyone's picture of himself as an innocent seeker. The voice is never an imposture,* something I do feel about the professionally enraged black nationalist, already satirized in *Invisible Man* as Ras the Destroyer shouting at the hero from a Harlem street corner. Ellison still believes in the sufficiency of art. His own voice in *Invisible Man* conveys his faith in the tradition, from *Benito Cereno* to *Light in August*, that race differences have made the strongest writing in this country. *Our* mythology is based on nature, hardship, and the struggle between people who may have nothing and everything in common by being Americans. The hero's grandfather, before dying, dropped his Uncle Tom

---

* Or as Imamu Amiri Baraka (better known around City Hall in Newark as LeRoi Jones) puts it in his "essays since 1965," *Raise Race Rays Raze*:
"We pull the reins of a nation, a whole people, and were it not for this humbling weight, we would sail meaninglessly into the firmament, too swiftly to sample the enlightening enriching scum of lower spirit higher humanistic feeling. . . ."

mask and called himself "a spy in the enemy's country ever since I give my gun back to the Reconstruction." The grandfather instructs him to play a part. "I want you to overcome 'em with yeses, undermine 'em with grins, agree 'em to death and destruction, let 'em swoller you till they vomit or bust wide open." But the hero does not really believe this or practice it. He emerges from the anonymity of Negro experience only through his gift for getting rushed to the platform, where he makes speeches held together by emotions expected of him. President Bledsoe is never anything but crafty, and the white Establishment is so sadistic that the hero's naïveté can be taken only for the continuing effects of slavery. And in fact he goes on to the North and stays dumb even in the communist "Brotherhood" as a Chaplinesque figure whose mad gift for rousing a crowd relates only to his own loneliness. The hero's voice in the book first innocently then mordantly reproduces many other voices; finally it tunes out all voices but its own. At the end he just barely saves himself by holing in from everything. But his last words are still an effort to connect, "Who knows but that, on the lower frequencies, I speak for you?"

In terms of the old tradition — the Negro as stooge, clown, sacrificial victim — he does. And in the course of the novel itself this generic figure does go on, in one of the many silent shifts of the book, to become an artist. At the end of the book he recalls the solitary figure in that half-light of the frontier that Faulkner caught in *The Bear*, for the best American writing is still a raid on the primitive. Ellison did not know how much he believed in the American frontier — in art's necessary struggle with history and nature as hardship — until he had achieved *Invisible Man*. Since 1952, faced with the problem of transcending his triumphant first book, Ellison has been too often embattled, first with Jewish literary critics who in the 1960s tried to interest him in their pro-Black militancy, later with Black militants who are interested in literature as exhortation. Ellison has become a solitary and wistful exhorter himself — of High Art.

But *Invisible Man* endures because it is representative, truthful, "real." It came just before the great age of derision. So much of the whole modern urban Negro experience is included in the life cycle of the hero! The believable element of absurdity — of a life situation thoroughly presented in all its contradictions to human sense — does not lie in the histrionic shifts of consciousness portrayed at the beginning (where the whipped-up Negro sermons remind one too much of famous sermons in *Moby-Dick* and *The Sound and the Fury*), or in the hallucinations and "illuminations" of the hero as he talks to us from his cellar while all that stolen electric light tapped from every circuit within reach makes a hideously bright operating room for us to stare right into his mind. It lies in the rushed total coverage of the book, which steams through so many improbabilities-as-actualities that the reader gets as trapped in the lunacies of history as the hero does.

Where to go from here? What to do? In the lobby of the YMCA the hero (just now in overalls) looks around him and ticks off, one after another, the counterfeits of middle-class success — the would-be gentlemen, the self-imagined businessmen, the janitors and messengers "who spent most of their wages on clothing such as was fashionable among Wall Street brokers, with their Brooks Brothers suits and bowler hats, English umbrellas, black calfskin shoes and yellow gloves. . . ." By the end of the book, the hero has also exhausted the possibilities in the Communist Party, in the Black Nationalist movement of Ras the Exhorter (now Ras the Destroyer), and in trying to burn Harlem down. Chased by the police into a manhole and there cursed by them and left for dead, he feels that he has also exhausted even the eloquence in hatred and must now wait life out in his hole.

So, for Ellison's "hero" in 1952, there was the absurdity indeed of running round and round the track to the same fear and rejection of one's black skin. But after 1954 "Black" became such a mighty interrogation and refutation of white middle-class existence that it was taken up by many Blacks as the mystique of blackness. "Our terribleness," said LeRoi Jones in a dithyramb called *In Our Terribleness*, "is our survival as beautiful things, anywhere. Who can dig that?" Blackness for Blacks; blackness in the form of "black humor" was now taken up by many whites as the shortest way of mocking a way of life, their own, that more and more seemed without point, security, joy. Many a white writer now wanted to gain strength and point by becoming what Mailer in a typical demonstration of "until you see what your ideas lead to, you know nothing," had in 1957 called "The White Negro: Superficial Reflections on the Hipster."

One is Hip or one is Square (the alternative which each new generation coming into American life is beginning to feel), one is a rebel or one conforms, one is a frontiersman in the Wild West of American night life, or else a Square cell, trapped in the totalitarian tissues of American society, doomed willy-nilly to conform if one is to succeed.

Knowing in the cells of his existence that life was war, nothing but war, the Negro (all exceptions admitted) could rarely afford the sophisticated inhibitions of civilization, and so he kept for his survival the art of the primitive, he lived in the enormous present, he subsisted for his Saturday night kicks, relinquishing the pleasures of the mind for the more obligatory presents of the body. . . .

. . . . To be a real existentialist . . . one must be religious, one must have one's sense of the "purpose" — whatever the purpose may be — but a life which is directed by one's faith in the necessity of action is a life committed to the notion that the substratum of existence is the search, the end meaningful but mysterious; it is impossible to live such a life unless one's emotions provide their profound conviction. . . .

As opposed to the patient in psychoanalysis, who "can conform to what he loathes because he no longer has the passion to feel loathing so intensely," two strong eighteen-year-old hoodlums beating in the brains of a candy-store keeper do have courage of a sort,

for one murders not only a weak fifty-year old man but an institution as well, one violates private property, one enters into a new relation with the police and introduces a dangerous element into one's life. The hoodlum is therefore daring the unknown, and so no matter how brutal the act, it is not altogether cowardly.

Mailer, we know, has tried to live some of this search for "purpose" through positive personal action. The deepest part of this belief in action has been not only his commitment to writing — and his willingness to risk failure and ridicule through the use of any new form — but his need to be a personal example of "existential courage." "Blackness" never interested Mailer, even in *The White Negro*, except as a synonym for the "hipster or psychopath." It was orgasm as the path to a wilder, freer personal sensation of life that made Mailer romanticize the *white* Negro as the "outlaw" who could find purpose only in sex.

"Black humor" was the typed derision of society in the name of a mythical Black nihilism that Blacks, at a time when they were gaining enough power to put up mass protest, could hardly relish. The "black humor" novelist was a white, often Jewish, totally middle-class writer who felt himself to be the last individualist in an increasingly regimented society. A totally cutting, profane, proudly frantic style of monologue had developed among pent-up comics like Lenny Bruce. It gave unlimited play to the Jewish outsider who acted out his anti-Establishment *and* anti-Jewish feelings, commemorated his sacred rage as a rebel too complex for the times, and died a martyr to the society whose insanity he had not been able to ridicule out of existence by ritualizing its once dirty words. Bruce's nightclub audience found more thrills in this would-be destruction than they did in a pornography that had already been thoroughly domesticated.

The Black writer — James Baldwin was especially strong on this — liked to say that America was driving him crazy; the writer of "black humor" liked to say that America was crazy. It was all crazy, man, crazy;* but that "all" was an intellectual fiction circulating among English departments, advertising agencies, girlie magazines and other instruments of mass sophistication that made one remember Harold Rosenberg's description of "the herd of independent minds." In any event, "black *humor*" was often just that; it had to entertain with jokes, gags, violent inversions and transpositions of the expected rather than to produce the kind of "black comedy," like Evelyn Waugh's, which by definition had always been heartless, mocking, and elegant. A British novelist living in America, Wilfrid Sheed, noted about the hero of his novel *Max Jamison*, "He had sensed that in educated America, humor was the number one language for criticism, passion, even cooking; and he set about learning it with grim intelligence." Not comedy but funniness may have been the price the American humorist paid for being so much part of the system that made it possible for him to entertain it.

But one function of the "black humor" novelist, especially if he was Jewish — Stanley Elkin, Jerome Charyn, Joseph Heller, Leonard Michaels — was to assist his

---

* American stories, novels, fiction collections now bore such titles as *Courting Disaster* (Philip Roth), *Debris* (Brock Brower), *Confusions* (Jack Ludwig), *Sick Friends* (Ivan Gold), *Desperate Characters* (Paula Fox), *Poor Devils* (David Ely), *Bad News* (Paul Spike), *Bad Characters* (Jean Stafford), *Going Nowhere* (Alvin Greenberg), *Losing Battles* (Eudora Welty), *A Bad Man* (Stanley Elkin), *A Thirsty Evil* (Gore Vidal), *Going Down Fast* (Marge Piercy), *The System of Dante's Hell* (LeRoi Jones), *The Death of the Novel and Other Stories* (Ronald Sukenick), *Lost in the Funhouse* (John Barth), *Welcome to the Monkey House* (Kurt Vonnegut, Jr.).

258

audience in throwing out its old moral baggage, and thus to get rid of his own. One key to these gifted, harsh, derisive writers is their sense of Jewish absurdity after the Holocaust in a world where their own denial of any purpose or comfort made them feel that Jews were simply the freaks of history. The tradition found them without joy in it, but ready to mock the actuality of things. They were naturally edgy satirists haunted by the different sounds made in the world by non-Jews and Jews. The strongest element in their work was always their mimicry of the guile, hysteria and sheer human extravagance of the single voice. In one of Stanley Elkin's best stories, "The Guest," the mad homeless trumpeter Bertie, occupying an apartment while its owners are on vacation, constantly talks to absent friends, ancient radio "personalities" forgotten by everyone else, conjures up every old situation in which he can now have the last word. All alone in the apartment but talking, talking, he is soon too far gone to keep some burglars from emptying the apartment. Elkin's stories often deal with some last-ditch madness in which the hard-pressed protagonist acts out his impossible situation by constantly talking and hearing voices. This emphasis on voice can get a little wearing, for the mimicry, after all, is usually of a dying man. But death is now a favorite idea. As another gifted and overintense novelist, Jerome Charyn, wrote in the preface to his anthology *The Single Voice*, "Terror is now the norm. . . . In a murderous, mechanical society, love and death have become interchangeable." Literature, said Charyn echoing Roland Barthès, is now necessarily "the language of hysteria. . . . Whatever place the black humorists ultimately hold in our literature, they have shown us the brittleness of the human heart and have warned us of the emptiness we will have to endure in a society that has devoted itself to hate rather than to love."

There was a typed extremism to this that sometimes made it difficult to tell one practitioner of black humor from another. These were all terribly intellectual writers, brought up like so many young novelists on academic criticism and its fashionable rejections. The habit of studiously never loving anything in sight, the passion for collecting all possible accidents, oddities, lunacies and giving them an enormous presence in one's own mind* was a stronger factor than the actual sadism, injustice, cruelty of what on every hand was felt to be, in the words of Elizabeth Bishop, "our worst century so far." The more exacerbated the writer felt by the strains, compulsions and legalities of an overorganized technical society, the more the writer felt like a specialist in a world of specialists — and so condemned to go unheard and neglected.

Novelists were in fact getting as special as poets, and feeling as outside everything as poets; which was why one now saw so many novels describing society as just "sick," while the protagonist's fantasy was of a total eccentricity and independence, an anarchism primitive,

---

* "What it really comes down to is the *New York Times*, which is the source and fountain and bible of black humor. . . . A mid-flight heart-attack victim is removed from an airliner, suddenly slides from the stretcher and cracks her head on the runway. We bomb North Vietnam and nervously await the reaction of Red China, scourge of the Free World. . . ." [Bruce Friedman, preface to his anthology *Black Humor*]

venomous and enraged. This itself was entertaining — the novelist as the last frontiersman, limiting himself to contempt and parody. The trouble with society, as the end of the century approached, was obviously society itself. With the loss of the old bourgeois confidence came an expectation on every hand of dissolution. No one felt this so keenly as the novelist, who had depended so long on a social furniture that, as the century's accelerating wars showed, could be carted off in one of those quick changes of scene that have led us to think of contemporary history as macabre entertainment. To come so close to social death, death as an idea on every hand, the actual extinction of those values that were once so real to the modern writer-as-rebel that his criticism depended on their existence — to think familiarly of planetary destruction — is to absorb the tough frivolousness so marked in contemporary novelists as opposed to both the literary ardor and the social wit so marked in novels of the modern period. Thus it was soon felt, as Lionel Trilling said on the occasion of Riesman's *The Lonely Crowd*, that social science was developing an increasingly acute and subtle "sense of social actuality" which contemporary fiction sadly lacked. Sociology seemed to be "in the process of taking over from literature one of literature's most characteristic functions, the investigation and criticism of morals and manners."

The new and now necessarily comic novelist, working in the current mode of monologue and parody, was too often his only embodiment of value as well as narrator and hero. Somehow he found the spur to his hoped-for creative energy in the idea of society as trash and of himself as a sentinel of the expected "catastrophe." One of the key feelings in so much fiction now was a sense of the tenuousness of life in a time when so many people were indeed unstrung by incessant change and so much destruction of community, nature, whole peoples. Americans, the people *par excellence* of the "future," were suddenly terrified of the burdens they had accumulated in their progress. But the accusation that society was "crazy, all crazy," was perhaps less urgent than the conviction that no one was any longer "free." So even the novel, that grand instrument for illuminating social relations, could be allegorized into the plight of the novelist alone.

Yet with all this, the novel exerted its traditional flexibility. It had the rare power to suggest the torment of freedom in a mass society. Even in the most absurdist monologue, the most clownish dramatization of "the literature of exhaustion," "the end of the novel" as an obsessive barrier, prose fiction could pick up the social comedy of a mass society in which so many wills competed for attention. In point of fact, fiction was now a free extension in every direction of prose. It was indispensable even when the aim was to turn the writer on, to capture the perfect freedom of a mental life uninterrupted by action — the perfect freedom of a dream.

> this tired death route
> — *The Naked Lunch*

This would seem to be the case with William Burroughs, who in an interview noted: "My mind moves in a series of blank factual steps without labels and without questions. . . . The new way of thinking is the thinking you would do if you didn't have to think about any of the things you ordinarily think about if you had no work to do nothing to be afraid of no plans to make." Burroughs is the great autoeroticist of contemporary fiction, the man who writes to stock up his private time machine. The "absurdity," the world-craziness which he claims to reproduce in its comic disorganization, consists in dislodging all the contents of his mind in a spirit of raw kaleidoscopic self-intoxication. These rapid shifts and indiscriminate couplings of scenes take place in Burroughs's books as if they were violently oscillating and exploding in the telescopic eyepiece of an astronomer who just happens to be gloriously soused. He writes scenes as fluently as other people write adjectives, so that he is always inserting one scene into another, *turning* one scene into another. Burroughs's fiction happenings are a wholly self-pleasing version of what D. H. Lawrence called the "pure present." Lawrence meant that the act of creation could renew the world. What Burroughs means by it is reverie, a world forever being reshuffled in the mind, a world that belongs to oneself like the contents of a dream.

Burroughs has written a meditation on the famous last words in pure stream-of-consciousness produced by the gangster Dutch Schultz as he was dying. "Morphine administered to someone who is not an addict produces a rush of pictures in the brain as if seen from a speeding train. The pictures are dim, jerky, grainy, like an old film." Burroughs likes to reproduce that indistinctness as well as the rush. In *The Naked Lunch*, his best book but a prototype of all the rest, you get in addition to the wildly funny indiscriminateness of what Burroughs calls the "cut-up novel" (which arbitrarily splices fragmentized memories, pictures, notes), instructions on the possible use of the drugged subject by outside control. Burroughs is himself a great cutup, and he declaims the supposed death-throes of our totalitarian and doomed society with the wildest possible imitation of solemn manipulation. "The biocontrol apparatus is prototype of one-way tele-pathic control. The subject could be rendered suscep-tible to the transmitter by drugs or other processing without installing any apparatus."

Burroughs is a comedian who gets his astral kicks by composing in wild blocks of scenes, in wild fantasies, in the excited mixing of remembered pictures and his own words with the derisive echoes of popular speech. It is impossible to suspect him of base erotic motives in his innumerable scenes of one shadowy stranger servicing another like a piece of plumbing. Nor, since he described at the beginning of *The Naked Lunch* his struggle with drugs and then went off into a beautiful tailspin of fan-tasy that showed how much he delighted in memories of his addiction, should one expect from *The Soft Machine*, *Nova Express, The Ticket That Exploded, The Wild Boys*, books different from his others.*

---

* Burroughs is a stimulating obsessive writer; he is to serious novelists what a money crank is to an economist. *He is different* and he writes out of his difference. The stale cult of provocation in contemporary fiction sometimes reaches very boring lows, espe-cially when it is exploited by journalists looking for a new angle. Thus Richard Kostelanetz, presenting some new novelists under the heading *The End of Intelligent Writing*:

"Many young writers cultivate an imaginative interest in areas

The square world is of course "mad." But the closer fact, to the amused appreciative witness of Burroughs's wild gift for *continuous* fantasy, is that he is mad about anything he can get down on paper. To judge from his obsession with "The Job," Burroughs would seem to be the victim of a mad impatience with the dullness of existence. He loves being taken up by the act of writing, filling up paper from the scene immediately present to his mind as he writes. His private memory theater is staggering. He is so evidently consumed by this that he convinces the reader that oddity, drift, spacelessness are the real sensations. The "outside" world, the agreed-upon world, the supposedly constituted world with some logical and/or

---

of experience either neglected, or clichéd, or rendered superficially in previous writing:

". . . the hysteria of Ishmael Reed's best fiction, the obsessive scatology of Ed Sanders' *Shards of God* (1970), the fragments in rectilinear space of G. S. Gravenson's *The Sweetmeat Sage* (1971), or the narrator's radically varying penmanship (photographically reproduced) in Nancy Weber's *Dear Mom and Dead* (1970). An extreme of another kind appears in Kenneth Gangemi's scrupulously uninflected novel, *Olt* (1969), whose narrator suffers a total inability to discriminate in his experiential responses:

" '[In an art museum] he looked at a painting of the skeletons of American presidents on exhibit in a Chinese museum; a painting entitled *Naked Schoolgirls Bathing in a Stream*; a series of photographs showing the transformation of a five-year old girl into a fifty-year old derelict; a framed blueprint of the Auschwitz raping harness; a reproduction of Rembrandt's *Man Seated Reading at a Table in a Lofty Room*; an aerial photograph of Coney Island on the 4th of July; a painting of Attila choosing from the virgins of a captured village; a model of a one-family tropical island, with mountain, orchard, farm, beach, and lagoon.' "

At a recent art exhibition in New York, there was a photograph of turds in a toilet bowl. Nowadays the representation of any object makes us "creative." Yet at the same time the trivialization of the art object proclaims the comic as parody of itself. Which leaves us with the "irony" of the artist as his own intelligence.

legal order to it — this is less significant to Burroughs than the delicious bouillabaisse of his internal sensations. We no longer have to trek back and forth between the square world and our own drunkenness. We are at home, where consciousness is king.

The effect of a purely internal, swooshed-up medium is to speed Burroughs up and down, across and every which way, past all the mental countries that do emerge in Burroughs's self-hypnosis. The vividness of the chase is startling even when we don't know how we got from one fold of the inner life to the other — or which one we are in:

> *There is only one thing a writer can write about:* what is in front of his senses at the moment of writing . . .* *I am a recording instrument . . . I do not presume to impose "story" "plot" "continuity". . . . Insofar as I succeed in* Direct *recording of certain areas of psychic process I may have limited function . . . I am not an entertainer. . . .*
>
> *"Possession" they call it . . . Sometimes an entity jumps in the body — outlines waver in yellow orange jelly — and hands move to disembowel the passing whore or strangle the nabor child in hope of alleviating a chronic housing shortage. As if I was usually there but subject to goof now and again . . . Wrong! I am never here . . . . Never that is fully in possession, but somehow in a position to forestall ill-advised moves . . . Patrolling is, in fact, my principle* [sic] *occupation. . . . No matter how tight Security, I am always somewhere* Outside *giving orders and* Inside *this straight jacket of jelly that gives and stretches but always reforms ahead of every movement, thought, impulse, stamped with the seal of alien inspection. . . .*

* The dots are in the text [author's note].

Burroughs gives us an extravaganza version of the noticeable speedup created by literature's relentless documentation of internal consciousness. Generally in twentieth-century literature, the more "advanced" the poet, the more mind space he seems to travel for us. This process, assisted by the endless "circuits" (Burroughs's key word) created by technology and ubiquitous "communications," encouraged by our idea of life as a continuum of moments, has made this mental speedup — the writer's temptation to think of himself as effecting total coverage of his internal world — very important to our contemporary literary rites. Consciousness has in truth become king, separating itself from the external world that it has learned to treat as flashes of light along the pathways of the mind.

No one has carried this stress on the private movie theater to such lengths as has Burroughs. Self and world become utterly opposed places. The mind has an illusion of infinite freedom, playfulness, caprice, that the body — especially when drugged and subject to the mind — cannot sustain. There develops, as an absolute joke on the "world," the difference between the speed of thought and the slowness of the body. The mind leaps at will through all space and time as naturally — a recurring theme in Burroughs — as a man being hanged leaps through all his memories and has an ejaculation with the total relaxing of his body into death.

This speedup is taken by Burroughs as a criticism of the world: the world becomes a nut place simply because it is the opposite of the private movie theater. Hence the addict, the homosexual, the odd man out still in touch with his feelings is pursued by what Burroughs in *The Wild Boys* calls the "thought-control mob," the narcotics cops and the despots of the communications monopoly who are the villains in *Nova Express*. The "wild boys" who come into the book of that name are not important except as a culmination of the continual fantasy of boys in rainbow-colored jockstraps coldly doffing them and turning their totally impersonal couplings into a piece of American science fiction. But they do express this fantasy of perfect freedom and Burroughs's fond reverie over adolescent sex around the golf course and the locker rooms in his native St. Louis in the 1920s. "Freedom" is mostly freedom from women; the wild boys have such an aversion to women that the boys continue the race by artificial insemination, and thus "a whole generation arose that had never seen a woman's face nor heard a woman's voice." But this idiosyncratic sense of freedom reproduces Burroughs's typical "fun"-scene — an undirected daydream, a fusion of *Amazing Stories* and porno-sade thriller that effects a high degree of fiction as personal performance; the different items suddenly get animated with a marvelously unexpectable profusion and disorder. Anything can get into a Burroughs novel, lead its own life for a while, get swooshed around with everything else.

Burroughs became an imaginative force in our self-indulgent literature of disaster with *Naked Lunch*. He was able to turn his addiction to morphine, "junk," into a startling ability to report the contents of his marvelously episodic imagination. His expressed aversion to hallucinogens is significant. He did not want to have *his* mind changed — Burroughs does not need inspiration! He wanted, in the tradition which is really his own — transcribing open sexual fantasy into literary energy — to make the fullest possible inventory and rearrangement of all the stuff natural to him. He wanted to put his own mind on the internal screen that is his idea of a novel.

More than anyone else I can think of in the fiction that is now written as a parody of the "system," Burroughs showed himself absolutely reckless in writing for his own satisfaction only. One recognized a novelist interested in nothing but self-expression. He had gone very far in his own life and had put just about everything into the personal system that is his novels. He was an addict from thirty to forty-five. He had an insatiable sort of mind; he was well educated, made a point of being specially well informed — the intelligent crank in action — obviously had a taste for slumming, yet his mind had some marked resemblance to his inventive grandfather and namesake Burroughs, who did not invent the adding machine but thought up the little gadget that kept it steady, and to his uncle Ivy Lee, the public relations man for old John D. Rockefeller who helped to sweeten that fetid reputation.

Burroughs worked in advertising and, typically, was an exterminator. His descriptions of Latin America and North Africa show an unmistakably upper-class American taste for practicing discomfort (rather like Theodore Roosevelt proving that he was no weakling). He has for all his flights into the ether a great shrewdness about American racketeering, political despotism, police agencies, plus a real insight into how machines work and

269

how the innumerable technical objects, stimuli and drugs in contemporary America affect the organism. He has put himself to some ruthless tests, for his compositions show the natural curiosity of a scientist, a fondness for setting up ordeals, and above all an utterly idiosyncratic gift for reliving technical operations, for subjecting himself to anything as an experiment.

"Experiment" of a peculiarly trans-literary, personal, Edison-inventive kind is indeed the big theme in all of Burroughs's work. So it is all a game, even when the material reminds you of Frank Kermode's saying that the counterlogical devices of the modern novel treat time and cause as it is treated by a totalitarian interrogator. Burroughs indeed writes his books as if he were responding to a totalitarian interrogator who, like a nineteenth-century detective, has only one person to investigate. But the self, taken as nothing but itself, its memories, fantasies, random cruelties, is a depressive, even when it rejoices in its unintelligibility.

Like so many American social theorists of fiction, who believe that society is nothing but a swindle, a racket, a "thought-control mob," Burroughs seems to me a victim of solitude. No situation, no line, no joke, lasts very long with him. Everything turns in on itself. Outside, the planets and constellations reel to prove that life has no meaning, that there is not and cannot be anything but our own sacred consciousness. Everything outside is *hell*. And after writing this, I open the Sunday *Times* at random and find an advertisement for the "Capitalist Reporter" that cries out: "Money! Opportunity Is All around You! American treasures are all around you — attic, church bazaar, house-wrecking yards, thrift shops, etc. Old bottles, obsolete fishing lures, prewar comics . . . names and addresses of people who buy *everything*, from old mousetraps to dirigibles to USED ELECTRIC CHAIRS. . . ."

The "system" as such is the obsession and the favorite subject of so much parody. To a writer who is mainly a satirist, Donald Barthelme, this system is made up wholly of cant, clichés, stale quotations, so that words now lead a life of their own, entirely outside the powerless-feeling people who are dragged along by them and who can no longer even recognize their dreams in the wantonly rubbed-thin currency of their lives. The myth of the totalitarian "system," all power over its subjects, is a favorite image of Americans satirizing our cultural dependency. And Barthelme amusingly evokes a cliché system, one in which clichés grow monstrous like airless plants to face us in our fierce self-consciousness with the "intellectuals' " word game. This is put together from the cultural fatigue of advertisements, slogans, counter words, cocktail party chatter, the museum without walls, the news magazine without end, the "end of the novel" and of practically everything else. The junk that the educated man has to carry around with him and constantly pay his respects to!

And hello! to our girl friend, Rosetta Stone, who has stuck by us through thin and thin. . . .

I am sorry to inform you that the Bauhaus no longer exists, that all the great masters who formerly thought there are either dead or retired, and that I myself have been reduced to constructing books on how to pass the examination for police sergeant.

"Ask us anything about our thing, which seems to be working," the chief engineer said. . . . "Do you want to know about evaporated thin-film metallurgy? Monolithic and hybrid integrated-circuit processes? The algebra of inequalities? Optimization theory? Complex high-speed microminiature closed and open loop systems? Fixed variable mathematical cost searches?"

We don't know how to lose a war. That skill is not among our skills. Our array smashes their array, that is what we know. That is the process. That is what is.

The cliché system is basic because everyone is an intellectual now, especially in advertising agencies, the Pentagon, and other centers of expertise. But it is basic to all mimicry and lampoon in our writing now because it conveys the wistfulness proper to dependents on "totalitarian" power. The words we use are outside us, the roles we play through words are outside us, our emotions become as strange to us as anything else on earth. Our life has been denuded, stripped down to patter. We have been reduced to a banal, repetitious, totally standardized gobbledygook. We are comic-strip characters whose most ordinary conversation has been manufactured.

And Barthelme? Literature itself? This too has been denuded, stripped down to the absurd, reduced to its consumers. What is exotic in so much banality is the fact that we consumers of "culture" naturally stick our attentive inquisitive consciousness into everything. Nothing that will be put into a paperback is alien to us. The comic in Barthelme is this extreme unrelenting reference system — match us up with any subject! — without any free choice. We are computers.

The last sentence in "Sentence" (*City Life*) reads,

> *and Ludwig falls through the Tugendhat House into the history of man-made objects; a disappointment, to be sure, but it reminds us that the sentence itself is a man-made object, not the one we wanted of course, but still a construction of man, a structure to be treasured for its weakness, as opposed to the strength of stones. . . .*

Kenneth Burke says somewhere that "we have been sentenced to the sentence," and Barthelme sentences us right back again to sentences constructed vindictively of American newspeak. Is Barthelme a "novelist?" He is one of the few authentic examples of the "antinovelist" — that is, he operates by countermeasures only, and the system that is his own joy to attack permits him what an authoritarian system always permits its lonely dissenters: the sense of their own weakness. The almighty state is always in view. So Barthelme sentences us to the complicity with the system that he suffers from more than anyone. He is wearingly attentive to every detail of the sophistication, the lingo, the massively stultifying secondhandedness of everything "we" say. Barthelme is outside everything he writes about in a way that a humorist like Perelman could never be. He is under the terrible discipline that the System inflicts on those who are most fascinated with its relentlessness. He is so smart, so biting, himself so unrelenting in finding far-flung material for his ridicule that his finished product comes out a joke about Hell. We go up sentence, down sentence, up and down. What severity we are sentenced to by this necessary satire! That is because Barthelme the anti-novelist is based on the perfect inversion of all current practice, and keeps too many records. This is the way Salinger's characters would write *if* they were writers, for it is all based on books.

Barthelme is funniest and even touching in *Snow White*, where the multifaceted plenty of sex (as opposed to the old economy of scarcity) does not bring happiness to our raven-haired heroine and her seven boyfriends. Parodying fairy tales, anti–fairy tales, the captions in Godard movies, market research questionnaires, Barthelme makes it clear that everyone is now so mired in cultured explanations of his and her plight that it is hard to get to bed. Meanwhile, the "electric wastebasket is overheating," Snow White "has taken to wearing heavy blue bulky shapeless quilted Peoples' Volunteer trousers rather than the tight tempting *how the West was won* trousers she formerly wore, which we admired immoderately," the wicked stepmother writes to a stranger that "even a plenum can leak," and with so many referents to live up to, there is (for once) tenderness to one's weakness as opposed to "the strength of stones." We have been cut off by the words hanging over our heads; our poor little word-riddled souls are distributed all over the landscape.

Another totally shown-up System now is History, that fraud of frauds, whose purposelessness is so manifest to late twentieth-century man that the repetitiousness of man's power-madness and self-destruction is reflected in the peculiar jauntiness and formlessness of the new comic fiction. Anthony Burgess noted in *Re Joyce* that "the real comic novel has to do with man's recognition of his unimportance in the universe; comedy in the current sense has to do with instructing the mass audience." The "real comic novel" had in fact to do with man's gift for disbelief; but even in a time of mass atheism, which in any event would seem to reflect rather than to produce man's inability to control the social and technical forces he has unleashed, "comedy in the current sense" has to do with man's social sense of frustration. This *is* a didactic point, and explains why the "absurd" is such a popular concept among people who love concepts more than the dramatic figure. Nothing is clearer to the generation that knows society to be the nexus of all realities, that has combined the nineteenth-century gift of social prophecy with the iciest distrust of man, than that "History" is full of "cunning passages," that nothing is what it seems, that "all identities are multiple masks," that the many shifts and ruses demanded of a contemporary demand illustrations for the common reader.

In Thomas Pynchon's *V* and *The Crying of Lot 49* the protagonist is History itself — History as a mystification, perhaps deliberate! that operates as a whirligig. In *V* it is operated by a woman, "V" herself, who is a woman of our time and is actually the mother of the questing seeking Englishman Herbert Stencil, who discovers and imagines her fantastic journeys and quick changes through twentieth-century history without learning that she is his actual mother as well as the Great Mother who can supply the thread of History he has been looking for. "V" appears at intervals, as does the Queen of the Night; she is a kind of antigoddess, a key to the bewildering modern Wheel of Fortune. But she is also a nineteen-year old Yorkshire girl named Victoria Wren who is deflowered by a British agent in Cairo during the Fashoda crisis in 1898; in Florence in 1899, she seduced Herbert Stencil's father on a couch in the British consulate; in Paris in 1913 she is a Lesbian in love with a young ballerina; in Malta in 1919, she is Veronica Manganese, and she now has a star sapphire sewn into her navel and a glass eye with a clock for a pupil; in 1922, she pops up in what had been German South-West Africa as Vera Meroving of Munich; in 1939, she is in Malta disguised as a nameless priest, and, unconscious after an air raid, is mauled to death by some children trying to dig out her star sapphire.

Fashoda, Malta, the South-West Africa in which the Germans before World War I practiced genocide on the natives, and many other points of modern imperialism make up one track round and round which we go while Herbert Stencil retraces and/or dreams the cruelties, betrayals, abductions, tortures to which he *thinks* he has a key in the reappearances of "V." Another track is one round and round which the ex-Navy Italian-Jewish drifter Benny Profane and his pals seek in many ports a perfect night out on the town; another is the unending violence to the body meticulously described in a nose operation on a Jewish girl, the "accidental" impaling of "V's" beloved ballerina onstage in Paris in a horrible parody of the sexual act, the "extermination" of natives in South-West Africa by German officers.

In *The Crying of Lot 49*, a subtler, tighter, impressively dramatic version of Pynchon's fascination with History as a puzzle game, Oedipa Maas is the pilgrim, quester, seeker of meaning in this proliferatingly insane world. Her superrich monopolistic ex-lover, Pierce Inverarity, made her executrix of his will, and by way of trying to settle his mysteriously tangled effects she is sent off on a mad treasure hunt and by the end of the book has good reason to believe, like Ellison's "Invisible Man," that "History" is just a conspiracy to keep *her* running and floundering. *The Crying of Lot 49* is a brilliant and compassionate book. Its compassion is as impressive as the fact that it is an imaginatively integrated narrative, both qualities generally missing from the "absurdist" convention — one that generally permits any manipulation of the reader's intellectual balance. But the comic devices are carried over from *V* — the constant shifting of ground, of names, and so of identities. (Herbert Stencil in *V* always refers to himself in the third person. "This helped 'Stencil' appear as only one among a repertoire of identities.")

The key to Pynchon's brilliantly dizzying narratives is the force of some hypothesis that is authentic to him but undisclosable to us. There is a felt mystery, a communicable unsolidity, to our human affairs. Herbert Stencil practices "forcible dislocation of personality" as a "general technique . . . the rest was impersonation and dream." What is also striking in *V* is the proliferation of dummy characters who come up from anywhere and may be anything. The network of consciousness in the world is more widely spread now than it ever was; the ambiguity of who-is-thinking-what gives the uncertainty an added touch of the sinister. But too often in *V* Pynchon's

exuberance settles on the high jinks of juvenile names
— Stencil, Benny Profane, Mafia, Charisma, Murray
Sable, Bloody Chiclitz. Profane and his rambunctious
friends clouting each other in every port are wearisome
merriment; there is also "The Whole Sick Crew" — Slab
the painter devotes his life to painting a series of cheese
Danishes; Esther Harvitz is the mistress of her plastic
surgeon, who starts with her nose but wants to remodel
the rest of her. . . . There are set-ups that do honor to
Pynchon's wild inventiveness, but add nothing to the
book: Father Fairing, a Jesuit priest convinced that the
rats are about to take over New York City, moves down to
the sewers to convert them to Roman Catholicism, blesses
and exorcises all the sewer water between Lexington
Avenue and the East River and between 79th and 86th,
and so creates Fairing's Parish.

But Pynchon is a keener as well as slyer mind than
most current practitioners of absurdity. *The Crying of
Lot 49* is a very short novel but imaginatively and stylistically the fable of the wild-goose chase that *something*
now sets up for minds that still seek order, source, tradition, divinity. Pynchon's comic exuberance is often
merely smart, but it also reflects a mind distinctly attuned
to the proliferating confusions he writes about. In V his
rhythms, though distinct, are still rhetorical; in *The Crying of Lot 49* there is a most satisfactory matching-up of
his quickness of mind with the needlessly deceitful *thing*
he is writing about. There seems to be a private mail
delivery system all over the United States that may very
well be a network for other purposes. People are secretly

exchanging messages all the time, and the symbol that identifies them all is a muted post horn.

This may be conspiracy, it may be delusion, it certainly reflects the distinct American feeling that the power grid by which we live is out of our control. Pynchon is an expert at identifying all traces of the thing-dominated, apparatus-laden, Disneyland-looking southern California that seems to be all cardboard, and isn't. Oedipa and the lawyer Metzger, making love in the motel, come together just as the electric guitars calling themselves the "Paranoids" blow all the fuses and off goes the TV set showing old science-adventure films in which the lawyer appeared when he was a pretty child actor. Pynchon has the ubiquitous culture scene — "We're the only bar in the area, you know, has a strictly electronic music policy"; he has above all, for all his smartness, the essential ability not only to make art of our confusion, but also to show the threat of this confusion to human leftover feelings. She may be called Oedipa Maas, but we come to believe that she is real — and that especially so is San Narciso (St. Narcissus), Calif. Near the end of the book, when Oedipa has been numbed by her failure to discover the terms of her quest, there is in capsule Pynchon form — we *shall* give you blood to drink! — the enormous social prophecy of our increasing disorientation that is being registered in American fiction:

> *Either you have stumbled indeed, without the aid of LSD or other indole alkaloids, onto a secret richness and concealed density of dream; onto a network by which X number of Americans are truly communicating*

whilst reserving their lies, recitations of routine, arid betrayals of spiritual poverty, for the official government delivery system; maybe even onto a real alternative to the exitlessness, to the absence of surprise to life, that harrows the head of everybody American you know and you too, sweetie. Or you are hallucinating it. Or a plot has been mounted against you, so expensive and elaborate, involving items like the forging of stamps and ancient books, constant surveillance of your movements, planting of post horn images all over San Francisco, bribing of librarians, hiring of professional actors and Pierce Inverarity only knows what-all besides, all financed out of the estate in a way either too secret or too involved for your non-legal mind to know about even though you are co-executor, so labyrinthine that it must have meaning beyond just a practical joke. . . .

She . . . hoped she was mentally ill; that that's all it was. That night she sat for hours, too numb even to drink, teaching herself to breathe in a vacuum. For this, oh God, was the void.

But of course even this goes too far. As Nigel Dennis said in praise of Samuel Beckett's *End-Game*, because it is so short, "In all absurd cases it is better not to explain at all." But our American absurdists do explain and explain, for unlike the Europeans who invented the term because they have a quarrel with existence, ours have merely realized the limitations of our own power. So the absurd becomes the transmissible:

"Nothing has any intrinsic value," I remarked, as coolly as though I had known it for years. . . . I delighted in it like a child turned loose for the first time in the endless out-of-doors, full of scornful pity for those still inside." [*John Barth,* The Floating Opera]

And it was there that I simply ran out of gas. There was no reason to do anything. . . . It is the malady cosmopis, *the cosmic view.* [*John Barth*, The End of the Road]

The trouble, I suppose, is that the more one learns about a given person, the more difficult it becomes to assign a character to him that will allow one to deal with him effectively in an emotional situation. Mythotherapy, in short, becomes increasingly harder to apply, because one is compelled to recognize the inadequacy of any role one assigns. [*John Barth*, The End of the Road]

And one volume of Ranke's History of the Popes, *the latter with marginal annotations in the Fuhrer's hand, often simply* Scheisse!, *souvenirs from a broader range of Nazidom; and finally a sheaf of small paintings on cardboard by an old man who lived under a heap of rubble in the Soviet Sector, whose wife had been killed in the bombings, whose daughter was raped and VD'd by the Russians, and whose pictures — calendar landscapes painted in saccharine and molasses — were moving slowly even with Ami soldiers. . . .* [*Thomas Berger*, Crazy in Berlin]

. . . . there is nothing intelligent to say about a massacre. Everybody is supposed to be dead, to never say anything or want anything ever again. Everything is supposed to be very quiet after a massacre, and it always is, except for the birds.

And what do the birds say? All there is to say about a massacre, things like "Poo-tee-weet"? [*Kurt Vonnegut*, Slaughterhouse-Five]

9

A PERSONAL SENSE OF TIME
Nabokov and Other Exiles

I confess I do not believe in time. I like to fold my magic carpet, after use, in such a way as to superimpose one part of the pattern upon another. Let visitors trip. And the highest enjoyment of timelessness — in a landscape selected at random. . . .

> — Vladimir Nabokov, *Speak, Memory*

Peculiar to Sirin is the realization, or perhaps only a deeply felt conviction, that the world of literary creativity, the true world of the artist, . . . conjured out of apparent simulacra of the real world, consists in fact of a completely different material. . . . So different that the passage from one world into the other, in whichever direction it is accomplished, is akin to death.

> — Vladislav Khodasevich, "On Sirin"

1

In a significant paper, "The Writer as Illusionist," the fiction editor of *The New Yorker*, William Maxwell, a novelist notably intelligent about fiction, located its enduring importance in the narrative writer's ability to perform tricks, to create illusions — and to be taken in by his own tricks.

So far as I can see, there is no legitimate sleight of hand involved in practicing the arts of painting, sculpture, and music. They appear to have had their origin in religion, and they are fundamentally serious. In writing — in all writing but especially in narrative writing — you are being continually taken in. The reader, skeptical, experienced, with many demands on his time and many ways of enjoying his leisure, is asked to believe in people he knows don't exist, to be present at scenes that never occurred, to be amused or moved or instructed just as he would be in real life, only the life exists in somebody else's imagination. If, as Mr. T. S. Eliot says, humankind cannot bear very much reality, then that would account for their turning to the charlatans operating along the riverbank — to the fortune-teller, the phrenologist, the man selling spirit money, the storyteller. Or there may be a different explanation; it may be that what humankind cannot bear directly it can bear indirectly, from a safe distance.

Maxwell's altogether charming lecture-portrait of the novelist as not "serious," a "shoddy entertainer," wholly a performer, was given at a large academic gathering in 1954 met to discuss the contemporary novel, and it was most gratefully received by an audience that needed no persuading that the creation of illusion, a finespun professionalism, is the essence of the novel — and that it is indeed playful, with many tricks up its sleeve. For nothing was more common now in the many universities over this broad land than to discuss novels selected as masterpieces, teachable as esthetic effect, to celebrate what Mark Schorer in a central essay of this period called "Technique as Discovery," and indeed to celebrate in unimpeachably well-executed novels, taken over from the New Criticism's structural analysis of dependable poems, the novel as structure, tension, imagery, form.

Among students and other specimens of "the common reader," the modern novel (whose other arm was necessarily the American novel) had never been more important as what Henry James called it: "an expression of life." The modern novel, the American novel, narrative as the fruition of prose, had indeed become for the obstinate, humble, ordinary reader of novels one of the great keys to the freedom of life, to life as unhinderable human experience. This was what James, in his great essay of 1884 on "The Art of Fiction," had hoped for the novel. James had seen the fiction of the future as the successor of history and the heir of painting, serious and demanding as any other fine art, but distinctly itself, something new in consciousness, because it was necessarily *a personal, a direct impression of life. . . . Experience is never limited and it is never complete; it is an immense sensibility, a kind of huge spider web of the finest silken threads suspended in the chamber of consciousness, and catching every airborne particle in its tissue. It is the very atmosphere of the mind; and when the mind is imaginative — much more when it happens to be that of a man of genius — it takes to itself the faintest hints of life, it converts the very pulses of the air into revelations.*

The novel of the future, which James had put up against the old-fashioned moralistic limitations on fiction, against the English upper-class fear of representing every possible social experience in fiction, against Zola's restriction of fiction to a programmed determinism, had in truth turned out — more than James would have liked!* — a great central avenue for the expression of man's life, man's hope, man's fate. Gatsby, Bloom, Nick Adams, Joseph K., Mrs. Dalloway, Miss Lonelyhearts, the Consul, the Compsons, had become the touchstones of "reality" — of our shared consciousness — for many young people who also recognized in the "heroes" of Salinger and the "villains" of Flannery O'Connor the spiritual plight of a generation that had to find its own stoic defenses against a vast emptiness, this encompassing sense of evil that was indeed "the absence of seriousness."

The common reader, the doggedly faithful reader, still read fiction for experience. A story was something he could add to his own life. But expert criticism of the novel, touring the achieved splendors of the museum of

* In 1914 James touched on *Sons and Lovers* in an omnibus review of "new novelists" only to put Lawrence down.

modern novels, tended to identify the end-product with his esthetic vocabulary, with the absence of "flaws," with that anxious consumerism in the arts that is possible only when all the creative returns seem to be in. The museum of modern literature enabled people to walk through it without regard for the different struggles that had led Joyce, Woolf, Kafka, Faulkner to create the now chic teachable art object called "the modern novel." By the 1950's modernism had become its memory of itself; criticism of the novel tended to extract the essence of itself as "form," "antirealism," "sensibility," to stress what was now astonishingly an academic cliché, "performance," even to instruct the new mass audience for art in "techniques of fiction" as if selected short stories or prescriptive excerpts from novels would themselves bring one nearer, ever nearer, to the mysterious thing-in-itself that made for dependable effect despite the great babble of so many stories being told at once.

Brilliantly informed on technical matters as this post-modernist criticism was — a criticism of elites for a mass culture! — it could not deal with the intellectual crisis behind modernism, the dizzying relativity and fragmentation of all traditional ideas. Against this, Proust had posited the great claim which he above all others was to realize in one great book: "the only truth of life is in art." It was this belief in art as a model of the transcendent truth to be found within existence, in art as *la vraie vérité*, in fiction as the largest rhythmic manifestation of the life within us that ties us to what is out there, that had been behind the lonely individual struggles, early in the century, of those great artists for whom the novel was visible and invisible reality realized. James had seen that the novelist "succeeds to the sacred office of the historian." Conrad had said that his aim as a writer was to render the highest possible justice to the created universe. Lawrence, in his amazing dithyramb, "Why the Novel Matters," had written exultantly,

The whole is greater than the part. And therefore I, who am man alive, am greater than my soul, or spirit, or body, or mind, or consciousness, or anything else that is part of me. . . . For this reason I am a novelist. And being a novelist, I consider myself superior to the saint, the scientist, the philosopher, and the poet, who are all great masters of different bits of man alive, but never get the whole hog.

The novel is the one bright book of life. Books are not life. They are only tremulations of the ether. But the novel as a tremulation can make the whole man alive tremble. Which is more than poetry, philosophy, science, or any other book — tremulation can do.

It was this openness to life, to life in any direction and in any volume, to literature as the height of knowledge and the novel as its Great Form, that novelists born at the end of the nineteenth century had stuck to amid the brilliant new specializations of knowledge that were to compete with literature in the twentieth. Virginia Woolf was so overcome by Chekhov's stories and by *A Portrait of the Artist as a Young Man* as higher forms of truth than the literalness of nineteenth-century realism that in her great essay of 1919, "Modern Fiction," she described the vision that these prophetic fictions had given her:

289

Life is not a series of gig lamps symmetrically arranged. . . . Life is a luminous halo surrounding us from the beginning of things to the end. . . .

The twentieth-century novel's claim to truth had withstood the challenge of positivism and even of relativity by absorbing them. Tolstoy had given up fiction because it seemed frivolous compared with the burden of human suffering and the need to find God within yourself. But with Proust, Joyce, Kafka, Woolf, Faulkner, fiction was to become the great secular voice of man — the Kingdom of God was now the knowledge within *you* as the link between all inner and outer worlds.

Suddenly the "end of the novel" hung over every novelist like the sword of Damocles. A "drastic reduction has taken place in the status of narration," Lionel Trilling noted, so that even historians have "repudiated the ancient allegiance of their craft to the narrative mode." This was so much an issue with critics of the novel that the necessary solitude of the novelist, compared with science as "the mind of the race," was now taken as weakness. There were no longer any common standards of manners to guide novelists, ran one critical refrain; no upper class, no ascertainable standards of judgment. But meanwhile a young, hip critic noted of Bellow, Styron, Salinger, Malamud, *et al.*,

their talents were formed at an unfortunate moment in history. They labored in the backwash of a dying historical era. . . . Society was dead at its very center . . . and the real life of it — the very raw material of novels — was to be found in the unorganized fringes. . . .

290

There was safety only in numbers. *"I would argue,"* wrote Pauline Kael,

> *that what redeems movies in general, what makes them so much easier to take than other arts, is that many talents in interaction in a work can produce something more enjoyable than one talent that is not of the highest. Because of the collaborative nature of most movies, masterpieces are rare . . . but the interaction frequently results in special pleasures and surprises.*

And in fact the bloodless esthetization of fiction was concurrently so much more important to critics of the novel than modern fiction's claim to truth that it was odd to look back to James's "The Art of Fiction."

> *The only reason for the existence of a novel is that it does attempt to represent life. When it relinquishes this attempt, the same attempt that we see on the canvas of the painter, it will have arrived at a very strange pass. It is not expected of the picture that it will make itself humble in order to be forgiven; and the analogy between the art of the painter and the art of the novelist, is so far as I can see, complete.*

Compare this with William Maxwell's saying in "The Writer as Illusionist" that painting may have had its origin in religion, and so is "fundamentally serious," while "in writing — in all writing but especially in narrative writing — you are being continually taken in." Why should the manifest fact that "life exists in somebody else's imagination," that all art involves the manipulation of appearance, the use of illusion, involve us in the belief that the novelist is exclusively an illusionist, a performer, and even (most charmingly) a "charlatan"? Why should

it be supposed that the creation of illusion is something
wholly deliberate? James had said, in apology for the
dubious ending of *The Portrait of a Lady*, "The whole
truth about anything is never told. You can only take
what groups together."

What "groups together" is what is brought together
under the necessity of the artist's belief in his own creation. He is, as Maxwell noted, the first to be taken in.
And it is interesting indeed, when one turns to Maxwell's most "achieved" novel, *The Folded Leaf*, a wholly
expressive novel of young love between two boys and a
girl at a large Midwestern university, to see how much
the success of this beautiful novel follows from Maxwell's
assured "grouping together" of all possible details of
place, character and age rather than from "sleight of
hand" divorced from the devastating emotions within the
book. *The Folded Leaf* was a novel of attachment, of the
profoundest personal tenderness toward every surface
and object. There was a vindication of experience, a positive sacredness about one's attachments, that became a
sense of loss among the characters themselves as they
moved out of the story. The force of feeling in Maxwell's
best novel shaped everything, prepared the reader for
the sequences. There was a rhythm, a pressure of passionate restraint that one misses in the forced energy of
many contemporary novels. The integrity of feeling behind *The Folded Leaf* was an event.

So one could say of another fine and undemonstrative
contemporary, J. F. Powers, that his favorite subject, the
personal triviality of many a Midwestern parish priest
compared with his spiritual office, was solidly rooted in

Powers's strength of feeling. In *Prince of Darkness, The Presence of Grace, Morte d'Urban*, Powers's knotted observation of the wry, inescapable contradiction between human nature and the formal religious profession, his interest in mediocrity and fascination with sin as the unconscious dramatic urge of people, gave his people a modest, dry, obstinate moral edge.

But in the "plight of the novel," supposedly redeemed by the sudden cult of the novel as a series of difficult propositions, modesty often wrote its own epitaph. It was easier for the novelist William Gass, a brilliant but exhaustingly self-conscious theoretician of the novel, to get attention with a showy construction, *Omensetter's Luck*, a book that showed every sign of great personal intelligence, curiosity, mimicry, but was brilliantly unconvincing — an act. Gass was a restlessly inventive, loquacious writer whose sharp critical writing showed that he knew as much about different minds operating in fiction as a philosopher is likely to know. But as a fiction writer Gass could stimulate many other critics without conveying any honest necessity about the relationships he described. He was like the man Kafka described who walked just above the ground. Everything was there in *Omensetter's Luck* to persuade the knowing reader of fiction that here was a great step forward: the verve, the bursting sense of possibility, the gravely significant atmosphere of contradiction, complexity of issue at every step. But it was all in the head, another hypothesis to dazzle the laity with. Gass had a way of dazzling himself under the storm of his style. In a book of essays, "Fiction and the Figures of Life," Gass called for a fiction in which.

his characters, "freed from existence, can shine in essence and purely Be." Perhaps Gass was, then, a mystic or absolutist of the novel? To have one's characters "freed from existence" is not a sensible wish for a novelist. The seeming unlimitedness of the novel as a form does tempt extraordinarily bright people into identifying their many "figures" for life with life itself on the page.

Gass was an event in the boggy history of the postwar novel. The overpowering classroom demonstrativeness of his skill at "construction" — of argument, of situation with voices — showed insight into the human mind and its fictions, in the current style that so much stressed the secret compartments of the mind, the counterfeit, the duplicity. But Gass's own fiction was make-believe fiction, not the real confidence game which takes in, to his supreme delight, the confidence man himself. The real-false thing had been around in America for some time. A major illusionist and trickster was at hand, still inexhaustibly delighted with every performance after fifty years. "The plight of the novel" was absorbed and parodied by a major writer who did not believe in it, but used it for his own purposes.

2

When Vladimir Vladimirovitch Nabokov arrived in America from France in May 1940 (with his first novel in English, *The Real Life of Sebastian Knight*), he probably did not altogether expect that the freest and gayest period in his creative life since his enchanted boyhood in

Russia was about to begin. Two separated periods of creative innovation, two exhilarations, were in fact now to join each other in the endlessly revolving life and mind of Vladimir Nabokov. A gifted poet as well as novelist, an accredited expert on butterflies, the much-cherished son of an aristocratic, wealthy Russian liberal and Anglophile, Nabokov had fled Bolshevik Russia in 1919 and Hitler's Germany for Paris in 1937. In 1922, his father had been shot to death by Russian fascists at a public meeting in Berlin of democratic Russian émigrés. Nabokov had taken a degree at Cambridge, had been in Berlin variously a tennis coach, English tutor, and composer of Russian crossword puzzles. After growing up as a young princeling in a St. Petersburg mansion and on a great private estate, he had in exile experienced "fifty or sixty" different lodgings, and under the pen name of Sirin, had by his cheerful admission become the only major novelist among the Russian émigré writers until Sirin had "disappeared" in Europe, leaving "a vague uneasiness" behind him.

By 1940, Nabokov's already well-stocked mind might well have seemed positively top-heavy to itself with images of the succession of lives he had led in Russia, England, Germany, France — and was now leading as a college teacher in America and as an "American" novelist. By contrast, Joyce (soon to die in Zurich) had been a stationary figure even in exile, which in any event was voluntary and in which he had written in his own language about a world located nowhere but in Dublin. Conrad had never, as a novelist, been forced to shift from Polish to English — and this at forty. The famous expatriates of Nabokov's end-of-the-century generation, the first consciously modernist generation — Hemingway and Fitzgerald, older writers like Gertrude Stein, D. H. Lawrence — had in their comfortable "exile" always kept up direct relations with their own country, language and people, and indeed had written *to* them.

Nabokov was thus a harder and more complex case of displacement than any other in his generation.* (Even the Danish Isak Dinesen, who wrote in English, freely chose to live in Africa, and was never, for all her talent, so thoroughly committed to writing as a way of life and to fiction as the art of arts.) The only counterparts of Nabokov's experience were among his fellow escapees from Russia. But though Russian exiles were his only real audience before he turned to English, "Sirin" left a "vague uneasiness behind him" because his mind was contentious yet not polemical. It was professedly apolitical, scornful of all public causes and "general ideas," uninterested in the famous Russian "spirituality" on the right and in the famous Russian passion for human betterment on the left. It was committed to art as "esthetic bliss." Nabokov would always elude transcendental doctrine, the famous Eureka! of romanticism as a key to knowledge. He was concerned with the surface phenom-

---

* Or the next. Some of the best contemporary novelists have moved from their country of origin — V. S. Naipaul, Malcolm Lowry, Anthony Burgess, Doris Lessing, Samuel Beckett, Brian Moore. Several African, West Indian and Indian writers have (like Naipaul of Trinidad) left colonies for cosmopolitan centers. But whatever the political pressures or personal urges behind these moves, these writers have not been condemned by their native countries — as was Nabokov, and the German literary emigration from Hitler. But neither Brecht nor Broch nor Werfel, etc., etc., wrote their "exile" works in anything but German.

ena in nature fascinating to an expert in butterflies, with working out unexpected combinations and patterns, as in chess, rather than with any "liberating" idea.

Nabokov made fellow Russian exiles "uneasy" by his disdain for *all* doctrines of salvation, whether by politics or the religion of the word. Nabokov was not sociological and "humanitarian" in the well-worn style of Russian progressive thought; he was equally indifferent to the God-hunger and the various esoteric and mystical traffick-ings among Russian poets. And despite his self-conscious virtuosity of style, he was not a symbolist looking to pro-claim a system of meaning through his own enraptured word-juggling. Nabokov gained disciples at Cornell by directing the attention of his students to "what hangs on the wall" in one chapter of *Anna Karenina*. Once he brought to class a diagram of an old St. Petersburg–Moscow railway carriage. He was distinguished in several fields by this pressing sense of fact. He was a very able and dedicated lepidopterist, a zealous scholar of prosody who in America was, characteristically, to make a pointedly faithful translation of Pushkin's *Eugene Onegin*. In Berlin he had translated *Alice in Wonderland* into Russian. As a novelist in Russian he had a peremp-tory, altogether sovereign way of describing the surface phenomena of life — a man dreamily walking a Berlin street, people restlessly occupying their seats in a railway carriage — at a bewilderingly sly tempo. The patterns this achieved seemed directed just to the eye and mind of the delighted Nabokov. The literal face of things, the arrested surface! This for Nabokov was not picture, as it was for Hemingway; not a clue to some "higher" human destiny, as it had been for Conrad; not rhythmically akin to human thinking, as it was for Lawrence and Faulkner. It was more like Poe's use of any situation to show its subservience to his intelligence. Nabokov already regarded himself as a Faust or magus of the novel. All material was there for him to transpose into new shapes, and his noticeable pride in his own powers was like a scientist's trust that he can depend on nature. Nabokov the novelist was anything but a realist trying to make literature correspond to life, and despite the pointed interposition of himself, very far from being a subjective romantic. Even his striking immodesty would have a humor all its own, for Nabokov did not so much praise himself as he did a world rich in the many things that waited for Nabokov to "seize" them in words.

What was also distinctive about Sirin before he became Nabokov again in America was that each of his books tended to be a case history, a straight-faced but mocking biography of an obsession. In the best Russian books, *The Defense, Invitation to a Beheading, The Gift*, the subject was an individual's unalterable way of looking at reality *and* the alternative. This was suspended in the minds of those relating to the doomed man, could be felt in the atmosphere surrounding him. But the alternative could be seized only if, like Cincinnatus C. in *Invitation to a Beheading*, the man doomed by the totalitarian state recognized himself not as "their" object but as a living power, could look behind the elaborate terror rigged against him to the mere show, and so could walk away from his own execution as one to which puppets were invited.

The different orders of consciousness made the supreme fact. In *Despair, King, Queen and Knave, Laughter in the Dark*, something rooted, some splintered individual consciousness, represented a person's destiny, for consciousness gave a pattern to the outside world from which, as the wretched chess master Luzhin discovered, there was no "defense"; Luzhin finally jumped to his death *into* an "outside world" that now looked like a chessboard. So each case history represented a critical revision of so-called "reality." In *Mary* and *The Gift* the protagonist clearly spoke for Nabokov himself; in *The Defense* and *Despair* the protagonist was a madman. But as Nabokov was to say in *Ada* apropos of Van Veen's ecstatic lovemaking up to old age, "Reality lost the quotes it wore like claws — in a world where independent and original minds must cling to things or pull things apart in order to ward off madness or death (which is the supreme madness)." The operative pattern was the gift or despair of some particular consciousness. We are nothing but what we see and think. This is the only hierarchy in nature. The supreme fact of life is the inviolate patterning of each single "reality." This renders any common measure meaningless and makes all social prescription, like Communist Russia's, a terror that must be supported by terror. But the infinitely various patterns put a supreme value on "independent and original minds." The man of genius may alone escape the solitude that holds lesser men obsessed — Luzhin, Herman in *Despair*, . . . and Humbert Humbert.

The conflict that a novel sets up, Nabokov was to say, is not between the characters but between the author and his readers. The illusionist in charge must "trip up" the reader, outwit him at every turn, and in fact unseat him as the condition of the author's keeping control. As Nabokov's Russian novels mounted up in English versions, their barbed prefaces said explicitly (with a certain innocent pomposity characteristic of the swagger in his English), what his American novels — *Pnin, Lolita, Pale Fire, Ada* — had already hinted. My fiction, dear reader, is a cunning and systematic revision of your reality. Fiction is the most urgent game, a contest of minds: if I win, the reader must surrender. There is no equality in nature, only endless adaptation. The novelist is supreme, and the novel brings out the different shimmering patterns — a contrast between those who cannot see beyond the bars of their cage and a mind that is free, lordly, momentous, ranging in nature just wherever it likes. And so is in command of the comedy inherent in the clash of appearances.

Nabokov demonstratively brought up characters wholly imprisoned by their intellectual specialties. Luzhin the chess master in *The Defense* sees nothing but chess patterns; locking himself into the bathroom, he jumps into the pattern outside the window as if he were making the supremely brilliant move of his life. Nabokov has always had an extraordinary ability to match the situation to his bizarre characters. In one of his greatest novels, *The Gift*, made unusually attractive by a hero altogether close to Nabokov, the young poet Fyodor Godunov-Cherdyntsev, living among grumbling half-alive Russian exiles in Berlin, writes a satirical biography of the famous Russian ideologue, Nikolai Chernishevsky, a hero of Lenin's but a stereotype in Nabokov's mind of the clumsy style and abstract idealism of Russian reformers. Chernishevsky becomes a model case of the futility and self-deception that the young poet despises in Russian liberalism. Against this he counterpoints every loving memory of his father, a great naturalist and explorer, and the openness and exultant freedom of his own "untrammeled"* perceptions as he discovers them walking about Berlin. Even young Godunov-Cherdyntsev's longing for dearly remembered places in Russia brings out Nabokov's belief that imagination is not just a form of memory, but a working-back to our connection with nature:

> Perhaps one day, on foreign-made soles, . . . I shall again come out of that station. . . . I reach the sites where I grew up . . . still make out something infinitely and unwaveringly faithful to me, if only because my eyes are, in the long run, made of the same stuff as the grayness, the clarity, the dampness of those sites. . . .

Nabokov plainly circumscribes the novel as a form to the *quality* of his own perceptions. In his beautiful memoir, *Speak, Memory*, he says of his boyhood raptures as a young entomologist in Russia wandering about with his butterfly net,

> I confess I do not believe in time. I like to fold my magic carpet, after use, in such a way as to superimpose one part of the pattern upon another. Let visitors trip. And the highest enjoyment of timelessness — in a land-

---

* A favorite adjective of Nabokov's, especially for the Russian language.

scape selected at random — is when I stand among rare butterflies and their food plants. This is ecstasy, and behind the ecstasy is something else, which is hard to explain. It is like a momentary vacuum into which rushes all that I love.

This ability to find the world so resplendently at his nerve ends, this exalted quality of self-reference means for Nabokov the supremacy of fiction the "antiworld" over reality. All political and religious dogmatisms, all constructed systems that seek to be absolutist versions of "reality," are founded on lies. But his novels honestly seem to Nabokov more interesting, more valuable than others because they are so much *his*, express so much curiosity, playfulness, invention, subtlety, that they give more free exercise to the mind, fortify the constructing human imagination. There is no "world," no model or replica that will unify the various stands of our imagination. There are no "spots of time" in this world that are landmarks of eternity, no divine patience that will raise ordinary life to the sublimity of mythology, *pace* Joyce in *Ulysses*! Hemingway said that "one true sentence" was enough to get him started. But this world as an allegory of the truth has for Nabokov nothing to do with fiction; there is just the mundane and the other. Life is too complex, as we are too specialized, for any reflection or "epiphany" or symbol of something higher than itself to emerge from fiction. Life and death are fascinatingly patterned phenomena, endlessly foldable and unfoldable, the beautiful variousness of nature: the thing-in-itself.

Do what you will, said William Blake in "The Everlasting Gospel," *this life's a fiction/And is made up of con-*

tradiction. The self-annulment of all systems that claim to find their final destination in truth is so glaring that Nabokov cannot contain his joy. Nothing should be more deceiving (if it is no longer self-deceiving) than the "total truth" behind the total tyranny of Soviet Commuism. Nabokov has been immeasurably stimulated in his exile by the lies on lies that Bolshevik Russia presents as truths.* He has put his mind and gift against more than fifty years of terror-enforced lies. Only Orwell among novelists of totalitarianism has equally understood how much the State-in-complete-control must rewrite reality. But more essentially a novelist than Orwell, and hardly a wounded radical consciousness, Nabokov has gone on to show how much the consciousness in our time has been demented and damaged by the exaction of obedience. The unalterable solitude of the characters even in his American books is like the proliferation of "madmen" in nineteenth-century Russian novels: the obsessed men in his American books — Pnin, Humbert Humbert, Charles Kinbote — suggest the threat that Nabokov carried away with him. We never get away from the particular case, the haunted self, some central bat in the belfry. Pnin is altogether touching in his defenselessness, Kinbote in *Pale Fire* is horribly mad, Humbert Humbert is perversely appealing in his all-concentrated love for his nymphet. For each of them life is a vacuum into which rushes all that they love. As the gleeful shuffling of countries shows

---

* And by the total obedience that totalitarianism exacts, for this enforces the doubts that may yet lead to disrespect for the whole system. This is how Cincinnatus C. in *Invitation to a Beheading* can finally walk away from his death; the crowd invited to his execution turns out to be a picture on a backdrop.

in all these books, especially in the fantasy extravaganza where Russia and America become parts of each other in *Ada*, Nabokov, once settled in America, was able to have his Russia in America.

America was a second youth for Nabokov; in America he developed a bantering frolicsome sense of life exploding in all directions under his authority. In America he not only took off from the comic machinery of his Russian novels — he published them all in English with prefaces telling his supposedly abject audience how to read them and what not to think! He was in his element. As the Russian poet and critic Vladislav Khodasevich had said, "Sirin" was an illusionist who loved to show all his tricks, to put his machinery directly onstage. In Germany and France, Nabokov quietly noted in his autobiography, he had made hardly any friends and had found people "spectral illusions." In America, Nabokov become a college teacher — now his sense of authority, his intense Russian belief in literature, his aristocratic paternalism and the modesty of American undergraduates combined to make him the most mischievous and insistent of teachers. At Cornell he gained many disciples and future scholiasts of his work, some of whom, however, there is reason to believe that Nabokov created himself, just as he surely kidded some of his too-adoring explicators in the zany off-key notes that Charles Kinbote attached to John Shade's poem, "Pale Fire."*

In America, indeed, Nabokov became the princeling he

* "Is it only a coincidence that Kinbote's 'Foreword' to *Pale Fire* is dated 'Oct. 19,' which is the date of Swift's death?" [Alfred N. Appel, Jr.]

had not been since his childhood in Russia, the aristocrat of fiction in our battered mass society, the opulently flowing mind, the proud exhibitor of his gifts in all fields, the happy wizard-Poe that he could not have been in the coldness of Cambridge and the loneliness of those European cities in which his only friends were Russians and Jews. The shaky pre-Hitler atmosphere of Berlin had been intensified by the natural disarray of Russian exiles who alone seemed to know that they were not "white" monarchists but staunch Russian democrats. America pleased Nabokov by its freedom and openness, made him aware of the comic possibilities in so many new people and settings.

He would never own a house but rented a succession of faculty houses like the most avid of eavesdroppers. America also enabled him to contribute to the collections of Cornell and Harvard. One day in Colorado, while not confined to *Lolita* by bad weather, he made the greatest single scientific discovery of his life — the first known female of *Lycaeides sublivens Nabokov*.

Nabokov's novels had always stressed the obsessional case — the single character that with him even more than with the "autobiographical" personae of Joyce and Proust expressed self-hypnosis, life dominated by a quest for necessarily misleading evidence. His first novel in English, *The Real Life of Sebastian Knight*, was another derision of biography, since it involves the search for a "truth," a "real" life, which did not exist, since Sebastian Knight was not the good writer his half-brother thought he was. Nabokov's characteristic stock-in-trade was all here — the artist as subject, the false clues, the "serious" tone applied to a career that was really the negative of what it was supposed to be. Above all, there was Nabokov the puppeteer gleefully rubbing his hands at how much he could put over. The "put-on" as "put-down" — emblems of a generation fascinated with the impersonation of roles, "the games people play," winners and losers at every moment of life — were to be combined by Nabokov with a slyness that hid the proud anguish behind it. *He* would always have to come out the winner — especially over his most zealous annotators. In Nabokov's mind life came in so many guises that the explicators could never come up with enough explanations.

Lolita, Nabokov's most famous book, had had its inception in Europe. A monkey was taught to draw — and drew the bars of its cage. Even a zoo made the requisite setting for the Nabokovian dilemma! But the American highway, the American motel, motor court, tourist home, the depthless American chumminess with strangers — all this floating, farcical easiness of America made a perfect setting for Humbert Humbert the European uprooted from his earliest, most fabled image of bliss. A nymphet as the supreme love-object is characteristic of Nabokov's heroes: they all have special requirements. Then Nabokov brought out in the maddened sex chase, so unrelated to actual physical possession, the usual theme and obsession of the exiled man's attempt, through Lolita as intermediary, to rejoin his earliest image of bliss. There is a lot of activity but no believable physical rapture. Nevertheless, Humbert Humbert must pursue this bliss in bed, in repeated but unreal possession of Lolita. He becomes a great collector of his own sensations; to his own eyes, an unlimited field of psychic folly whose only analogy is overbusy America looking for *something*.

Humbert Humbert can never rejoin his early, blissful self no matter how many times he takes his prize, his nymphet, his unpossessable "little girl." She is of course not a "symbol," as Nabokov would haughtily say with his insatiable hatred of Freud. She is an Other from the man who pursues her. Vladislav Khodasevich had noted that "Peculiar to Sirin is the realization, or perhaps only a deeply felt conviction, that the world of literary creativity, the true world, consists in fact of a completely different material. So different that the passage from one world into the other, in whichever direction it is accomplished, is akin to death." So Lolita herself, now the most celebrated prize in Nabokov's collection, is another discrete phenomenon of life on the endlessly shifting scale of being. She is so very like the pulsating surface, the wonderful differentness, of *Lycaeides sublivens Nabokov* that pride and obsession become equal in Humbert Humbert. The pursuit and the supposed pathology of the pursuit are colors of the mind marvelously blended in Nabokov's adoration of his own theme. This is the superlative cunning, the passionate effort, the directness with which the Nabokov hero escapes "the real world" — *their* world — to concentrate on what will alone answer to the spirit of his nature. And this must be lived to death.

The pursuit is so deeply etched in love, in ultimate feeling, in wonder, that the other side of it is the comic surface that Humbert Humbert presents to himself, the inevitable embarrassment and guilt at having another human being become an object of the oneness he loves and pursues so mightily. The comedy of *Lolita* is the ridiculousness of loving some one "thing" beyond anything else. It is the singling out that comes to dominate one's whole existence. The victim is nevertheless an artist laughing at the ludicrous figure his excessiveness makes. He sees himself from every side. But he must live one choice so thoroughly that far from explaining it, he can only transpose it from false lead to false lead.

To be a nut like Humbert Humbert, to pretend that one is anything to one's beloved but that, to be so devoured by the necessary chase that one's lies become more cunning and far-seeing — this is to raise the artist's glory in his tricks, the exile's sense that the false world and the real one exist side by side, the gifted man's dependence on his childhood passion . . . to the most glowingly happy terms. The excruciation is joy, for no one else in the wide world is living this. Edgar Allan Poe's ambition was also to express pure omniscience, the singular poet as wizard not priest. But Poe did not know, as Nabokov does, the pleasure of turning an obsession into comedy without sacrificing its glory. Poe had his "nymphet" to dwell on, but he was so mixed up and insanely proud that he thought he was spied on and misused by his inferiors. He could not have used the delicious comedy of Nabokov's Russian ploy — the "double." Clare Quilty, Q, Cue, unlike Poe's many sinister *Doppelgänger*, cannot be fully done away with. Quilty, after being shot by Humbert Humbert, lingeringly expires amidst drunken friends who do not grasp what is going on, and who exuberantly cheer on the murderer. Then Humbert

Humbert finds that he can just barely squeeze his car out of the parking space.

Nabokov's incidental achievement in *Lolita* was to make the reader identify with Humbert Humbert's obsession rather than with Humbert Humbert himself, who is one of Nabokov's quicksands. The obsession, as Humbert Humbert is the first to complain, is intolerably selfish. But though Nabokov leeringly talks about his art in the book if only to mislead the reader in a fashion that would have been inconceivable to Joyce (who said that the artist should be present in his creation but invisible, like God), Nabokov does have the artistry to make the reader feel entirely at home with and on the side of what he does not accept intellectually. Nabokov's work firmly expresses his own need to be left alone with what he loves. The exceptionality of this gives an impressive self-sufficiency to his characters. The reader finds himself wholly in Humbert Humbert's corner, and makes fun of all those, like "John Ray, Jr. Ph.D.," who will never understand him. So the reader wholly takes in the life-style and the life-tone of such ideal artists as John Shade, the elderly poet in *Pale Fire*, who is pursued and totally misunderstood by the mad scholiast, Charles Kinbote, who thinks that he adores him and that he alone understands him.

Nabokov's own allusiveness has its charm, and it has provided work for several humorless disciples, brought up on the difficulties of modern fiction and the gamesmanship of Russians. Their highest praise for Nabokov, no end to the snares he leaves for the reader, falls in with his open admiration of himself as a man who can

think in several languages and fields of knowledge. It is
bizarre, coming from the creator of Charles Kinbote, the
exiled "king" and lunatic annotator in *Pale Fire* who is
always getting away from the text he intends to clear up,
to see how much Nabokov encourages pedantic irrele-
vance on his behalf. But Nabokov's sense of himself is
like nothing else in contemporary art. It is not cosmic
conceit but a cosmos. He *necessarily* proclaims himself
the grand master of modern fiction, the pure artist opposed to such "idea-mongers" and creators of "trash" as
Dostoevsky, Balzac, Conrad, Mann, Faulkner. For all his
admitted cleverness, no one would read Nabokov except
assistant pedants if it were not for his extraordinary
ability to make you *side* with certain heroes. It is because
the love for certain persons is positively Nabokov's craft
that he can also create such driven lunatics and enemies
of genius as Charles Kinbote.

What moves us, indeed, is fiction *as* Nabokov's reality,
the insistency of the emotional loyalties that his elaborate
wary mind likes to conceal. There is no "reality" except
as we divest it of the "quotation marks it wore like
claws"? There is no central truth, only a supreme fiction
created by that matching relationship of subject and
artist, that appropriation of reality for oneself? That
matching, that coming together of "mimetic subtlety,
exuberance and luxury far in excess of a predator's
power of appreciation" made Nabokov discover in nature
and art the same "nonutilitarian delights. . . . Both were
a form of magic, both were a game of intricate enchantment and description." Fiction even for this exile was not

time recaptured but the sought-for thing in itself; fiction was the antiworld that could take one out of "exile."

This has been Nabokov's peculiarly personal achievement. He has in fact been so living and existential a storyteller in making us identify with his protagonists, all those shades of and jokes on Nabokov, that one irony of his career is that despite his refusal to belong to anything but his art and his family, he is the one twentieth-century master novelist whose mind and heart we know best — whose every personal opinion we know better than we have ever known Joyce and Proust. This is because of the extraordinary expressiveness with which Nabokov has itemized his sense of exile — and therefore what he holds on to. The consistency of his affections is openly at variance with the seeming concealment of his means. Only fiction, as Nabokov practices it, could so much bring home the personal aspiration behind it: which is not to remake life into fiction, but to celebrate the conclusive evidence of his own heart.

So, with Nabokov, we come back to something that everyone else has doubted: the indissolubility of life with fiction. When we see life as purely a story, and story as the natural projection of a mind wholly curious rather than moral, we grasp what Nabokov has gained by seeing life wholly as the truth of what *seems*. We escape the clutching at relevance, the effort to *establish* relations between life and art. Perhaps this unusual freedom is possible only when a writer is so deep in his exile that exile becomes his life — not "life" in general, not anyone else's life. Then, from the depths of his exile, he is able to see everything as necessarily a fiction, to tell *the* story over and again to himself as if there were nothing but the shapes made by the unfolding of the story.

Some day it will perhaps be seen, conclusively, what Nabokov has insisted on about the Bolshevism he fled at twenty: that it has been the enforced victory of illusion over reality, of words over truth. But Nabokov himself is often guilty of this kind of "victory." When the tie between fiction and reality is not absolute, as it is in his best work, one sees Nabokov the "illusionist" straining and making lordly gestures without convincing us. It may be that the great uneasiness, the totality of the age that is treading hard on our heels, is as hard on Nabokov as it is on the many imaginations in our time who have felt themselves pressed beyond "art." There is an indissolubility, too, with the human condition in our time that leaves its "shadow" on our "mirror" — to use two Nabokov key words. Certainly *Pale Fire* at first reading is awe-inspiring, gives the reader a sense of the solidity behind the shadows it describes. The madman chases the great poet after his death *into* his work. The pursuit is described on so many levels, to force us into the necessary inferences, that a real spirit-world is created, and we see, through the madman's mythification of his own mysterious identity, the marvelously engaging (because so much *loved*) figure of John Shade the poet, who on the brink of death writes this superbly relaxed poem in valedictory to his life. But read again and again because of the puzzles and jokes it proudly offers in every page, the book leaves us with the Nabokov showiness. Are we supposed to give this gifted man, at his age, prizes for being clever? Does the modern novel result in perceptions totally new or just in *perform-ance*?

Performance is certainly one of Nabokov's vanities. And the more one unravels the tangled skein of Kinbote's madness, and the variations which Nabokov plays on his obsession with exile, kingship, true poets and false scholars — Nabokov always seems to be defending himself from the annotators he has called into being — the more the book comes to lack surprise. The stress on real and false angles of vision, the spoof (considerably overdone) of the scholarly notes on the poem that can lead back only to Kinbote's madness, cannot make more supple than they are the already fixed figures of John Slade and his antithesis Charles Kinbote. And whenever, as in *Ada*, Nabokov's need to show the indissolubility of *his* life with his fiction comes over him, we become aware that the many puns, allusions, hoaxes, refer only to Nabokov's self-hypnosis. There is no continuing human interest — the one thing Nabokov can certainly not afford to do without — in his brilliant transposition of Russia into America and of the nineteenth century into the twentieth.

Of course: Nabokov is the last of his century, the last of the "moderns," perhaps the last of the great Russian novelists — for in Russia itself only poetry, a voice from the moon, has not been totally ground down. But in *Ada*, the backward-running and dizzyingly mixed up novelistic film which spoofs Russia, America, and so many modern writers, even the pleasures of love on the old country estate, while enchanting in their display of Nabokov's mental richness, are too narcissistic to be more than brilliant. We already know all about "the world we have lost," the enchantment that Nabokov has written his way back to in exile. The repetition gives us nothing of that development which makes Proust the greatest of all "autobiographical" novelists. Nabokov at seventy reminds us too much of what he was at twenty. Shift rather than growth is his strategy; the performance is terrific, but at this point, why should *we* care when so much of the effort goes into demonstration and when Nabokov's frank pleasure in his own mind becomes part of the act?

Certainly Nabokov's ideas about the final simultaneity of all events in time are not original. Baudelaire said it all: "Talent is nothing more nor less than childhood rediscovered at will — a childhood now equipped for self-expression, with manhood's capacities and a power of analysis which enables it to order the mass of raw material which it has involuntarily accumulated." Or as the painter Claes Oldenburg recently put it: "Everything I do is completely original. I made it up when I was a little kid."

Self-sufficiency, for our time a major form of freedom, is Nabokov's real genius. And freedom as it expresses itself in and through the creative act is its object. There is finally no "truth," just this sense of freedom. Love is the pleasure of freedom. Even in lovemaking, genius is the only actor.

> *What, then, was it that raised the animal act to a level higher than that of even the most exact arts or the wildest flights of pure science? Reality lost the quotes it wore like claws — in a world where independent and original minds must cling to things or pull things apart*

in order to ward off madness or death (which is the supreme madness).

The reciprocal love of Van Veen, Ivan Demonovitch Veen, for his sister Ada, his only possible double, is like the privilege of gods. Van's sexual prowess — he first makes love to Ada in 1884 and is still going strong up to age eighty-six — is just another aspect of his universal genius. He can rearrange our stale concepts of time and place, walk on his hands, pop up in different disguises as a magician, card expert, variety artist, scientist, doctor, philosopher, writer. In a key passage Nabokov says of his walking-on-his-hands:

The essence of the satisfaction belonged . . . to the same order as the one he later derived from self-imposed, extravagantly difficult, seemingly absurd tasks. When Van sought to express something, which until expressed had only a twilight being . . . nothing but the illusion of the backward shadow of its imminent expression. . . . It was Ada's house of cards. It was the standing of a metaphor on its head not for the sake of the trick's difficulty but in order to perceive an ascending waterfall or a sunrise in reverse: a triumph, in a sense, over the ardis of time. Thus the rapture of young Mascodagama [his stage name] derived from overcoming gravity was akin to that of artistic revelation in the sense utterly and naturally unknown to the innocents of critical appraisal, the social-scene commentators, the moralists, the idea-mongers and so forth. Van on the stage was performing organically what his figures of speech were to perform later in life — acrobatic wonders that had never been expected from them and which frightened little children.

Nabokov can never write without scorning the other, some other, be it Balzac, Dostoevsky, Mann, Conrad, Faulkner — or the Freud whom he attacks in every preface. Freud would have doubted Nabokov's unlimited sovereignty over his own life. Fiction for Nabokov is unmotivated imagination resting in the pure freedom of his exiled state. The non-Nabokov world must always be shown up as unnecessary to Nabokov's freedom.

At the same time Nabokov is saying something encouraging about our irreversible skid through time, and this is demonstrated in *Ada*'s virtuosity. Time is essentially personal: we are its only creators. Past, present and future leak into our consciousness from every side; we live a creative disorder unpredictable, unassembled, witty and gay. The recouping of life through the imagination of time is happiness, enchantment, the delicious absurdity of rising above all stated connections. Time is the open reality of our senses, space the deception, death a misinterpretation. Van's half-sister Lucette jumps off a liner for love of him, and the sea becomes the "accidental home she was about to leave." Drowning, Lucette "thought it proper to inform a series of receding Lucettes that what death amounted to was only a more complete assortment of the infinite fractions of solitude." The "world" most people know is a substitution for themselves. As opposed to a "green world rotating in space and spiralling in time, which in terms of matter-and-mind were like cut-outs or the dreadful Siamese coupling of space and time," Nabokov propounds the simultaneous existence in time of our different selves as that moment in which all the languages he has used, the countries he has lived in, join to make the antiworld that every novelist needs.

Ada is striking as a summing up of all the resources of Nabokov's thought. It is a counterdemonstration to the mass society that sometimes seems to make up contemporary fiction. Obviously Nabokov recognizes no hindrance to his own absolute freedom — *e s'è non è vero, è ben trovato*. But *Ada* will not mean as much to us as *Pnin, The Gift, The Defense, Speak, Memory, Pale Fire.* Nor will it live as long as *Lolita*, which in Humbert Humbert's pursuit of the unattainable is one of the great fables of man's inability to know the whole truth until he becomes part of it in the form of death. Nabokov's best books are like invisible writing slowly brought up to the fire. They exert their spell as a legend of madness and the madman's destructive pursuit. This is no longer Poe's romantic quest but the most urgent of themes in our world: man afraid of himself.

The artist's perfect freedom in *Ada* is a fantasy too lovely — and therefore imperfect — as opposed to a perfect nightmare. Nabokov is a novelist of madness, that great contemporary subject. In *Ada* his vanity, nourished by noncontact in exile, has become diffuse. It is too much about himself, his life, his Russia-America, rather than an extension of the art that bears his name. Its self-celebration slops all over the planet. Nabokov has certainly not saved himself. Nor has he wanted to. But he has saved *us* from being always at the mercy of the age.

INDEX

321

Lonely Voice, The (O'Connor), 166

"Looking for Mr. Green" (Bellow), 125

"Los Angeles Notebook" (Didion), 191

Losing Battles (Welty), 258n

Lost in the Funhouse (Barth), 258n

"Lottery, The" (Jackson), 174

Love and Friendship (Lurie), 187

Love in the Ruins (Percy), 66

Low Company (Fuchs), 130

Lowell, Robert, 123

Lowry, Malcolm, 18–19, 296n; *Under the Volcano*, 18–19

Luce, Henry, 229n

Ludwig, Jack, *Confusions*, 258n

Lurie, Alison, 186–188; *Love and Friendship*, 187; *Real People*, (quoted) 188

Lytle, Andrew, 38, 65

Macdonald, Dwight, 103

Magic Barrel, The (Malamud), 104

Magician of Lublin, The (Singer), 161

Magic Mountain, The (Mann), 18, 19

Mailer, Norman, 71–77, 86, 147, 149–157, 190, 211, 232, 233, 236–241, 255–257; *The Naked and the Dead*, 71, 74, 76–77, 151, 154, (quoted) 77; Hemingway on, 71; *The Armies of the Night*, 149, 228, 240; *Barbary Shore*, 151, 154; *The Deer Park*, 152, 154, (quoted) 153; *An American Dream*, 154, 155, (quoted) 155n; *Why Are We in Viet Nam?*, 154, 156; "The Time of Her Time," 155n; *Advertisements for Myself*, 155n; *Of a Fire on the Moon*, 238, 240; *The Prisoner of Sex*, 240; "The White Negro," 255–257, (quoted) 256

Malamud, Bernard, 104, 127, 139–144; *The Magic Barrel*, 104; "Take Pity," (quoted) 139; "Fidelman" stories, 140; *The Natural*, 141; *The Assistant*, (quoted) 141, 143; "The Mourners," (quoted) 142; criticism of, 289

Malcolm X (Malcolm Little) 233; *The Autobiography of Malcolm X*, 221, 224–226

Malraux, André, 25, 231

"Manners, Morals and the Novel" (Trilling), 107n

Mann, Thomas, 309, 314

Mansion, The (Faulkner), 33, 34

"Man Who Went to Chicago, The" (Wright), 243

Mary (Nabokov), 299

Max Jamison (Sheed), 258

Maxwell, William, 285; *The Folded Leaf*, 292–293; "The Writer as Illusionist," (quoted) 285, 291

McCarthy, Mary, 188–189; "America the Beautiful," 107n; *The Groves of Academe*, 189; "The Oasis," 189; *A Charmed Life*, 189; *The Group*, 189; *Birds of America*, 189

McCullers, Carson, 38, 46, 49, 50, 51–54; *The Heart Is a Lonely Hunter*, 52, 53, 54; *The Ballad of the Sad Café*, 53; *The Member of the Wedding*, 53

McNamara, Robert, 75n

Melville, Herman, 246, 248

Member of the Wedding, The (McCullers), 53

Men Without Women (Hemingway), 6

Michaels, Leonard, 258

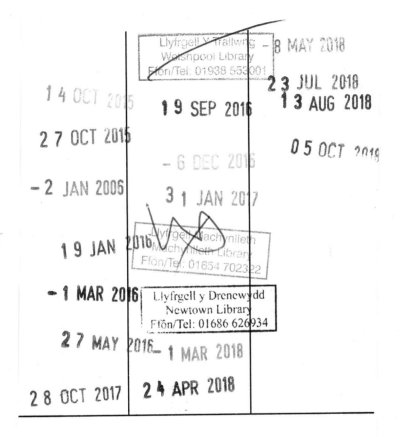
**Please return by the last date shown
Dychweler erbyn y dyddiad olaf uchod**

LLYFRGELLOEDD POWYS LIBRARIES

www.powys.gov.uk/libraries